Social Thought in America

SOCIAL THOUGHT
IN AMERICA:
The Revolt Against Formalism

BY MORTON G. WHITE

NEW YORK

The Viking Press

1949

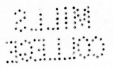

Grateful acknowledgment is made to the *Journal of the History of Ideas* in which Chapter II appeared as an article and to *The Philosophical Review* which published the essay "Value and Obligation in Dewey and Lewis," parts of which appear in this book.

To My Mother and Father

Preface

THIS book originated in a plan to write a history and criticism of liberal social philosophy in twentieth-century America. Because it will take more time to carry out this plan than I had expected, I have decided to present what is essentially the first part of the study as originally conceived. In it I have tried to trace the development of the leading ideas of Charles A. Beard, John Dewey, Oliver Wendell Holmes, Jr., James Harvey Robinson, and Thorstein Veblen, and to analyze critically some of their key philosophical views. I have left the consideration of a number of detailed problems in the methodology of social science and political philosophy for another book.

Many have helped me, and I want to record my debt and my gratitude to them. My wife, Lucia Perry White, has read and heard the manuscript and its discarded forerunners for several years; without her suggestions, her criticism, and her encouragement, I would never have finished it. Without the kindness and interest of B. W. Huebsch of The Viking Press I would never have begun it. Rosamond Hart Chapman has prepared the manuscript for publication; she has relentlessly checked the text and the notes and in several places has saved me from serious error.

A number of teachers, colleagues, and friends have helped me

without having read through the entire manuscript, though
some of them may be surprised or disappointed by part or all of
it. I want especially to record the inspiration I have received
from the friendship and intellectual companionship of Henry
D. Aiken, James T. Farrell, Nelson Goodman, Ernest Nagel,
Benjamin N. Nelson, and Meyer Schapiro. I also want to thank
many students at Columbia University, the University of Penn-
sylvania, and Harvard University for their interest in the lectures which formed the basis of this book.

                                                    M. G. W.

Cambridge, Mass.
April 24, 1949

Contents

Social Thought in America

Introduction

CATASTROPHES are peculiarly suitable aids in tracing the history and development of ideas and intellectual currents. Wars and atomic bombs become devices for the dating of other events. They make so much seem absurd and so much seem old-fashioned that they serve as convenient reference points. When they do not literally force us to put down all our books, they make us pinch the corners of pages, and send us off in new directions. It seems obvious that our most recent calamities have done just that. Abroad books were destroyed; here they glided out of public view. I have in mind the submersion of a certain style of thinking which dominated America for almost half a century—an intellectual pattern compounded of pragmatism, institutionalism, behaviorism, legal realism, economic determinism, the "new history." When we consider the illustrious names in these traditions we become even more aware of the end of an era—John Dewey, Thorstein Veblen, Justice Holmes, Charles A. Beard, James Harvey Robinson.

It might be argued that these movements are not dead, but one cannot avoid feeling that they are past the peak of their influence. These are days in which Dewey's views are being replaced by Kierkegaard's in places where once Dewey was king; when Robinson is dismissed as a pleasant popularizer; when Keynes comes in triumph over Veblen; when Beard's work is divided into "periods" so that his later views can be consistently anathematized by those who once made him a hero.

Some may deny that the demise or decline is connected with the war and the atomic era. Maybe not. But surely it took place in the popular mind sometime during the ten years before we were engulfed by war, and most likely the decline was connected with the forces that overwhelmed us. But I shall not argue these points here; here I shall be satisfied with marking the change in American intellectual fashion. I want to examine the older tradition, the early twentieth-century pattern, show that it was a pattern, and critically consider its philosophical foundations. When I say "philosophical foundations" I cannot be precise; indeed I would rather do what I plan to do and let the reader decide in what sense the enterprise is philosophical. Only one thing ought to be said in advance: an encyclopedic compendium of economics, history, law, political science, and ethics is not to be expected. Rather, for example, I shall consider the philosophical aspects of Veblen's institutionalism because it claims to have a method different from that of its predecessors and a distinctive attitude toward the relation between moral value and economic theory. I shall consider the elements of Holmes' legal realism, particularly his conception of the nature of the law. I shall examine Robinson's demand for a new conception of the nature of history (which he shares with so many American historians who are more respected as technical monographers). All of these, it seems to me, are philosophical claims in an elementary sense. They are concerned with method, with value, and with the nature of fundamental concepts. And what is more, in these different fields these men make claims which have striking ideological affinities with each other and with the distinctively American movement in philosophy—pragmatism. The main purpose of this study, then, is to follow the course of liberal social philosophy in America from the end of the nineteenth century to the nineteen-thirties.

In a sense the exploration which I set myself in these pages is not new. Parrington, in the very last section of his *Main Currents in American Thought,* was interested in a related theme. He begins his "Chapter in American Liberalism" with the following:

> Liberals whose hair is growing thin and the lines of whose figures are no longer what they were, are likely to find themselves today in the unhappy predicament of being treated as mourners at their own funerals. When they pluck up heart to assert that they are not yet authentic corpses, but living men with brains in their heads, they are pretty certain to be gently chided and led back to the comfortable arm-chair that befits senility. Their counsel is smiled at as the chatter of a belated post-Victorian generation that knew not Freud, and if they must go abroad they are bidden take the air in the garden where other old-fashioned plants—mostly of the family *Democratici*—are still preserved.[1] *

Now this, we must remember, was written before the crash of 1929 and before the Second World War. The figures we shall treat were already considered intellectually arteriosclerotic—charming elder statesmen of a movement, deans who were to be visited occasionally. This, even before the belligerent attacks upon their movement made by Marxism in the thirties, before the short-lived challenge of neo-Thomism, before the half-critical, half-supporting writings of logical positivism, sane semantics, and operationalism. And, most important, before the atomic bomb was to discredit, according to some, the scientific outlook which these men shared and hoped to extend to all spheres of human action.

Parrington was concerned in 1929 to show that the liberalism of this older generation was not dead, that it was firmly rooted in American history, that it would supply the last and most perfect expression of the tradition in American thought which he hoped to chronicle and justify. But Parrington was being defensive before the tradition had suffered its hardest blows, for a depression and a war lay in waiting. Today most of these

* All notes will be found at the end of the book, beginning on p. 247.

liberals are no longer with us, and in Washington a whole generation which looked to Veblen and Holmes has already disappeared from political power. If in 1929 Parrington thought
he was looking at something in twilight, we may feel as though
we look at it in darkness and eclipse. But this raises a question
the answer to which might come more easily as a result of carefully probing the roots of this tradition. Are we faced with a
dead tradition—a chapter in American thought that is already
behind us? Are we to perform an analysis or an autopsy? Others
have tried to answer the questions raised in this last section of
Parrington's book, among them John Chamberlain in his *Farewell to Reform,* and Max Lerner in *Ideas Are Weapons.* But
they have been concerned mainly with its literary connections
and its impact upon political action. Here I shall attempt a more
limited task—that of examining what I have called its philosophy, its conception of its method and its values.

Pragmatism, instrumentalism, institutionalism, economic determinism, and legal realism exhibit striking philosophical kin-
ships. They are all suspicious of approaches which are excessively formal; they all protest their anxiety to come to grips
with reality, their attachment to the moving and the vital in
social life. Most of those who founded or represented these
movements started their serious thinking in the eighties and the
nineties of the last century, a period of ignition in American
thought which was followed by the explosions (and duds) of
the present century. The eighties and nineties saw the growth
of science and capitalism, the spread of Darwinism, socialism,
industrialization, and monopoly. Holmes was directly confronted
with truculent capitalism in cases involving concrete social
questions. Veblen, interested in unmasking the effects of absentee
ownership upon industry, and the role of the leisure class in
American life, was brought face to face with the pattern of
exploitation. Dewey met it when he examined the touchy relations of science, morality, and society and urged the scrapping
of outworn theological and metaphysical creeds. Beard was the

scholarly product of a progressive age bent upon raking muck and fulfilling the promise of American life.

The general patterns of this intellectual culture are known to most students of American society. I have mentioned the work of Parrington, the literary historian who parallels the others and who hoped to chronicle their work, and the attempts of John Chamberlain and Max Lerner. But not much has been said systematically on the ideas of the older generation of liberals viewed as a group. There are isolated studies like Dorfman's *Thorstein Veblen,* Sidney Hook's *John Dewey,* Lerner's useful commentary on and collection of Holmes' writings, and Joseph Ratner's anthology of Dewey's work; but no one has tried to present a unified picture of the intellectual growth of this exciting movement in American thought. By a unified picture I mean, as I have already suggested, a study which would emphasize the fundamental philosophical positions implicit and explicit in their work. Although Dewey is the only professional philosopher of the group, every one of the others has given considerable thought to the larger aspects of his own work, to general considerations of method and value. They were actively interested in the logic of their inquiries, and all of them, with the possible exception of Veblen, explicitly adopted certain values which, when put together systematically, lead to a moral philosophy.

If one were to try to express succinctly the basic ideas to be examined, I think a first approximation would run something like this:

1. Instrumentalism is Dewey's doctrine which holds that ideas are plans of action, and not mirrors of reality; that dualisms of all kinds are fatal; that the method of intelligence is the best way of solving problems; and that philosophy ought to free itself from metaphysics and devote itself to social engineering.

2. Veblen's institutionalism is a doctrine which insists upon the importance of studying empirically the connections between economic institutions and other aspects of culture. It rejects

classical political economy as abstract in a way that supposedly condemns it, and it offers instead a programmatic theory of economic development in terms of two fundamental institutions: the engineers and the price system.

3. Holmes' realism consists in rejecting the view that law is an abstract entity present as *the* meaning of a given statute, waiting to be found by a judge. On the contrary it is, in great measure, *made* by the judge.

4. Beard's most serious contribution to the pattern is a development and elaboration of Madison's view in the tenth Federalist paper, the view that faction is the great problem of modern democratic society and that property is the source of faction. Beard, therefore, looks with Madison for underlying economic forces that determine the acceleration of social life, and urges the historian to chart the process of civilization as a whole.

5. James Harvey Robinson was the literate American representative of the view that history is not merely a chronicle of the past, but rather a pragmatic weapon for explaining the present and controlling the future of man, a doctrine which he named the "new history" in contradistinction to recitations of royal and military intrigue. .

These, as I have said, are parts of a first approximation. A good deal of the study will be devoted to clarifying these doctrines, judging their truth, relating them to other movements in American thought, and placing them, as it is said, in their "cultural context." By and large, when I say my emphasis will be philosophical I mean that it will be analytical and critical. As I understand it, one task of the philosopher is the clarification or analysis of fundamental concepts. What is law? What is history? What is science—in particular, economic or legal science? What is "the good"? The key figures of this study are remarkably fruitful for any philosopher who wishes to investigate these problems concretely. Needless to add, these questions might very well be studied by practitioners of the particular disciplines. But unfortunately they are too often occupied, and rightly so, with their special problems, and unable to devote themselves carefully to these more general questions. It is obvious, for example, that a detailed study of a particular branch of mathematics need not wait upon clear and definite answers to the questions, "What is mathematics?" and "What is deduction?" Nor does a fruitful study of physics depend upon being absolutely clear about what is meant by the words "physics" and "causality." Nevertheless, these questions are perfectly reasonable so long as we continue to use these words, and tradition has assigned their elucidation to philosophers—in many cases, of course, to philosophers ignorant or even contemptuous of the sciences. But there is obviously a mean between hostility or indifference to the concrete disciplines and total absorption in them. In urging the importance of analysis I do not say that the *sole* task of the philosopher is analysis. I think that general questions of a political and moral character have and ought to be considered by philosophers. It has been said that "ethical philosophers have, in fact, been largely concerned, not with laying down rules to the effect that certain ways of acting are generally or always right, and others generally or always wrong, nor yet with giving lists of things which are good and others which are evil, but with trying to answer more general and fundamental questions such as the following: What, after all, is it that we mean to say of an action when we say that it is right or ought to be done?" [2] Now this may be true historically of many ethical philosophers, but surely Dewey has concerned himself with questions like "Is freedom good?" and "Is democracy good?" These are not merely analytical questions, for they call for judgments of practice and morality. Indeed, most of our American social thinkers, in so far as they devote themselves to moral questions at all, devote themselves to questions of the less analytic kind. I will try to consider these as well, but my basic concern will be to trace the growth of the philosophical ideas and assumptions which have formed a canon for several generations of American intellectuals and serious laymen.

My method, it will appear quickly, is not that of mere textual analysis. Rather I have tried to treat the subject historically; I have tried to present a school of thought in development from its earliest beginnings through the twenties of this century. The reasons for stopping at the end of the twenties are complex, but a few may be set down. First of all, and most important, is the fact that the twenties were the last decade in which the figures with whom I deal acted as participants in anything like a single school of thought. Veblen died in 1929 (as did Parrington). Holmes retired from the Supreme Court in 1932 and died in 1935. Robinson reached the height of his popularity in the twenties and died in 1936. When we reach the thirties, the depression marks the first important break in the influence of the movement as a movement. Much is said and done after that, chiefly by Beard and Dewey, but it takes place in a new world. By 1930 a line had been broken, and the remaining soldiers marched in different directions and enlisted in new regiments. To follow these new moves would bring us onto new terrain and would demand a study easily as large as the present one. What I have attempted here is a preface to that as yet unfinished story.

CHAPTER II

The Revolt Against Formalism

THE movements of thought with which we shall be most concerned cannot be fully understood without some sense of their relation to the ideas which dominated the nineteenth century. That century transcended the eighteenth through its concern with change, process, history, and culture. It was the century of history, evolutionary biology, psychology and sociology, historical jurisprudence and economics; the century of Comte, Darwin, Hegel, Marx, and Spencer. It is not surprising, therefore, to find American intellectuals ranging themselves, in the eighteen-nineties, against formalism, since they had been convinced that logic, abstraction, deduction, mathematics, and mechanics were inadequate to social research and incapable of containing the rich, moving, living current of social life. So convinced had some American intellectuals become that their earliest work touched off a large-scale revolt against formalism in philosophy and the social sciences. The battle for history and culture may have been won on the Continent, but here in America it was only beginning, and the last bastions of formalist philosophy, economics, law, and political science were being besieged. Dewey, Holmes, and Veblen were the leaders of a campaign to mop up the remnants of formal logic, classical economics and jurisprudence in America, and to emphasize that the life of science, economics, and law was not logic but experience in some streaming social sense.

It is very hard to give an exact definition of the word "formalism," but I think its meaning will become clearer as we consider examples. It may be that the term as applied to movements in different fields—in law, philosophy, and economics—does not retain precisely the same meaning, but there is a strong family resemblance, strong enough to produce a feeling of sympathy in all who opposed what they called formalism in their respective fields. Anti-formalists like Holmes, Dewey, Veblen, and Beard called upon social scientists in all domains, asked them to unite, and urged that they had nothing to lose but their deductive chains.

This attack on formalism or abstractionism leads to two important positive elements in the thought of these men—"historicism" and what I shall call "cultural organicism." These are frequently identified in discussions of nineteenth-century thought, but it seems to me that they can be distinguished in a rather simple way. By "historicism" I shall mean the attempt to explain facts by reference to earlier facts; by "cultural organicism" I mean the attempt to find explanations and relevant material in social sciences other than the one which is primarily under investigation.[1] The historicist reaches back in time in order to account for certain phenomena; the cultural organicist reaches into the entire social space around him. In many cases these two tendencies exist side by side in the thought of a single man, and in fact this is precisely what happens with most of the figures we shall treat. They are all under the spell of history and culture. Holmes is the learned historian of the law and one of the heroes of sociological jurisprudence; Veblen is the evolutionary and sociological student of economic institutions; Beard urges us to view political instruments as more than documents; Robinson construes history as the ally of all the social disciplines and the study of how things have come to be as they are; Dewey describes his philosophy alternately as "evolutionary" and "cultural" naturalism. All of them insist upon coming to grips with life, experience, process, growth, context, function. They are all products of the historical and cultural emphases of the nineteenth century, following, being influenced by, reacting from its great philosophers of change and process. The present chapter is an attempt to delineate somewhat specifically the early roots of this outlook. It lays great stress upon the fact that Dewey violently attacked formal logic in his earliest writings, that Veblen devoted great energy to deprecating the abstract-deductive method of classical political economy, that Beard fought against the formal-juridical approach to the Constitution, that Holmes proclaimed in 1881 what later became the slogan of generations of legal realists: "The life of the law has not been logic: it has been experience." [2]

In the case of Dewey the roots are very clear. His early thought began under the domination of neo-Hegelianism with its unqualified condemnation of the formal and the mechanical. It was supported (in his own mind) by the results of Darwinian biology.[3] Dewey was first a disciple of G. S. Morris, the obscure American idealist. His first philosophical work was also under the influence of Thomas H. Green and Edward Caird. Not only his views of logic and metaphysics but also the earliest expression of his political philosophy found their roots here.[4] Veblen, by an interesting coincidence, was also a graduate student at Johns Hopkins, and he too listened to Morris.[5] Although Veblen did not go through a serious early Hegelian stage with Dewey, he shared Dewey's tremendous admiration for Darwin. It is interesting to observe that Veblen constantly compared the Hegelian and Darwinian conceptions of change, always to the detriment of the former, whereas there was a period in Dewey's development when he tried to defend his Hegelianism with arguments from Darwinism.[6] In spite of their early differences on Hegel, Dewey and Veblen were part of a reaction against English and Scottish empiricism, and their early thought expressed this quite vividly. One berated the philosophical wing of the tradition, the other attacked the economists. And sometimes, of course, they converged on the same figures—Hume, Adam Smith, Bentham, or John Stuart Mill.

It is extremely important to take into account this aversion to British empiricism—a phenomenon which can surprise only those who casually link Dewey and Veblen with all "empiricists." The paradox, if any, was almost solved by Leslie Stephen when he remarked in his study of the utilitarians that, although the latter were frequently appealing to experience, they had a very low opinion of the value of historical study. Now Holmes was certainly less opposed to the British tradition. Nevertheless Holmes selected for his special attack the prime exponent of utilitarian jurisprudence—John Austin. Holmes was disputing as early as 1874 Austin's view of the law as the command of the sovereign.[7] For if the law is the command of the sovereign, then the judge is to find it rather than make it, and this conflicted with Holmes' main positive view. I emphasize the fact that Austin was a Benthamite in order to indicate the centrality of Bentham in the camp of the enemy. When Dewey first published books on ethics, it was hedonism, and utilitarianism, which he most severely attacked;[8] when Veblen criticized the foundations of classical economics, it was Bentham's calculus of pains and pleasures that he was undermining; when Holmes was advancing his own view of the law, it was the tradition of Bentham he was fighting against; when Beard came to treat the Constitution as a social document and not simply as an abstract system to be logically analyzed, he found Bentham's shadow, made longer by Austin on Bentham's shoulders. That Robinson, the historian, should not have found a comparable sparring partner among the utilitarians does not destroy the generality of my thesis; on the contrary, it confirms it, for there were no utilitarian historians of comparable stature. And it was precisely utilitarianism's alleged failure to deal with social phenomena in a historical-cultural manner that led to the attack on the tradition of Bentham. Dewey attacked utilitarian ethics, psychology, and logic for failing to study the actual workings of the human mind; Veblen attacked the hedonic calculus as well as the failure to study economic institutions in their wider cultural setting; Beard opposed the analytical school for treating the Constitution as if it were axiomatized geometry rather than a human, social document; and Holmes regarded Austin's theory as an inaccurate account of law as it was practiced.

These general reflections give a fair idea of what I mean when I connect all of these men as anti-formalist revolutionaries; I turn now to some concrete expressions of this attitude in their early writings.

I. *Oliver Wendell Holmes, Jr.*

Because Holmes was the oldest of these men, and because he was the first of them to present a mature and clear statement of his position, I want to treat him first. I want particularly to consider some of the more general aspects of his work *The Common Law* (1881) in order to focus upon its important role in the revolt against formalism.

His purpose, Holmes tells us on the first page, is to present a general view of the subject. And then, as if to dissociate himself from a view which he might have expected his readers to assign to him, he announces that "other tools are needed besides logic" in order to accomplish this task.[9] May we infer that there were some expositors of the common law who believed that *only* logic was necessary as a tool? I doubt it; but certainly there were some who conceived of logic as the fundamental tool.[10] Of what logic is Holmes speaking? If it were not for the fact that he published his book in 1881, when the world was being swamped with two-volume studies in idealistic logic, such a question might not be raised. But I raise it only to make explicit the fact that he was not referring to these works or to the discipline which they claimed to expound, but rather that he had in mind traditional Aristotelian logic. It was syllogistic logic that did not suffice for presenting a general view of the common law. Moreover, we can be sure that Holmes was not rejecting Aristotelian logic because of any failure which might be remedied by modern, mathematical logic. Of the latter he knew almost nothing, and in it he had little interest.[11] No enrichment of syllogistic logic in the modern manner would have changed the situation for Holmes' purposes. It was simply his conviction that deductive logic did not suffice, no matter how enriched. Holmes was not about to give a list of legal axioms in the manner of Euclid and promptly to deduce theorems with the help of logic. If this had been his sole purpose, logic would have been the sole tool necessary in addition to the legal principles expressed in his axioms. But on this he says: "The law embodies the story of a nation's development through many centuries, and it cannot be dealt with as if it contained only the axioms and corollaries of a book of mathematics." [12]

We see at once the historical emphasis in Holmes. It is because the law embodies the *history* of a nation that it cannot be treated deductively. Although Holmes does not explicitly formulate them, we may indicate at least two questions which are introduced by his statement, in order to be clearer about what he is saying. 1. Can we formulate the law accepted at a given time in a deductive fashion, beginning with legal axioms or fundamental principles? 2. Has the law in its actual historical course developed in a logico-deductive manner? In other words, did the axioms, for example, reveal themselves to man before the theorems? Now we must not forget that in this place Holmes is concerned with the latter question, and his answer is that we cannot explain legal history in terms of logical processes alone. Legal history does not unfold as if it were created by a logician. The life of the law has not been logic in this sense.[13] He follows this statement with a statement of other factors to which we must refer if we are to understand why and how certain legal rules were developed: "The felt necessities of the time, the prevalent moral and political theories, intuitions of public policy, avowed or unconscious, even the prejudices which judges share with their fellow men, have a good deal more to do than the syllogism in determining the rules by which men should be governed." [14] The theory, we see, is predominantly a theory of historical development of law, and it is anti-formalistic in so far as it rejects the view that the law evolves in accordance with a formal-logical pattern.[15]

The positive implications of this attack on formalism are fairly obvious. Holmes is led to an intensive study of the history and theories of legislation in order to explain the meanings of certain legal terms and rules and why they emerged when they did. The first chapter of *The Common Law*, for example, is an exercise in historical explanation; it is a study of early forms of liability in order to show that they are rooted in passion and vengeance. The entire study, the details of which we need not consider, is permeated with a historical outlook, specifically with the spirit of an epoch-making work in anthropology. *The Common Law* followed the publication of E. B. Tylor's *Primitive Culture* by ten years, and the impact of the latter was still considerable. Not only is Tylor cited by Holmes on certain factual questions,[16] but some of his general ideas are also absorbed. For example, Holmes remarks on what he calls a "very common phenomenon," and one which is "very familiar to the student of history": "The customs, beliefs, or needs of a primitive time establish a rule or a formula. In the course of centuries the custom, belief, or necessity disappears, but the rule remains. The reason which gave rise to the rule has been forgotten, and ingenious minds set themselves to inquire how it is to be accounted for. Some ground of policy is thought of, which seems to explain it and to reconcile it with the present state of things; and then the rule adapts itself to the new reasons which have been found for it, and enters on a new career. The old form receives a new content, and in time even the form modifies itself to fit the meaning which it has received." [17]

The point of view expressed here is closely related to Tylor's conception of survival, treated at length in the third and fourth chapters of *Primitive Culture*. In the case of Tylor, the study of primitive culture is motivated, in part, by a desire to ferret out just those elements of his own culture which are mere survivals of a more backward and less civilized age. The study of the past is not exclusively archaeological or antiquarian for Tylor. He urges that we try to get rid of those practices which have nothing to commend them but the fact that they are survivals of the past. It is for this reason that he concludes his great work with the following statement: "It is a harsher, and at times even painful, office of ethnography to expose the remains of crude old culture which have passed into harmful superstition, and to mark these out for destruction. Yet this work, if less genial, is not less urgently needful for the good of mankind. Thus, active at once in aiding progress and in removing hindrance, the science of culture is essentially a reformer's science." [18]

Tylor's conception of the science of culture as a reformer's science must be underscored if we are to appreciate the link between the historicism and the liberalism of our American thinkers. Tylor's view shows conclusively that historicism is not necessarily associated with a veneration of the past. Here the study of the past is construed as instrumental to the solution of present problems—to the elimination of contemporary irrationality. The student of the past need not have a stake in the past.[19] If the example of Marx is not sufficient to show this, certainly that of Tylor is worth mentioning. The statement of this idea is of great value in helping us to understand the evolutionary and historical orientation of Holmes, Veblen, Dewey, Beard, and Robinson. It helps us to distinguish the motivation of their historicism and organicism from that which inspired European reactionaries in the nineteenth century.

II. *John Dewey*

In 1882, one year after the publication of *The Common Law*, Dewey's first published contribution to philosophy appeared.

With it he began a series of investigations into philosophy and psychology, under the influence of British neo-idealism. This influence was to continue until the emergence of his distinctly instrumentalist, pragmatist, or experimentalist outlook.[20] Dewey was even more anti-formalist than Holmes. Under the more direct influence of Morris he came to scorn the epistemology of the British empiricists, and to single out for criticism their dualistic separation of mind from the object of knowledge. This separation was construed by Dewey as "formal" and "mechanical" and hence attacked in the manner of Hegel. The "new psychology" was a movement, according to Dewey, which was to free psychology from the analytical dissections of associationism.[21] Hegel provided him with the concept of a universal consciousness which embraced everything and which provided the link between individual consciousness and the objects of knowledge, the link which supposedly showed them to be more than formally related. The *objective mind* of idealism was made central,[22] and, as Dewey tells us later, it was the ancestor of his insistence upon the influence of the cultural environment in shaping ideas, beliefs, and intellectual attitudes.[23] It was this which united him with the spirit of *The Common Law*—this emphasis on the need for regarding human action (in Holmes the special case of legal action) as part of what Dewey later called a "cultural matrix." Although Holmes was not a Hegelian, I think there is no doubt that he and Dewey were motivated by similar considerations in their attack on formalism. In the light of this great similarity in their early years, and their mutual respect in later years, the convergence of pragmatism and legal realism should occasion little surprise.[24] It was in the eighties that Dewey was also attacking formal logic. Now Holmes was no admirer of Hegel's *Logic;* certainly he would not have agreed that it represented "the quintessence of the scientific spirit," as Dewey maintained in 1891.[25] But the classic excerpt from *The Common Law* about the life of the law not being logic can be matched with several from Dewey, the most striking being Dewey's claim in 1891 that formal logic was *"fons et origo malorum* in philosophy." [26]

In addition to sharing Holmes' attitude toward the role of formal logic, and toward what I have called cultural organicism, Dewey shared his respect for the historical or genetic method.[27] We have seen how this functioned in Holmes' early work. In Dewey's thought the use of genetic method is positively motivated, whereas his opposition to formalism is the product of a polemic on Hegelian grounds against British empiricism. This is not to say that his historicism had no connections with his Hegelianism. What must be emphasized is the fact that Dewey's Hegelianism directed him against formalism, and that this was fortified by his study of Darwin. It is not surprising, therefore, to find his use of genetic method taking on an evolutionary cast. This links him not only to Holmes but also to Veblen, as we shall see when we examine the latter's regretful complaint in 1898 that economics was not then an evolutionary science.

Dewey's application of evolutionary method to morality not only is useful for establishing his connection with Holmes and Veblen; it also helps to illuminate some of the ties between his historicism and his experimentalism, between his early Hegelian emphasis on change and history and his later pragmatic emphasis on experiment and control. In expounding the nature of evolutionary method he tries to formulate the sense in which experimental method is itself genetic. His answer is rather simple. In conducting experiments on the nature of water, to use his own example, we perform certain acts of combination and we see that water is formed as a consequence. The entire process is one in which water is "called into being." The experimental process, therefore, is viewed as genetic in character, precisely because it "calls into being" certain phenomena as a result of experimental manipulation. Now there are some domains, Dewey thought at the time, in which experimental control is impossible. We are able to use experiment in chemistry, he argues, but we cannot apply it to "those facts with which ethical science is concerned. We cannot," he says, "take a present case of parental care, or of a child's untruthfulness, and cut it into sections, or tear it into physical pieces, or subject it to chemical analysis." What we can do, however, is study "how it came to be what it is," that is, study it historically. History, therefore, is construed, according to Dewey, as "the only available substitute for the isolation and for the cumulative recombination of experiment. The early periods present us in their relative crudeness and simplicity with a substitute for the artificial operation of an experiment: following the phenomenon into the more complicated and refined form which it assumes later, is a substitute for the synthesis of experiment." [28]

We see then that for Dewey at this time history was the only available substitute for experiment and, moreover, that he viewed experiment itself as a kind of historical enterprise. The notion of history as a possible alternative for experiment was not original with Dewey; in fact his whole argument is reminiscent of the kind of discussion one finds in *A System of Logic,* especially where Mill considers the various methods and their applicability in the social sciences.[29] Mill also concluded that experiment was not possible in at least one of the "moral sciences," namely, economics, but he argued that the best substitute was the deductive method, and not history. That Mill and Dewey should have divided in this way is quite understandable in the light of Dewey's avowed opposition to formalism. It is important to see, moreover, how this permits Veblen to enter the picture. For it was precisely this aspect of Mill's methodology which Veblen attacked in his own critique of classical economics. And Veblen, like Dewey, appealed to history, to the need for an "evolutionary science."

III. *Thorstein Veblen*

Like Holmes and Dewey, Veblen was strongly influenced by new developments in anthropology. If anything, he was more in-

terested and more learned in that field than they were. So strong
was this influence that he began his famous attack on all previous schools of economics by approving the following statement: "Anthropology is destined to revolutionize the political
and the social sciences as radically as bacteriology has revolu-
tionized the science of medicine." [30] But economics, he complained, was not then in tune with this new note. In short, it
was not an evolutionary science.

But why wasn't it an evolutionary science? To understand this
we might best turn to John Stuart Mill for the light he sheds on
Veblen's lament, and in this way observe concretely how Mill
represents, with Bentham and Austin, the ideology against which
so many of the pioneers of American social science revolted. The
doctrine of economic method associated with Mill is well expressed in *A System of Logic,* but it is even more sharply defined in a brilliant essay which he wrote in 1830 when he was
twenty-four years old, "On the Definition of Political Economy;
and the Method of Investigation Proper to It."[31] For Mill, political economy is to be distinguished from what he calls social
economy or speculative politics—the latter treating "the whole
of man's nature as modified by the social state." Political economy
is rather a branch of social economy, because it does not deal
with the whole of man's nature. It is concerned with man "solely
as a being who desires to possess wealth, and who is capable of
judging of the comparative efficacy of means for attaining that
end. It predicts only such of the phenomena of the social state as
take place in consequence of the pursuit of wealth. It makes entire abstraction of every other human passion or motive; except
those which may be regarded as perpetually antagonizing principles to the desire of wealth, namely, aversion to labour, and
desire of the present enjoyment of costly indulgences." [32] The important point in Mill's statement of the nature of political
economy is his use of the subjunctive conditional mode of assertion in the following passage (the italics are mine): "Political
economy considers mankind as occupied solely in acquiring and

consuming wealth; and aims at showing what is the course of action into which mankind, living in a state of society, *would* be impelled, *if* that motive, except in the degree in which it is checked by the two perpetual counter-motives above adverted to, *were* absolute ruler of all their actions." [33] I emphasize the subjunctive mood of the statement, for it is clear that Mill is not saying that in fact the pursuit of wealth is the sole motive of man. Indeed he goes on to say that the economist does *not* put this forth as a description of man's actual behavior. He denies that any "political economist was ever so absurd as to suppose that mankind are really thus constituted." [34] But later critics of Mill, pre-eminently Veblen and his followers, have treated this view of the economic man as though it were an unconditional assertion in the indicative mood about man's actual psychology. We can see, therefore, why Veblen rejected the view and why he should have found himself in agreement with Dewey on this point. For Veblen this is the acme of "faulty psychology," and what is worse than faulty psychology for an institutionalist? It is simply not true to say that man is governed by this single motive (even where the qualifications about counter-motives are made). And since this is an "assumption" of classical economics which is false, everything which is "deduced" from it is suspect in the eyes of a Veblenian.

There are other aspects of Mill's methodology of economics which contribute to an understanding of what was troubling Veblen. Mill suggests that the economist ought to treat man much as the astronomer treats planets. The astronomer frequently talks about what *would* happen to a planet if it were not subject to the sun's attraction. (This, of course, occurs when he considers it as a particle subject only to Newton's first law of motion.) In such a case, Mill says, he *abstracts* and considers the planet *as if* it were a body outside the sun's gravitational field (although he knows it is not). Just as astronomers pursue this method successfully, so, it is urged, may economists. By considering first how men *would* behave if they were simply dominated by a single motive, Mill believes that economists will come to a good approximation of how they do in fact behave. "This approximation," he points out, "is then to be corrected by making proper allowance for the effects of any impulses of a different description, which can be shown to interfere with the result in any particular case.[35]

There can be no doubt that this was the tradition against which Veblen was rebelling when he rejected the method of classical economics. I don't think he ever clearly formulated for himself the methodological tenets of Mill in a way that left them defensible, but it was a doctrine of this kind that he rejected. I say "of this kind," not to exclude the possibility that there were classical economists who were less able than Mill in methodology, and less cautious in what they asserted about the actual psychology of man. In any case, it should be evident that classical economics was formalistic for Veblen in a sense related to that in which formal logic was formalistic for Dewey, and Austin's jurisprudence was formalistic for Holmes. Dewey in his earliest attack on it construed formal logic as a description of how we think, and contemptuously dismissed it. Holmes insisted that when we study law "we are not studying a mystery but a well-known profession," [36] and what could be more mysterious than the abstract dicta of Austin, formally conceived and having nothing to do with the "bad man"—the man who pays the lawyer to advise him how to keep out of jail? It is for this reason that Holmes, Dewey, and Veblen found themselves arrayed against three apostles of empiricism—Bentham, Mill, and Austin: they weren't empirical enough.

When Veblen complained that economics was not an evolutionary science he was voicing precisely this attitude. Now what was evolutionary science as Veblen understood it? In his essay on it he is, unfortunately, too occupied with asserting that all the traditional schools were not evolutionary, and little concerned with saying what an evolutionary science is. He insists that some things which might be expected to make a science evolutionary really don't. Hence the historical school—Schmoller, Hildebrand, Ashley, Cliffe-Leslie—was "realistic" in so far as it dealt with "facts," but this is not enough, according to Veblen. It failed, in his opinion, to formulate a theory concerning those facts. For him an evolutionary science must present a "theory of a process, of an unfolding sequence." [37] When he comes to the classical economists he finds that even where they do refer to empirical data, and even where they try to present a theory of process, they still fall short of the evolutionary ideal.[38] What, then, is the difference? As we press on we find a statement to the effect that the difference is one of "spiritual attitude"—a rather tender expression for one so tough-minded as Veblen. We press further and find that what he is disturbed about in the classical economists is their addiction to natural law. He is opposed to their formulating an ideal situation and generalizing about that situation without attending to actual economic facts. In some of Veblen's writings this amounts to an objection to the use of a subjunctive conditional like that used by Mill. We cannot, Veblen seems to urge, use hypotheses like "If man were subject to only one motive," "If perfect competition prevailed," because they are false. At other times Veblen seems to be objecting not so much to the use of such hypotheses in science but rather to the fact that certain classical economists also had a moral attitude toward them. They thought either that these hypotheses formulated socially and morally desirable states, or that society was tending toward those states. In both cases Veblen held that some kind of belief in natural law was present. The first alternative involved a moral judgment on society; the second a faith in progress.

We may become a little clearer about Veblen's objection if we compare the situation of the student of mechanics with that of the classical political economist. The former tells us how the distance fallen by a freely falling body depends on the time it takes to fall. He points out, of course, that this law holds only in a vacuum. Thus far his procedure is analogous to that of the economist who insists that his laws hold only for economic

vacuums, so to speak—cases where only one motive is in operation. But the physicist does not add, "And indeed the vacuum is
a highly prized state," or, "The atmosphere tends more and more
toward a vacuum." But the analogous economist, according to
Veblen, not only uses ideal concepts like "economic man" and
"perfect competition," but also admires these kinds of men and
states of society, and looks upon them as ends toward which man
and society are moving.

Thus far we have considered Veblen's attack on the use of abstraction in classical economics, but we have not considered his
attitude toward the use of a priori method in economics. To
understand this we must return to Mill's view.

Mill distinguished between two types of minds—the "practicals" and the "theorists," as he called them. The difference between them may be exhibited by his own illustration. Suppose
we were faced with the following question: Are absolute kings
likely to employ the powers of government for the welfare or
for the oppression of their subjects? How would the practicals
go about settling it? They would try, Mill says, to examine the
conduct of particular despotic monarchs in history and to find out
how they behaved. But the theorists, he says, "would contend
that an observation of the tendencies which human nature has
manifested in the variety of situations in which human beings
have been placed, and especially observation of what passes in
our own minds, warrants us in inferring that a human being in
the situation of a despotic king will make a bad use of power;
and that this conclusion would lose nothing of certainty even if
absolute kings had never existed, or if history furnished us with
no information of the manner in which they had conducted
themselves.[39] The practical uses the a posteriori method, the
theorist the a priori method.[40]

We see how Mill regarded economics as both abstract and a
priori in method—abstract because it abstracted one aspect of
man's behavior and tried to discover how he would behave if he
had only one motive; a priori because it avoided the laborious

and painstaking methods of statistical research. To verify hypotheses by reference to history was for Mill "not the business of science at all, but the application of science." It should be evident why Mill's doctrine was opposed by historicism and institutionalism. It is plain how Dewey's early views also ran counter to Mill's. Dewey's suggestion that we use history as a substitute for experiment where the latter is not possible was clearly the method of the "practical" for Mill—a label which the later Dewey would have accepted gladly.

It is evident how much the historical, evolutionary, cultural attitude united Dewey and Veblen against the abstract and a priori method of Mill. It is also clear why American thinkers rejected so much of the "empiricism" of Bentham and Mill: they were revolting against the least empirical elements of the tradition—apriorism, abstractionism, the hedonic calculus, formal jurisprudence. The grounds of Veblen's rejection of the method of classical economics are very similar to those which led Dewey to reject what he called scholastic formalism in psychology and logic. They also resemble the considerations which led Holmes to reject the so-called mechanical theory of the law as existing in advance and awaiting the judge's discovery of it. Furthermore, to complete the pattern, Veblen also turned to history and culture, to a cross-sectional study of the institutional context of economic behavior as well as to a study of the temporal development of society.[41] Like Dewey and Holmes, he looked to temporal antecedents and cultural concomitants. For this reason we may say that Dewey, Holmes, and Veblen were united in an attempt to destroy what they conceived of as three fictions—the logical, legal, and economic man. In this way they began a tradition in recent American thought which Beard and Robinson continued in political science and history.

IV. *James Harvey Robinson and Charles A. Beard*

The connections between Robinson, Beard, and the revolt against formalism are evident as early as 1908—the year in which

they delivered lectures on history and politics respectively at
Columbia University, in a series devoted to science, philosophy,
and art.[42] Considered in terms of the revolt, Robinson's work is
an expression of historicism, the evolutionary movement in social science, and genetic method. Robinson was anxious to establish the scientific character of history, but at the same time to
distinguish his own from Ranke's version of scientific method in
history.[43] According to Robinson, historians from Thucydides to
Macaulay and Ranke had examined the past "with a view of
amusing, edifying, or comforting the reader." None of these motives, however, can be described as scientific, according to Robinson. He says: "To scan the past with the hope of discovering
recipes for the making of statesmen and warriors, of discrediting
the pagan gods, of showing that Catholic or Protestant is right,
of exhibiting the stages of self-realization of the *Weltgeist,* of
demonstrating that Liberty emerged from the forests of Germany
never to return thither—none of these motives are scientific although they may go hand in hand with much sound scholarship.
But by the middle of the nineteenth century the muse of history,
semper mutabile, began to fall under the potent spell of natural
science. She was no longer satisfied to celebrate the deeds of
heroes and nations with the lyre and shrill flute on the breeze-
swept slopes of Helicon; she no longer durst attempt to vindicate
the ways of God to man. She had already come to recognize that
she was ill-prepared for her undertakings and had begun to
spend her mornings in the library, collating manuscripts and
making out lists of variant readings. She aspired to do even more
and began to talk of raising her chaotic mass of information to
the rank of a science." [44]

It is evident from this passage that Robinson was anxious to
free historical research from moralism and estheticism, a concern
which linked him with Holmes and Veblen in their attempt to
distinguish their disciplines from morals; it is also connected
with the early (though not the later) views of Beard, who held in
1908 that "it is not the function of the student of politics to

praise or condemn institutions or theories, but to understand
and expound them; and thus for scientific purposes it is separated from theology, ethics, and patriotism." [45] We must remember that this amoralism occurred at a time when the confusion
of factual and ethical questions was usually viewed as an instrument of conservatism and reaction. Objectivity was eagerly
sought. Social theorists wanted to expose, to rake the facts, and
to achieve scientific status. Indeed, on this point they were not
seriously opposed to the tradition of Bentham and Mill. Like the
utilitarians, they were part of a reforming movement, and they
too sought to distinguish between what was and what ought to
have been. Nevertheless it should be remembered that the desire
to make this distinction was not regarded as incompatible with
the view that moral judgments are theoretically capable of empirical verification. Certainly this was Dewey's view at the time.[46]

Although Robinson was anxious to exclude moral considerations from the writing of history, he was also anxious to go beyond a mere report of what actually happened. Past historians,
he said, "did take some pains to find out how things really were
—*wie es eigentlich gewesen,* to use Ranke's famous dictum."
Moreover, "to this extent they were scientific, although their motives were mainly literary, moral or religious." What they failed
to do, however, was to "try to determine how things had come
about—*wie es eigentlich geworden.*" And so Robinson concluded that history had remained for two or three thousand
years a record of past events—a definition, he said, which still
satisfied "the thoughtless." "It is one thing to describe what once
was; it is quite another to attempt to determine how it came
about." [47] The old history, he thought, functioned as a dead
formula rather than as a living picture of the past.

His view of history as itself a genetic account of how things
come to be emphasized the concept of development, and was
therefore part of the movement I have called historicism.[48] It
was quite like Holmes' conception of history as something which
furnished explanations of the emergence and meaning of legal

rules; it was wholly sympathetic with Veblen's critique of the historical school; it was like Dewey's view of history as a statement of "how the thing came to be as it is." How did it compare with Beard's view? Let us turn to the latter's lecture on "Politics," delivered in the same year, in the same place, and before much the same audience.

Beard's major complaint about his predecessors revolved about their error in studying juridical-formal relations in the abstract without attention to their roots in the social process. He warned his audience that "official performances are not really separable from other actions of the governmental agents themselves or from many of the actions of the citizens at large." Political facts are organically related to the social process as a whole. "The jural test of what constitutes a political action draws a dividing line where none exists in fact, and consequently any study of government that neglects the disciplines of history, economics, and sociology will lack in reality what it gains in precision. Man as a political animal acting upon political, as distinguished from more vital and powerful motives, is the most unsubstantial of all abstractions. The recognition of this truth has induced students of politics to search in many fields for a surer foothold than law alone can afford." [49] And now just one more quotation to give the flavor of Beard's early conception of political science: "We are coming to realize that a science dealing with man has no special field of data all to itself, but is rather merely a way of looking at the same thing—a view of a certain aspect of human action. The human being is not essentially different when he is depositing his ballot from what he is in the counting house or at the work bench. In the place of a 'natural' man, an 'economic' man, a 'religious' man, or a 'political' man, we now observe the whole man participating in the work of government." [50]

Robinson and Beard taken together present us with a historicist view of history and an organic view of political science. The connection with Dewey, Holmes, and Veblen is only too obvious. In the case of Beard, moreover, even the influence of some of the other historicists is evident. He was younger than they, and his work appeared later. One need only point to the fact that he cites Holmes, Pound, Goodnow, and Bentley in the *Economic Interpretation of the Constitution* (1913) in order to show the intimate ties between his own cultural organicism and that of the key figures in some of the most important intellectual trends of the century—legal realism, sociological jurisprudence, pragmatism. Many of them, of course, did not accept the main thesis of his book on the Constitution,[51] but this must not obscure the broad ground on which Beard was united with the rest in a struggle against what I have called formalism and in an attempt to break down artificial barriers between the social disciplines. Like them, he embarked on a historical and cultural study of man.

CHAPTER III

The American Scene

THE revolt against formalism broke out in a social and economic setting the contours of which were familiar to the revolutionaries, since it was part of their creed to insist upon historical awareness and perspective. And so, while Robinson was formulating methodological programs for the new history, Beard was writing a new history of the American past which came to dominate the minds of the men we are studying as well as the age in which they lived. In 1913 Beard finished two books: *An Economic Interpretation of the Constitution of the United States,* into which we shall look carefully later, and also his *Contemporary American History.* In this second book he presented a tough economic approach to the whole of American politics from 1877 to 1913. When the United States entered the First World War, therefore, the American liberal movement had already been treated to the hardheaded, debunking history which became standard fare in the twenties. In *Contemporary American History* Beard put on a larger canvas the same paints which he laid on so thickly and so intensely in his book on the Constitution. The latter became a more celebrated book because it challenged the intellectual old guard on a very delicate issue, but *Contemporary American History* in its quiet way helped shape the historical imagination of the coming generation. It drew the picture which became a religious icon to the readers of the *New Republic* and *The Nation* and which later was adopted by the *New Masses* after it had been slightly retouched.

Beard had not yet pushed the organicism of the new history to its furthest conclusion, for he did not emphasize the "idea of civilization." He did not attempt a sweeping survey of all art, religion, science, and philosophy; he was writing a modest text-book. It was hardly a study of all the social institutions of America from 1877 to 1913, but it did try to relate the growth of political institutions to economic processes in a way that would help people understand their morning newspapers—a favorite goal of Robinson and Beard. Beard's view of the past was spiritually linked with Veblen's work, as he pointed out, and with the work of Dewey in ethics, as we shall see later; and it described the historical setting of Holmes' legal realism. For this reason it provides a remarkably useful background for a view of all the social philosophies of the day.

Like so many histories, it reveals as much about the historian as it does about the period he describes, and because we are interested in the historian as well as in the period I shall let Beard speak for himself throughout this chapter; only in this way will the emotive nuances of his statements become evident. Beard's avowed purpose was to make more intelligible the leading issues of the politics of 1913, and he contemptuously rejected the task of writing an "artistically balanced" account of the period. Therefore he vigorously put aside "the methods of the almanac and chronicle . . . at the risk of displeasing the reader who expects a little about everything (including the Sioux War and the San Francisco earthquake)." [1] The usual items in history books were consciously omitted in order to treat more fully matters which seemed important to a thinking man of 1913; and a thinking man of 1913 was concerned with trusts, the money question, the tariff, imperialism, and the labor movement. Although Beard was primarily interested in the political problems of 1913, his book was certainly not born of the conviction that history is past politics. It was an attempt to survey the interconnections of the important political and economic aspects of the period between 1877 and 1913. Beard's concern with current history involved no little amount of self-consciousness, as can be seen in the conclusion of his preface: "It is showing no disrespect to our ancestors to be as much interested in our age as they were in theirs; and the doctrine that we can know more about Andrew Jackson whom we have not seen than about Theodore Roosevelt whom we have seen is a pernicious psychological error." [2]

The opening theme in Beard's history is the restoration of white dominion in the South. During President Hayes' administration, which began in 1877, federal troops were withdrawn from the last states in which they were quartered and from that time on the Negroes of the South had to depend on the generosity of the whites and on their own collective efforts for the preservation of their civil and political rights.[3] The first thing to be fought was the disfranchisement that began with the poll tax and a series of ingenious constitutional and statutory provisions of which the "grandfather clause" was the most notorious. The move for disfranchising the Negro was supplemented by intimidation and social discrimination, which was heightened and encouraged by the declared unconstitutionality of legal attempts to ease the situation. In the famous Civil Rights Cases of 1883 the Supreme Court invalidated provisions for social equality and prepared the way for further Jim Crow legislation. So long as radical Republicans held the center of the stage in the aftermath of the Civil War, they "gave to politics a flavor of talk about 'human rights' which was foreign to practical statesmen like Clay and Webster." But soon, Beard tells us, history again supplied practical men who were "primarily interested in economic matters—railways, finance, tariff, corporations, natural resources, and western development. The cash nexus with the South was formed once more, and made far stronger and subtler than in olden days. Agitation of the Negro question became bad form in the North, except for quadrennial political purposes." [4]

The antecedent of the Negro question—the agitation over slavery—had been the leading topic for public debate, and had distracted attention from what Beard, in a tone that foreshadowed his later views on the causes of the Civil War, called "the real staples of politics." [5] For the "real staples" were economic in character—or at least they became so after the Civil War. After presenting some confirming statistics, Beard turned aside to say: "It would be easy to multiply figures showing astounding gains in industry, business, foreign trade, and railways; or to multiply stories of scandalous and unfair practices on the part of financiers, but we are not primarily concerned here with the technique of inventions or the history of promotion. The student of social and political evolution is concerned rather with the effect of such material changes upon the structure of society, that is, with the rearrangements of classes and the development of new groups of interests, which are brought about by altered methods of gaining a livelihood and accumulating fortunes. It is this social transformation that changes the relation of the individual to the state and brings new forces to play in the struggle for political power." [6] He proceeded to describe this great social transformation, after praising Veblen's *The Theory of the Leisure Class* and *The Theory of Business Enterprise* for the acuteness of the analyses they contained. This began a practice of thirty-five years of praise and respect for Veblen, and shows that the common outlook which I hope to consider in these pages was recognized early by those who shared it.

The great social transformation which followed the Civil War began with a battle in the perpetual and more basic war between capitalism and agrarianism. This theme was announced by Beard in his work on the Constitution, and was maintained through the *Economic Origins of Jeffersonian Democracy* and *The Rise of American Civilization*. The Civil War was an episode of this larger struggle in which capitalism triumphed. "The scepter of power now passed definitively from the masters of slaves to the masters of 'free laborers.' " [7] This social transformation was accompanied by an increase in wage workers and a rapid growth of city populations. The demand for labor stimulated immigration from Europe. "Industrial development meant the transformation of vast masses of the people into a proletariat, with all the term implies: an immense population housed in tenements and rented dwellings, the organization of the class into trades-unions, labor parties, and other groups; poverty and degradation on a large scale; strikes, lockouts, and social warfare; the employment of large numbers of women and children in factories; the demand for all kinds of legislation mitigating the evils of the capitalist process; and finally attacks upon the very basis of the industrial system itself." [8] The industrial proletariat came to be a political and economic factor in the decade after the Civil War, with the emergence of unions between 1860 and 1870 and the appearance soon after of the Knights of Labor. In 1877 a dispute between the Baltimore and Ohio Railway and its employees was the first of the great labor struggles at the end of the nineteenth century. Federal troops were called out to buttress ineffectual state militias. Where railways were in the hands of receivers, federal courts intervened, using injunctions, and "the first blood in the contest between the judiciary and labor was drawn." [9]

Beard emphasized that the last, but perhaps the most significant, result of the Industrial Revolution was the rise of enormous combinations and corporations in industry as well as in transportation. More and more business of the country passed steadily into corporate ownership, and the result was a change in the rights, duties, and economic theories of the owners of capital. The trust became a device for improving business organization, but on the whole the decades following the Civil War were characterized by economic anarchy—"laissez faire with a vengeance." After reciting the charges against the railroads which were enumerated by a Senate investigating committee of 1885, Beard concluded with a somewhat Veblenian observation: "In a word, the theories about competition written down in the books on political economy were hopelessly at variance with the facts of business management; the country was at the mercy of the sharp practices of transportation promoters." [10]

The economic revolution which Beard described so succinctly and directly became the central, dynamic factor in the rest of his history. The first subsidiary revolution which follows it is one which he calls "The Revolution in Politics and Law." Senators of the old school, like Clay, Webster, and Calhoun, were succeeded by "apostles of the new order"—Roscoe Conkling, Thomas C. Platt, James Donald Cameron, Leland Stanford, and others, a group described by Beard as "men of affairs—practical men, who organized gigantic enterprises, secured possession of natural resources and franchises, collected and applied capital on a large scale to new business undertakings, built railways, established cities with the advancing line of the western frontier—or represented such men as counsel in the courts of law." [11]

He observed their lack of learning, eloquence, and of understanding of European politics, and described their political philosophy as that of the Cobden-Bright school in England. "They believed in the widest possible extension of the principle of private property, and the narrowest possible restriction of state interference, except to aid private property to increase its gains. They held that all of the natural resources of the country should be transferred to private hands as speedily as possible, at a nominal charge, or no charge at all, and developed with dashing rapidity. They also believed that the great intangible social property created by community life, such as franchises for street railways, gas, and electricity, should be transformed into private property. They supplemented their philosophy of property by a philosophy of law and politics, which looked upon state interference, except to preserve order, and aid railways and manufacturers in their enterprises, as an intrinsic evil to be resisted at every point; and they developed a system of jurisprudence which, as Senators having the confirming power in appointments and as counsel for corporations before the courts of the United States, they succeeded in transforming into judicial decisions. Some of them were doubtless corrupt, as was constantly charged, but the real explanation of their resistance to government intervention is to be found in their philosophy, which, although consonant with their private interests, they identified with public good." [12]

This senatorial philosophy, it would appear from Beard's ironical description in 1913, was one of the major bulwarks of the established order confronting the generation of philosophers, economists, lawyers, historians, and political scientists with whom he allied himself. The rocklike forms of Roscoe Conkling, Mark Hanna, and their assistants loomed large before Dewey and Veblen and Holmes and their disciples. The first practical accomplishment of this new political phalanx, according to Beard, was "writing laissez faire into the Constitution," an action which began with Justice Field's dissent in the Slaughter House Cases of 1873, in which the Fourteenth Amendment was construed in a manner to be made popular later by Conkling.[13] The majority of the Supreme Court, however, did not share Field's view, and so those admirers of the Fourteenth Amendment who looked to the court to establish a federal defense of corporations and business enterprises were disappointed. But they were not permanently disheartened, for the court moved from the doctrine of noninterference with state legislatures to the belief that it had a duty to review all and every kind of economic legislation of the states. But the shift was not sudden, and Beard was bold enough to assert that "had a veto power of this character been suddenly vested in any small group . . . a political revolt would have speedily followed." Instead, the power was built up by gradual accretions, and it consequently took a long time for "the advocates of leveling democracy, leading an attack on corporate rights and privileges, [to discover] that the courts were the bulwarks of laissez faire and [to direct] their battalions in that direction." [14]

Although the account is made to sound as objective as possible, Beard's feeling is thinly disguised by the impersonal style of the textbook. He was not sympathetic with the court in its defense of corporate power, but, interestingly enough, allowed himself one political remark which showed that he was no extreme "advocate of leveling democracy." He urged a distinction between the power of the court and the manner in which it was exercised, and suggested that "it is possible to hold that the court has been too tender to corporate rights in assuming the power of judicial review, and at the same time recognize the fact that such a power, vested somewhere in the national government, is essential to the continuance of industries and commerce on a national scale." [15] Although the court had declared very little social legislation invalid and, in fact, had "been inclined to take a more liberal view of such matters than the supreme courts of the states," it did invalidate the ten-hour law in the case of *Lochner* v. *New York*. In this connection Beard cited Justice Holmes' celebrated dissent, underscoring his contention that the case "was decided on an economic theory which a large part of the country did not entertain," and quoting with obvious approval Holmes' gibe about the Fourteenth Amendment's failure to enact Herbert Spencer's *Social Statics*.[16]

The conditions created by the economic revolution described by Beard were not immediately reflected in political literature and programs. They were only vaguely understood by statesmen brought up in the days of the stagecoach and the water mill. And although the course of American capitalism might have been foreseen by turning to Europe, particularly to England, "American politicians believed, or at least contended, that the United States lived under a special economic dispensation and that the grave social problems which had menaced Europe for more than a generation when the Civil War broke out could never arise on American soil." [17] But arise they did, and the history of American party politics from 1877 to 1892 was full of issues that might have engaged the parties in decisive battle had they chosen to take opposing sides. The situation, however, did not develop until 1896.

Beard spoke for his own generation when he called 1896 a turning point in the development of American society. The monetary issue, around which the election battle was supposedly fought, was simply a manifestation of a broader and more deep-rooted crisis. "Deep, underlying class feeling found its expression in the conventions of both parties, and particularly that of the Democrats, and forced upon the attention of the country, in a dramatic manner, a conflict between great wealth and the lower middle and working classes, which had hitherto been recognized only in obscure circles. The sectional or vertical cleavage in American politics was definitely cut by new lines running horizontally through society." [18] Another line of conflict split society: the Eastern creditors were opposed by a wave of Western protest against the objectionable methods of great corporations, which had been exposed to the public view by fierce criticism and many legislative investigations.

After a survey of federal legislation from 1877 to 1896, Beard concluded that by and large there had been no decisive effort to placate the poorer sections of the population by distinct class legislation. As a consequence, "the accumulation of vast fortunes, many of which were gained either by fraudulent manipulations, or shady transactions within the limits of the law but condemned by elementary morals, and the massing of millions of the proletariat in the great industrial cities were bound in the long run to bring forth political cleavages as deep as the corresponding social cleavage. The domination of the federal government by the captains of machinery and capital was destined to draw out a counter movement on the part of the small farmers, the middle class, and the laborers. Mutterings of this protest were heard in the seventies; it broke forth in the Populist and Socialist movements in the nineties; it was voiced in the Democratic campaign of 1896; silenced awhile by a wave of imperialism, it began to work a transformation in all parties at the opening of the new century." [19]

This protest and dissent found political expression in a wave of third or minor parties—the Prohibitionist party, which held its first convention in 1872, the Labor Reformers, who met in the same year, the Greenbackers, and the Socialist Labor party of 1892. "Although the socialism of Karl Marx had by this time won a wide influence among the working classes of Europe, there are few if any traces of it in the Socialist Labor platform of 1892. That platform says nothing about the inevitable contest between labor and capitalism, or about the complete public ownership of all the means of transportation and production. On the contrary, it confines its statements to concrete propositions, including the political reforms of the initiative, referendum, and recall, all of which have since been advocated by leaders in the old parties." [20] Beard added that the small vote received in 1892 by the Socialist Labor candidate was no evidence of the strength of the labor protest, for the Populist party in that year also supported pretty much the same principles and appealed to the working class as well as to the farmers.

Agitation for free silver was so great that even the Republican convention of 1896 was split on the question. But once a group of silverites had walked out of the hall, the party declared itself without qualification for sound money. The division in the Republican party was mild compared to what happened at the Democratic convention. The election of 1892 served as an omen, for the agrarian party had polled a million votes and had elected members to Congress. It was well organized and had arisen "from a mass of discontent which was justified, if misdirected. It was no temporary wave, as superficial observers have imagined. It had elements of solidity which neither of the old parties could ignore or cover up. No one was more conscious of this than the Western and Southern leaders in the Democratic party. They had been near the base of action, and they thought that what the Eastern leaders called a riot was in fact the beginning of a revolution. Unwilling to desert their traditional party, they decided to make the party desert its traditions, and they came to the Democratic convention prepared for war to the hilt. From the opening to the close, the Democratic convention in Chicago was vibrant with class feeling." [21] We need not recite with Beard the details of the convention. Bryan was nominated on a platform which made bimetallism the central plank, and delivered his famous "cross of gold" speech. And in the nominating speeches the revolution in American politics was even more evident than it had been in the debates on the platform. The enemy had been defeated, and the convention was captured by the radicals, who no longer had to compromise or conciliate their opponents. "The campaign which followed the conventions was the most remarkable in the long history of our quadrennial spectacles. . . . Argument, party organization and machinery, the lavish use of money, and terror won the day for the Republicans." But "the attention of the country," Beard remarked, "shortly after the campaign of 1896, was diverted to the spectacular events of the Spanish War, and for a time appeals to patriotism subdued the passions of the radicals." [22]

The Republicans won in 1896, but the large vote for Bryan and his platform made it clear, according to Beard, that new social elements had entered American politics. "It was fortunate for the conservative interests that the quarrel with Spain came shortly after Mr. McKinley's election, and they were able to employ that ancient political device, 'a vigorous foreign policy,' to divert the public mind from domestic difficulties." And then one of those characteristically acid remarks for which Beard became well known: "This was particularly acceptable to the populace at the time, for there had been no war for more than thirty years, and, contrary to their assertion on formal occasions, the American people enjoy wars beyond measure, if the plain facts of history are allowed to speak." [23] But the war and the vigorous foreign policy were not simply political devices; they were expressions of imperialism. "There were not wanting . . . signs that the United States was prepared economically to accept that type of imperialism that had long been dominant in British politics and had sprung into prominence in Germany, France, and Italy during the generation following the Franco-Prussian War. This newer imperialism does not rest primarily upon a desire for more territory, but rather upon the necessity for markets in which to sell manufactured goods and for opportunities to invest surplus accumulations of capital. It begins in a search for trade, advances to intervention on behalf of the interests involved, thence to protectorates and finally to annexation. By the inexorable necessity of the present economic system, markets and safe investment opportunities must be found for surplus products and accumulated capital. All the older countries being overstocked and also forced into this new forms of international rivalry, the drift is inevitably in the direction of the economically backward countries: Africa, Asia, Mexico, and South America. Economic necessity thus overrides American isolation and drives the United States into world politics." [24] We see, then, that in 1913 Beard was advancing a view of imperialism very close to that of the Marxists, and was therefore armed with an interpretation when the First World War broke out. He was already presenting in popular form an economic approach to war which was to become almost a commonplace in the twenties and thirties, and to be forgotten by some in the forties of this century.

The years immediately following the war with Spain were years of great prosperity in business. The Dingley tariff law of 1897 had contributed to prosperity by raising protection to the highest point since the Civil War, and the Spanish War, of course, had stimulated trade. "But the real cause lay in the nature of the economic processes which had produced the periodical cycles of inflation and collapse during the nineteenth century. Having recovered from a collapse previous to the war, inflation and capitalization on a gigantic scale set in and did not run their course until a débâcle in 1907." [25] Corporate combination continued its hectic pace. "The formation of trusts and the consolidation of older combinations . . . were commensurate in scale with the gigantic financial power created by capitalist accumulations. . . . The period of the later seventies and eighties, as has been shown, was a period of hot competition followed by pools, combinations, and trusts. The era which followed the Spanish War differed in degree rather than in kind, but it was marked by financial operations on a scale which would have staggered earlier promoters. Perhaps it would be best to say that the older school merely found its real strength at the close of the century, for the new financing was done by Vanderbilt, Astor, Gould, Morgan, and Rockefeller interests, the basis of which had been laid earlier. There was, in fact, no break in the process, save that which was made by the contraction of the early nineties. But the operations of the new era were truly grand in their conception and execution." [26]

When McKinley was elected in 1900 populism had been pronounced dead, but, Beard insisted, this was the result of only a superficial examination of the social scene. True, the country had repudiated Bryan twice; it was high on a wave of prosperity created by the Spanish War, and congratulated itself on its success in an imperialist venture. But populism was far from dead. Defeated in the national elections, it set to work from the bottom up and campaigned for a series of reforms in the interest of "direct democracy." It stimulated the various movements for referendum, initiative, recall, the direct primary, woman's suffrage, the direct election of United States senators. When it accomplished some of its milder reforms it died naturally as an organizational factor in American politics. Those of its devotees who were satisfied with purely political gains trickled back into the old parties, but those who pressed further for economic reform soon found themselves in or close to the ranks of socialism.

In 1896 the Socialist Labor party had polled more than eighty thousand votes. Its small political pressure was supplemented by the pressure of events; the bloody struggles at Homestead, Coeur d'Alene, Buffalo, and Pullman in the eighties and nineties "moved the country as no preachments of abstract social philosophy could ever have done." [27] Labor was gathering its forces, and soon the Social Democratic party was formed with Eugene V. Debs as its presidential candidate. It polled ninety-six thousand votes; steps were taken to organize more permanently, and the Socialist party was formed in 1901. In 1904 it polled over four hundred thousand votes, a figure which was doubled in 1912. The IWW was also formed in 1904 and inaugurated its syndicalist appeal to direct action under the leadership of Bill Haywood.

At this point in American history, Beard says, a "counter-reformation" occurred, and it is important to have his own description of it:

Just as the Protestant Revolt during the sixteenth century was followed by a counter-reformation in the Catholic Church which swept away many abuses, while retaining and fortifying the essential principles of the faith, so the widespread and radical discontent of the working classes with the capitalist system hitherto obtaining produced a counter-reformation on the part of those who [wished] to preserve its essentials while curtailing some of its excesses. This counter-reformation made a deep impress upon American political thinking and legislation at the turning of the new century. More than once during his presidency Mr. [Theodore] Roosevelt warned the capitalists that a reform of abuses was the price which they would have to pay in order to save themselves from a socialist revolution. Eminent economists turned aside from free trade and laissez faire to consider some of the grievances of the working class and many abandoned the time-honored discussion of "economic theories," in favor of legislative programs embracing the principles of state socialism, to which countries like Germany and Great Britain were already committed.

Charity workers whose function had been hitherto to gather up the wrecks of civilization and smooth their dying days began to talk of "a war for the prevention of poverty," and an examination of their concrete legislative proposals revealed the acceptance of some of the principles of state socialism. Unrestricted competition and private property had produced a mass of poverty and wretchedness in the great cities which constituted a growing menace to society, and furnished themes for social orators. Social workers of every kind began the detailed analysis of the causes of specific cases of poverty and arrived at the conclusion that elaborate programs of "social legislation" were necessary to the elimination of a vast mass of undeserved poverty.[28]

Although Beard made no direct appeal for action, we can be sure that he was part of that social counter-reformation as it expressed itself on the intellectual and ideological level. In his concept of the American Counter-Reformation he formulated a category which embraced the generation of economists, philosophers, lawyers, historians, and political scientists who were represented by Veblen, Dewey, Holmes, Robinson, and Beard himself. They criticized some of the more glaring evils of capitalism, but their political affiliations were never revolutionary. Rather, each of them functioned as an American Erasmus, calling from his classroom or courtroom. This habit they first developed in the early years of the present century, when the country was faced with the possibility of a revolutionary political transformation. This was the period in which ethics and history were put to work in a new way, and the result was the outlook dominating the collaboration of Dewey and Tufts, and that of Robinson and Beard. American history and philosophy became concerned with the Negro problem, imperialism, the money question, the trusts, and the labor movement. To these problems the band of new scholars hoped to apply scientific method. They continued their hope with varying degrees of steadfastness through the wars and depressions that awaited them.

CHAPTER IV

The New History and the New Ethics

THE revolt against formalism was the intellectual forerunner of more positive ideas. Its supporters documented and supported their methodological convictions by writing on the concrete questions raised by the social, political, and legal problems of the early twentieth century. Their methodology was not to be wasted and developed for its own sake, and therefore they tried to apply it to specific problems in different fields. They proceeded to formulate a "new psychology," a "new education," a "new economics," a "new history," a "new philosophy," a "new jurisprudence." This was the age of "news," as Van Wyck Brooks observed, an age which was to see its first political expression in Wilson's New Freedom and its apogee in the New Deal.

The aspect of this era with which I am concerned is relatively philosophical. John Chamberlain in his *Farewell to Reform* devotes a chapter to what he calls "Philosophical Progressivism" and treats the period in some detail, but his conception of philosophy is less technical than mine, closer to what is meant when we speak of the philosophy of Theodore Roosevelt or of Woodrow Wilson. Ideas like historicism and organicism are not emphasized by Chamberlain, although he does note the importance of Marx and the Hegelian tradition. In the next few chapters I want to consider the uses to which these philosophical credos were put in the years before the First World War. The clearest indications are to be found in Holmes' epochal talk, "The Path of the Law," which he delivered in 1897; in Veblen's *Theory of the Leisure Class* and Dewey's *School and Society*, both of which appeared in 1899; in *The Development of Modern Europe*, the famous text which Robinson and Beard put out in 1907; in *Ethics* (1908) by Dewey and his Chicago colleague James H. Tufts. As textbooks reaching a wide audience, the two last were distinguished by their demonstration of the practical importance of history and of the theory of morality. In trying to link history and ethics with the concrete problems of society, Robinson, Beard, Dewey, and Tufts breathed new life into subjects which had become thin, dusty, and remote in the hands of their academic predecessors of the nineteenth century. History ceased to be a tale of regal insanity and political intrigue, and ethics was no longer a dreary catalogue of the virtues, having no connection with trusts, imperialism, and the labor movement. In spite of having come after the path-breaking work of Holmes and Veblen, these books written from the point of view of the new history and the new ethics formulate more clearly the social and intellectual context of the new movement of thought, and therefore it is useful to consider them first.

The Development of Modern Europe is a concrete expression of the views which Robinson urged in his 1908 lecture on history. He and Beard were dissatisfied with other history manuals for failing to connect the past with the present, and, in a tone which Beard continued in 1913, they chided other teachers of history for paying "a mysterious respect to the memory of Datis and Artaphernes which they deny to gentlemen in frock coats, like Gladstone and Gambetta." They openly confessed their association with the new history by admitting that they had "consistently subordinated the past to the present," and that it had been their "ever-conscious aim to enable the reader to catch up with his own times; to read intelligently the foreign news in the morning paper; to know what was the attitude of Leo XIII toward the Social Democrats even if he has forgotten that of Innocent III toward the Albigenses." [1] In their attachment to the frock coat and the morning newspaper they felt no guilt. In permitting the present to dominate the past they thought they hadn't "dealt less fairly with the general outline of European history during the last two centuries than they would have done had they merely narrated the events with no ulterior object." [2] And should anyone have accused them of disregarding evidence in preferring Leo to Innocent, they assured the reader that "there has been no distortion of the facts in order to bring them into relation to any particular conception of the present or its tendencies." [3] They construed history pragmatically, as a study which could and should contribute directly to the understanding and explanation of current affairs.

The view that history can contribute to our understanding and to the explanation of the present depends upon certain philosophical assumptions. One is the view, popular since Hume, that explanation is based on scientific law. To explain something is to present its causes, which, according to Hume, occur earlier than the event to be explained. To find out why we feel a sensation of heat we turn to our personal history and discover that we have just come in contact with a flame. But in order to know that this particular sensation of heat was caused by that particular flame we must know at least that touching flames is regularly followed by the sensation of heat. And to know that this regularly occurs is to know that some generalization or law holds. The view, therefore, that history can explain supposes that the historian is familiar with *laws* of social behavior, if the events he wants to explain are primarily social in character. It follows that the historian must be familiar not only with the isolated facts and events which form a bare chronicle; he must also be familiar with those generalizations which help us infer the occurrence of the event we call the effect from its cause. For this reason the new historical approach demands a greater familiarity with the social sciences, the disciplines which hope to establish important generalizations or laws of human, social behavior; and Robinson urged that all the social disciplines are indispensable allies of history.

The notion of cause, however, is not peculiar to the new history; the latter does not merely urge us to explain any and all events by reference to history. The new historian is particularly anxious to explain *present* events—those which are approximately contemporaneous with the historian himself. It is obvious that a twentieth-century historian who hopes to explain the advent of the medieval economy may, in a typically causal manner, describe the events leading up to the Arab control of the Mediterranean, and in this way try to explain the appearance of the Middle Ages. But, one sometimes suspects, Robinson would have regarded such a preoccupation as inconsistent with the basic tenets of the new history. Why? Certainly not because the medieval historian is forsaking the task of explanation. Clearly he uses the notion of cause. The answer, it would seem, is: precisely because *in 1907* the medievalist was interested in explaining medieval events rather than modern events; because he was more interested in explaining why Innocent III had the attitude he had toward the Albigenses than in explaining why Leo XIII had the attitude *he* had toward the Social Democrats. The distinguishing mark of the new history, then, is to be found, not in its concern with historical explanation alone, but in its concern with historical explanation of the *present*. The over-all effect of this concern upon the writing of Robinson and Beard is fairly obvious. They are bound to connect the past with the present, and so their histories must begin at the beginning and end with a description of the moment in history at which they put the last period to the last sentence. Consequently they trace things right through to the end—bitter or sweet. Whether they intended to impose this obligation on every historian is not too clear. What we must observe is the fact that the new historians were especially concerned with the present.

This concern represented the pragmatic tendency in their writing—"pragmatic" not necessarily in the technical sense of Dewey and James, but in the sense of demanding some useful accomplishment of the historian. "Useful," of course, in a limited sense; the historian must help his reader understand the morning newspaper.

Robinson, the more articulate spokesman of the new history, did not always maintain that the past must be directly connected with the immediate present or that all histories had to end with an explanation of events in the morning newspaper. On some relaxed occasions he found it possible to justify the activities of the medieval historian living in the twentieth century. How? Usually by pointing out that concern with the Middle Ages does have something to contribute to our understanding of the present. When pressed, Robinson did not urge his opposition to the study of something as remote as medieval history, but rather to concern with *trivial* events of the past, such as the murders, idiosyncrasies, and names of absurdly remote kings and warriors—Magnus VI (1263-1280), Erik II (1280-1299), Haakon V (1299-1319). If such data are trivial, what are the important elements of history? Institutions—"the ways in which people have thought and acted in the past, their tastes and achievements in many fields besides the political." [4] These are the important entities of history, and they are defined by Robinson as they were by Veblen. Since institutions are of primary importance according to this view, we may study remote ones as well as recent ones, and a history which concludes with the thirteenth century may well pass muster before the scrutiny of the new historian. If it should by any chance include Magnus VI, it should concern itself with him as a figure related to the institutions of his time. Only then can it be relevant to the problems of today, for the institutions of the past form a more significant chain with the present than the "kingly nexus." For this reason Beard's study of the Constitutional Convention was quite within the scope of the new history because the Constitution is definitely connected with the key institutions of colonial and modern American society. Robinson and Beard, at this stage in their development of the new history, combined a historical interest with a pragmatic reforming spirit. Like Marx and the liberal-radical wing of nineteenth-century historicism, they saw no inconsistency in their historical interest in the past and their anxiety to convert the present into a more decent future. Their study of history was not motivated by nostalgia for the past, but rather by concern for the future.

A similar combination of interests turned up in the *Ethics* which Dewey and Tufts published in 1908. It is composed of three parts, one on the beginnings and growth of morality, a second on the theory of the moral life, and a third on "the world of action." The second, it should be said in passing, is the only one devoted to the kind of question that most contemporary philosophers deal with in their ethical writings. It is the only section devoted to what has been called the analysis of ethical notions, the attempt to clarify the meaning of words like "good," "bad," "right," and "wrong." The first and third sections reveal a genetic and pragmatic interest in the new ethics, and here Dewey and Tufts were aware of the need for an explanation. Why deal with the history of morality and moral ideas?[5] Among the reasons given for examining earlier stages of moral behavior is the fact that they are simpler than our own, and by studying them we may come to understand our own complex society and moral situation better. Here, of course, Dewey and Tufts were using the evolutionist notion of development from the simple to the complex, and agreeing with a methodological viewpoint that dominated the sociology of their time. They argued in the manner of their sociologist friend, W. I. Thomas, who defended evolutionary studies on pedagogical grounds in his extremely influential *Source Book for Social Origins*: "In the lower orders of brain the structure and meaning are writ large, and by working up from the simpler to the more complex types, and noting the modification of structure

and function point by point, the student is finally able to understand the frightfully intricate human organ, or has the best
chance of doing so." [6]

The second reason for the concern of Dewey and Tufts with
moral history was connected with Tylor's notion of survival.
They pointed out that the moral life was filled with rudiments
and survivals. Some of our present standards and ideals were
formed at one period in the past, and some at another; some
applied to the conditions of 1908, some didn't; and some were
at variance with others. They hoped to explain apparent conflicts in moral judgments by showing how the judgments came
to be formed in the first instance. We shall see later how Veblen
turned this same notion to use in his examination of leisure-
class culture. We see now how this is bound up with some of
the early views of Holmes. Dewey and Tufts were clearly sub-
scribing to Tylor's conviction that anthropology was a reformer's
science; indeed they might have generalized this with Robinson
and Beard and concluded that history was a reformer's science.

Dewey and Tufts added other reasons for studying the history
of morality. They urged that a study of past moral codes was
broadening. They were inheritors of the cosmopolitanism of
the Enlightenment, Middle Western professors who did not suffer from xenophobia; and so they pointed out the dangers of
insularity to their students. "Until we have been led . . . to
compare our own conduct with that of others it probably does
not occur to us that our own standards are also peculiar, and
hence in need of explanation." [7] Thus Dewey and Tufts in their
quiet way endorsed the liberal, radical attitude toward history.
With Condorcet, they urged the study of history as a record of
endless change in society and as evidencing the growth and development of morality. "Merely to examine the present," they continued, "may easily give the impression that the moral life is not
a life, a moving process, something still in the making—but a
changeless structure. There is moral progress as well as a moral
order. This may be discovered by an analysis of the very nature

of moral conduct, but it stands out more clearly and impressively if we trace the actual development in history." [8] The first part of the *Ethics,* therefore, was to describe morality in the making.

Following this description of morality in the making, the second part of the work comes closest to what some contemporaries would call the analysis of ethical concepts. With this Dewey was mainly concerned. But in the third part both authors tried to show the relevance of all of this to "the world of action," and here their interest in the details of social morality emerged. It was here that they tried to apply ethics to social problems: ". . . if we can discover ethical principles these ought to give some guidance for the unsolved problems of life which continually present themselves for decision. Whatever may be true for other sciences it would seem that ethics at least ought to have some practical value. 'In this theater of man's life it is reserved for God and the angels to be lookers on.' Man must act; and he must act well or ill, rightly or wrongly. If he has reflected, has considered his conduct in the light of the general principles of human order and progress, he ought to be able to act more intelligently and freely, to achieve the satisfaction that always attends on scientific as compared with uncritical or rule-of-thumb practice." [9]

The reason for this concern with the world of action was made fairly explicit. Although Dewey and Tufts thought that questions of practical politics and economics were at that time "unsettled" as compared with those in "personal" or "individual" ethics, they felt obliged to discuss them because of their urgency. "When the whole civilized world is giving its energies to the meaning and value of justice and democracy, it is intolerably academic that those interested in ethics should have to be content with conceptions already worked out." [10] And what was the most urgent question in 1908 for academics trying not to be intolerably academic? The question was individualism versus socialism, and the plan of Dewey and Tufts was to show that both the extremes were pitting a priori claims against each other.

In the light of this Dewey said with Tufts then and forever after: "The need of the hour seems . . . to be the application of methods of more deliberate analysis and experiment. The extreme conservative may deprecate any scrutiny of the present order; the ardent radical may be impatient of the critical and seemingly tardy processes of the investigator; but those who have considered well the conquest which man is making of the world of nature cannot forbear the conviction that the cruder method of trial and error and the time-honored method of prejudice and partisan controversy need not longer dominate the regulation of life and society. They hope for a larger application of the scientific method to the problems of human welfare and progress." [11]

The similarity between the *Ethics* and *The Development of Modern Europe* is remarkable. It appears not only in the attempt to combine history, theory, and practice, but also in the conception of the problems which faced the world of 1908. The last chapter of Robinson and Beard dealt with "some of the great problems of today," very much as Dewey and Tufts concluded their work with the world of action. And just as the pragmatists felt that things were unsettled, so the new historians claimed to be ignorant of the likely outcome of the unrest and agitation which they saw. "Even if all of us cannot contribute directly to their solution," they said mournfully, "we should regard it as our duty," they added solemnly, "to grasp the main difficulties and dangers which Europe and the world at large now face, and to follow intelligently the discussion that goes on about them." [12] The great problems of the day, as viewed by Robinson and Beard, fell under three broad heads: the responsibilities of modern government, the war on poverty, and the progress and effects of natural science. Under the first fell the three great political questions of the day: "Who shall control the government? How far shall the government be forbidden to interfere with the independence of individual citizens in the conduct of their own affairs? What, on the other hand, shall be the responsibilities of the government in protecting the members of society, preventing them from injuring one another, and in promoting the general welfare?" [13]

The state of Europe in 1907 was described in the following words, and we may read them today with mixed feelings: "Rousseau, it will be remembered, declared in his popular little treatise, *The Social Contract,* that the will of the people should be law, and this great principle of democratic government was embodied in the first French constitution. It is now practically adopted in all the states of Europe with the exception of Turkey and Russia." [14] The specific political tendencies which Robinson and Beard found encouraging were the extension of suffrage for male adults, the agitation for woman's suffrage, the demand for written constitutions and for systems of responsible ministries, the demand for the right of the initiative and the referendum. They recalled that the French National Assembly was particularly impressed with the things that government was *not* to do, an observation which served to introduce a ticklish subject. But, Robinson and Beard continued, "It has . . . become clearer and clearer that the functions of government cannot be confined to merely observing the 'imprescriptible' rights of its citizens, maintaining the peace, and repelling the attacks of foreign powers. New responsibilities are constantly being laid upon the governments, both central and local." [15] These responsibilities had been increased by the Industrial Revolution, the development of transportation, and the demands for scientific sanitation. The great social problems of the day revolved about the distribution of wealth, the income tax, strikes, insurance for sickness and old age, unemployment, and the problems of urbanization.

In spite of advances in invention and science and in spite of attempts at the improvement of the condition of the working class, "a large part of the population of even the most civilized countries spend their lives in poverty, ignorance, and wretchedness, due principally to low wages, uncertain employment, and overcrowding in the great cities." [16] This was the stimulus for the "War on Poverty," and they recited the skirmishes which had already begun—the history of the trade unions, the cooperative movements, socialism from the Utopians through Marx and Engels. But in spite of all favorable signs, they concluded with doubts concerning the future. "Whether this mutual hostility of poor and rich will deepen in Europe and bring on a new social conflict, or whether there will be concessions on both sides resulting in gradual reform, the future alone can determine. It is clear in any case that the evils of our present organization are being more and more generally understood, and there is hope that many shocking inequalities may gradually be done away with." [17] And so the new historians, in spite of their genius and admiration for historical explanation, were noncommittal about the future. Yet they had faith in the growth of knowledge and understanding. Like Dewey and Tufts, they were content with *presenting* problems to college students of the pre-World War I generation. They urged peaceable reflection and the method of science upon those who were about to witness the first great war and the first great revolution of the twentieth century. This attachment to science was evident throughout the last section of the book. Its progress and its effects were praised throughout, and historians were urged to study its development, "to observe the ways in which it is constantly changing our habits and our views of man, his origin and destiny." [18] Indeed, the very last paragraph envisages "the possibility of a new kind of history in which kings and warriors will give place to men of science." [19]

One cannot read Robinson and Beard on Europe, or Dewey and Tufts on ethics, without deeply appreciating the atmosphere in which they lived, and the liberal humanitarianism which they wished so much to communicate. They tried their best to give a fair account of socialist ideas (duly supplemented, of course, by a report of arguments against them); they were enthusiastic if not wholly competent reporters of new discoveries in the natural sciences, and they hoped to apply similar methods to social problems. The last chapter of *The Development of Modern Europe* was appropriately decorated with two full-page portraits of the bearded prophets who dominated their age— Charles Darwin and Karl Marx.

CHAPTER V

The Path of the Law

EVEN before the historians and the philosophers of the new liberalism came to assert the need for a revolt against formalism and to give it concrete expression in their combination of history, theory, and practice, Holmes was finding another path to the liberalism which they all came to share. Holmes did not begin his public career as a tribune of the people, but rather as a Harvard professor and a solemn judge of the Massachusetts Supreme Court. In 1881 he had published his *Common Law,* which, as we have seen, was one of the landmarks in the revolt against formalism. As a friend of William James and Charles Peirce, he had come in contact with the new philosophy—pragmatism—even before Dewey, and his friend Brooks Adams had already introduced him to the theories of historical materialism and social revolution. When he came to deliver his speech, "The Path of the Law," in 1897 he was by no means a conscious spokesman of anything close to the populism of the times. But he was familiar with the history of philosophy and political science, and well read in the problems of traditional jurisprudence. He was concerned with the fundamental concepts of his discipline, and somewhat worried about the decay of the legal profession in a world of corporations. He had begun his interest in ideas "twisting the tail of the Kosmos" with his friend Bill

James, but soon he left idle speculation for the Army and the law court. There he hoped to maintain his ideals, and throughout his life he felt obliged to defend war and law as honorable professions. Small wonder that his first qualms about the law were evident in those years when Veblen could say: "The lawyer is exclusively occupied with the details of predatory fraud, either in achieving or in checkmating chicane, and success in the profession is therefore accepted as marking a large endowment of that barbarian astuteness which has always commanded men's respect and fear." [1]

"We all want happiness," Holmes said in 1897. "And happiness, I am sure from having known many successful men, cannot be won simply by being counsel for great corporations and having an income of fifty thousand dollars." And so he was interested in the philosophy of the law, in "the remoter and more general aspects of the law . . . which give it universal interest." [2] As a judge his concern with litigation was less than that of Veblen's specialist in chicanery, the corporation counsel, although Veblen would have found an equally damning description of the judge and scholarly legal philosopher. But Holmes was probably impervious to Veblen's attack on the leisure class, and besides, there was no corner to which one could flee in the nineties in order to escape Veblen's irony or contempt. The corporation counsel who was pilloried in one chapter of *The Theory of the Leisure Class* would have found himself pilloried in another, even after he had surrendered his fifty-thousand-dollar income for a life amidst all the wisdom of the past. But this is more an index of Veblen's mind than it is of Holmes', and Veblen's we shall look at later.

When Holmes called upon lawyers to think more about general concepts and less about secure incomes, he was not leaving this world. He was not asking for a return to the monastery and the mysteries of traditional jurisprudence. For he said very plainly in the opening sentence of "The Path of the Law": "When we study law we are not studying a mystery but a well-known profession. We are studying what we shall want in order to appear before judges, or to advise people in such a way as to keep them out of court." [3]

Unlike Dewey and Beard in 1908 and Veblen in 1899, Holmes was not manifestly disturbed by the state of American society. Nor did he ever become active in the movement to change it by political action and reformist polemic. His contribution was always from on high. As a Justice of the Supreme Court and a leisure-class New Englander, his occasional help was welcomed gratefully by those who were striving to change American society, but his liberalism was always phrased in the Olympian tones proper to the judge and the removed scholar. For this reason I consider his views not as an expression of political radicalism in the nineties, but rather as an expression of a methodological radicalism consonant with that of Beard, Dewey, and Veblen at the time. Holmes' direct political inspiration to this group came later—in 1905, for example, when he wrote his famous dissent in the Lochner case.

"The Path of the Law" is an important document for us because it presents Holmes' views on the definition of law, on the relations between law and ethics, history, economics, and logic. When Holmes urged that the law was not a mystery and that the study of the law was devoted, in part, to advising people how to keep out of court, he was revealing a concern with one meaning of the word "law" as it is used. Holmes recognized that all or almost all words are equivocal. In his essay, "The Theory of Legal Interpretation" (1899), he said: "It is not true that in practice (and I know no reason why theory should disagree with the facts) a given word or even a given collocation of words has one meaning and no other. A word generally has several meanings, even in the dictionary. You have to consider the sentence in which it stands in order to decide which of those meanings it bears in the particular case." [4] In effect, Holmes applied this rule to the word "law" itself in the early sentences of "The Path of the Law." Limiting its sense to that which clients pay counsel for knowing, he concluded that "the prophecies of what the courts will do in fact, and nothing more pretentious, are what I mean by the law." [5]

There are at least two things that ought to be observed here in connection with this definition of the law. First of all, it is eminently consistent with Veblen's view that a lawyer is expert in achieving or checkmating chicane, a task which demands great skill in predicting what the courts will do in fact. The second point of interest is Holmes' emphasis on *prediction*. The use of this is what has led many to insist that Holmes is a pragmatist and that legal realism, the school which grew up under him, is really legal pragmatism. With the epistemological connections between pragmatism and legal realism we shall not be concerned here, except to point out that philosophies other than pragmatism have seen the value of prediction, and that it is questionable whether the concern with prediction of itself makes Holmes a pragmatist. It is important to insist, however, that the closeness of Peirce, James, and Holmes in their youth as well as the "practical" character of Holmes' definition of the law suggests a very strong cultural and intellectual tie between our most distinctive philosophy and our most distinctive philosophy of law.

That Holmes was selecting only one use of the word "law" can be seen from the fact that most people (laymen and lawyers) construe law as something which directly refers to statutes, reports, treatises, and ordinances written or remembered. In Holmes' view, however, these are merely "means" of the study of law. In other words, the things which most people call laws are, in Holmes' view, simply instrumental to the lawyer's prediction of what the courts will do in fact. Whether those who hold that the statutes, reports, and treatises themselves constitute the law have more than a trivial verbal quarrel with Holmes is a nice question. It is customary to construe the debate between legal realists and their more traditional opponents as one between rival definitions of "the same concept," between com-

peting attempts to arrive at the "essence of the law," but this
is a doubtful construal of the controversy.

When the law is viewed as a set of predictions it becomes a
body of empirical statements, and the law itself aims to become
an empirical science in a very elementary sense. The lawyer
must predict judicial behavior, and his success as a lawyer
(scientific and financial) will depend on his ability to make
lots of good predictions. These predictions will, in turn, depend
upon his mastering a body of generalizations concerning what
the courts will do under certain conditions. The law is systematized, therefore, with economy in mind. "It is to make the
prophecies easier to be remembered and to be understood that
the teachings of the decisions of the past are put into general
propositions and gathered into textbooks, or that statutes are
passed in a general form." [6] It should be obvious from statements
like this that Holmes was not an opponent of generalization, or
of the deductive method, or of system. He was not motivated
by any irrational contempt for logical inference. The law, like
any other empirical science, deserves and needs the machinery
of deduction and valid inference, and Holmes fully recognized
this fact. Nevertheless he could consistently maintain that the
life of the law is not logic, and in 1897 he continued to speak
of "the fallacy of logical form."

Like Dewey, Tufts, Robinson, and Beard, Holmes believed
in the importance of historical study as a means to understanding why the law is as it is at any given time. We have seen that
this was his attitude in *The Common Law;* it continued to be
his attitude in 1897. "At present, in very many cases, if we want
to know why a rule of law has taken its particular shape, and
more or less if we want to know why it exists at all, we go to
tradition. We follow it into the Year Books, and perhaps beyond
them to the customs of the Salian Franks, and somewhere in
the past, in the German forests, in the needs of Norman kings,
in the assumptions of a dominant class, in the absence of generalized ideas, we find out the practical motive for what now

best is justified by the mere fact of its acceptance and that men are accustomed to it. The rational study of the law is still to a large extent the study of history. History must be a part of the study, because without it we cannot know the precise scope of rules which it is our business to know. It is a part of the rational study, because it is the first step toward an enlightened skepticism, that is, towards a deliberate reconsideration of the worth of those rules." [7] It should be plain that Holmes was sharing the view of history which we have already seen in Beard, Robinson, Dewey, and Tufts. He regarded it as the source of our causal explanations of the state of the law at a given moment, and as the basis of a critique of what is merely a rudiment or survival of the past. "When you get the dragon out of his cave," he continued, "on to the plain and in the daylight, you can count his teeth and claws, and see just what is his strength. But to get him out is only the first step. The next is either to kill him, or to tame him and make him a useful animal. For the rational study of the law the black-letter man may be the man of the present, but the man of the future is the man of statistics and the master of economics. It is revolting to have no better reason for a rule of law than that so it was laid down in the time of Henry IV. It is still more revolting if the grounds upon which it was laid down have vanished long since, and the rule simply persists from blind imitation of the past." [8] We need not produce any more evidence to show that Holmes shared the historicism of early instrumentalism and the new history.

Let us turn to another theme of considerable significance—law and morals.

Those who were brought up in America in the second half of the nineteenth century were young victims of a vast literature of social apologetics. One tradition of Hegelianism identified the real with the rational, one group of Darwinians regarded the survivor as the fittest. In other words, the very traditions upon which our figures drew most heavily had their conservative or reactionary wings. Right-Hegelianism and conservative social

Darwinism are expressions of this split within the historicism of the nineteenth century. It is of extreme importance to point out that American liberals of the twentieth century questioned these conservative inferences from the texts of Hegel and Darwin very early. None of them ever accepted the doctrine that whatever is, is right; indeed Veblen questioned it to the point of maintaining its perverse contrary: "Whatever is, is wrong." For this reason their early writings are filled with insistence upon the difference between that which exists here and now and that which ought to be. They would not be saddled with the obligation to justify the evil which they plainly saw. In the case of Holmes this is not a product of sympathy for the radical movements of his day, but rather of a clear and distinct idea of what the law is. He was very anxious, therefore, to make clear what it was not; it was not ethics.

The refusal to identify the law with ethics is evident in several parts of Holmes' view in 1897. It turns up, for example, in his conception of legal duty. To say that someone has a duty to do something is to say that if he doesn't do it, the court will make him pay damages. But this is the *legal* conception of duty; duty is simply a relation between a man and a kind of act which can be observed by examining the behavior of the courts. To say that someone has a legal duty to do something involves observing how the courts behave when a person does *not* do it. It follows that if a man is not penalized by the courts for a certain omission, then that omission is not a failure to do his legal duty. That it may be his moral duty is of no interest to the lawyer. Holmes was urging a mode of looking at the matter which, he said, "stinks in the nostrils of those who think it advantageous to get as much ethics into the law as they can." [9]

The origin of this desire to distinguish between the law and ethics was different from that which operated in the case of those who were more liberal and radical at the time. Liberals and radicals wanted to make it clear that this was not the best of all possible worlds, and therefore that the legal system was not what it ought to have been. Holmes' explicit motive, on the other hand, was basically that of the business lawyer. Let us not be sentimental, he urged; let us not suppose that we can establish the law by appealing to our moral convictions. The law is not a goody-goody affair, and we, as lawyers, are bound to advise our clients as to the likelihood of their being jailed. Our client may very well be a bad man, but as our client he is asking us to predict whether the courts *will* put him in jail. The simple point is that the law does not always punish a man for committing a morally wrong act. "If you want to know the law and nothing else, you must look at it as a bad man, who cares only for the material consequences which such knowledge enables him to predict, not as a good one, who finds his reasons for conduct, whether inside the law or outside of it, in the vaguer sanctions of conscience." [10]

Holmes was not given to blurring lines. In calling him an organicist I hope I have not given the impression that he would not make hard and fast distinctions when they were called for. After having urged the distinction between law and morals, he said, somewhat sardonically, "I do not say that there is not a wider point of view from which the distinction between law and morals becomes of secondary or no importance, as all mathematical distinctions vanish in presence of the infinite . . . . But I do say," he added forcefully, "that that distinction is of the first importance for the object which we are here to consider— a right study and mastery of the law as a *business* [my italics] with well-understood limits, a body of dogma enclosed within definite lines." [11] The business of the lawyer is to defend his client, just as it is the business of the soldier to defend his country, and Holmes' attitude toward his client was not unlike Stephen Decatur's toward his country: he hoped that his client would always be right, but *his* client, right or wrong!

Because Holmes was so occupied with distinguishing law from morals (rather than morals from law, so to speak) he said little positive about morals. At one point he distinguished between the rights of men in a moral sense and their rights in a legal sense. In the former case, he said, "we mean to mark the limits of interference with individual freedom which we think are prescribed by conscience, by our ideal, however reached. Yet it is certain that many laws have been enforced in the past, and it is likely that some are enforced now, which are condemned by the most enlightened opinion of the time, or which at all events pass the limit of interference as many consciences would draw it." [12] In this illustration at least, the distinguishing mark of a moral rule or right is the fact that it is established by "conscience." Holmes referred often to the fact that the legal notions of *malice, intent,* and *negligence* were rendered confusing by the use of moral concepts. His example is striking: "Three hundred years ago a parson preached a sermon and told a story out of Fox's *Book of Martyrs* of a man who had assisted at the torture of one of the saints, and afterwards died, suffering compensatory inward torment. It happened that Fox was wrong. The man was alive and chanced to hear the sermon, and thereupon he sued the parson. Chief Justice Wray instructed the jury that the defendant was not liable, because the story was told innocently, without malice. He took malice in a moral sense, as importing a malevolent motive. But nowadays no one doubts that a man may be liable, without any malevolent motive at all, for false statements manifestly calculated to inflict temporal damage. In stating the case in pleading, we should still call the defendant's conduct malicious; but, in my opinion at least, the word means nothing about motives, or even about the defendant's attitude toward the future, but only signified that the tendency of his conduct under the known circumstances was very plainly to cause the plaintiff temporal harm." [13] For Holmes the mark of the moral is its concern with *motives* and *attitudes.*

In general, Holmes' view here, as in *The Common Law,* was that morals and ethics are peculiarly subjective and internal in character. Hence the notions of conscience and motive were typical examples of subjective, moral notions which had no business in the law. "Morals deal with the actual internal state of the individual's mind, what he actually intends." The law moves, on the other hand, and ought to move, toward the use of *external* standards. "You see how the vague circumference of the notion of duty shrinks and at the same time grows more precise when we wash it with cynical acid and expel everything except the object of our study, the operations of the law." [14] One aim of the law was precision, and to accomplish this Holmes would wash away all its semantic sins with his brand of acid: "For my own part, I often doubt whether it would not be a gain if every word of moral significance could be banished from the law altogether, and other words adopted which should convey legal ideas uncolored by anything outside the law. We should lose the fossil records of a good deal of history and the majesty got from ethical associations, but by ridding ourselves of an unnecessary confusion we should gain very much in the clearness of our thought." [15]

Just as his view of the relation between logic and the law makes it possible for some to interpret Holmes as an irrationalist and others to regard him as an admirer of system and order, so his remarks on the relation between law and morals have been used to put him in opposing camps. Those who cite his demand for a purge of the legal vocabulary claim him as a brutal positivist who would eliminate all interest in morals, a stern advocate of (legal) justice under a falling heaven. Others cite him to prove his attachment to a more humane school of thought. Consider the following passage from *The Common Law:*

In substance the growth of the law is legislative. And this in a deeper sense than that what the courts declare to have always been the law is in fact new. It is legislative in its grounds. The very considerations which judges most rarely mention, and always with an apology, are the secret root from which the law draws all the juices of life. I mean, of course, considerations of what is expedient for the community concerned. Every important principle which is developed by litigation is in fact and at bottom the result of more or less definitely understood views of public policy; most generally, to be sure, under our practice and traditions, the unconscious result of our instinctive preferences and inarticulate convictions, but none the less traceable to views of public policy in the last analysis. And as the law is administered by able and experienced men, who know too much to sacrifice good sense to a syllogism, it will be found that, when ancient rules maintain themselves in the way that has been and will be shown in this book, new reasons more fitted to the time have been found for them, and that they gradually receive a new content, and at last a new form, from the grounds to which they have been transplanted.

But hitherto this process has been largely unconscious. It is important, on that account, to bring to mind what the actual course of events has been. If it were only to insist on a more conscious recognition of the legislative function of the courts, as just explained, it would be useful.[16]

We shall see later (Chapter XIII) that this passage, in its call for a more conscious recognition of the legislative function of the courts, urges an *introduction* of moral concepts into the law in a manner which is consistent with the amoralism of the Holmesian attitude discussed earlier.

Perhaps the most succinct statement of Holmes' attitude on the misuse of logic and ethics in the law can be seen in the following passage, in which he states the view he opposed: "Take the fundamental question, What constitutes the law? You will find some text writers telling you that it is something different from what is decided by the courts of Massachusetts or England, that it is a system of reason, that it is a deduction from principles of ethics or admitted axioms or what not, which may or may not coincide with the decisions." [17] This passage suggests that Holmes, in "The Path of the Law," rejects the view that the law is a set of statements which may be deduced by logic alone from "principles of ethics." Furthermore he argues that many legal words which are moral in origin are no longer moral in the current legal usage, viz., "duty," "malice," "intent." A modern logician might say that Holmes was denying two things: (1) that the rules of law could be deduced from the principles of ethics, (2) that the concepts of law could be defined in terms of ethics. But curiously enough one of the reasons he gives for denying (1) *seems* to reintroduce moral considerations by suggesting that the law is made by judges who do draw upon considerations of social and moral advantage in making the law. One of the great problems for Holmes' philosophy of law, therefore, is the demonstration of the consistency of these two propositions.

Independently of how we answer this question, we must observe that Holmes was all for the improvement of the law. We have already seen this in our discussion of his attitude toward the study of history. He was certainly interested in a study of the worth of the rules of law: "A body of law," he said, "is more rational and more civilized when every rule it contains is referred articulately and definitely to an end which it subserves, and when the grounds for desiring that end are stated or are ready to be stated in words." [18]

Holmes' ambiguity on the relation between law and morals also emerged in his discussions of the place of science in the law. He was, of course, one of the first of the figures treated in this book to feel the effect of the new technology and the scientific spirit in the social sciences. This effect was reflected in several speeches and essays on the place of history and science in the law. Out of these discussions several clear conclusions emerge, but the basic knot that should tie law to morals in Holmes' philosophy remains undone.

As the son of a physician and poet, Holmes moved within the scientific and the humanistic tradition; as a child of nineteenth-century Cambridge, he was pushed by all the forces which sponsored pragmatism, Darwinism, and Spencerian philosophy in America. He also moved within the genteel tradition's boundaries. As a result, his earliest work was characterized by a conflict between learning and science as well as one between law and philosophy. The second problem engaged a great deal of his attention, and he constantly solved it by assuring himself that he was right in leaving his friend William James to twist the tail of the

Kosmos by himself. Holmes' career moved steadily toward practice. He began thinking in cosmic bull sessions with James, moved on to law school, where speculation was almost impossible, became a noted legal historian and finally a judge. The movement was steadily away from preoccupation with learning and, as Holmes construed it, toward science. For this reason the relations between learning and science concerned him as much as the relations between philosophy and law.

The dichotomy between learning and science appears throughout Holmes' writings, especially in those early years when he was not yet through with legal history but when he had already assumed judicial responsibility for practical decision. His attitude toward learning has much of the quality of Veblen's contempt for dead languages and scholarly waste and of Dewey's distaste for the school curriculum, in which dead facts of the past were drilled into the passive spectator-child. Learning is identified with the study of the past. It has its function, of course, but it has a tendency to lead us astray. It gets in the way of evaluating the law in terms of its present worth; it is temperamentally the ally of the conservative. "The law, so far as it depends on learning, is indeed, as it has been called, the government of the living by the dead." "But the present," Holmes added, "has a right to govern itself so far as it can." "Historic continuity with the past," he said in a phrase that was to stick with him, "is not a duty, it is only a necessity." And when the present sees fit to govern itself, it will govern with science, for an "ideal system of law should draw its postulates and its legislative justification from science." [19]

Some of Holmes' critical views about legal history (or learning, or pure science as opposed to practical science), succinctly expressed in his essay, "Science in Law and Law in Science" (1899), grew out of a feeling that a good thing was being worked to death. Historical explanation as Holmes understood it arose in reaction to teleology. The latter he understood as an attempt to explain something by showing its fitness for certain ends or purposes in accordance with a providential scheme, whereas historical explanation consisted in "tracing the order and process of . . . growth and development from a starting point assumed as given." It was the great success of historical explanation in the law which led to the "feeling that when you had the true historic dogma you had the last word not only in the present but for the immediate future," and it was this feeling that led Holmes to put legal history in its place, and to argue that there are other more important problems in the law. While legal history pursued in the abstract scientific way is an honorable pursuit ("It is perfectly proper to regard and study the law simply as a great anthropological document"),[20] it is of minor importance compared to the practical problems of law. Learning in the history of law is, in this context, identified with pure science, while the critical evaluation of law is identified with practical science. The terminology is shifted somewhat, but the distinction between scholar and legislator remains. One looks to the past, the other to the present and the future.

Few practical men showed as much respect for the contemplative life as Holmes did, but his military training and his judicial responsibilities turned his attention and respect to the man of action. "I doubt if there is any more exalted form of life than that of a great abstract thinker, wrapt in the successful study of problems to which he devotes himself, for an end which is neither selfish nor unselfish in the common sense of those words, but is simply to feed the deepest hunger and to use the greatest gifts of his soul." But this praise is followed almost immediately by a peculiar kind of retraction, for "after all," he said, "the place for a man who is complete in all his powers is in the fight." The implication is that the scientific genius is not complete in all his powers, for the professor, according to Holmes, "surrenders one-half of life that his protected talent may grow and flower in peace." Holmes believed in carrying out the principles of pragmatism: "to make up your mind at your peril upon a living question, for purposes of action, calls upon your whole nature." [21] The conclusion was based on personal experience, for Holmes had been soldier, scholar, and then judge. His brief life of scholarship was merely an interlude; his basic interests lay elsewhere. Whatever scholarly and refined interests remained after he became a judge were left for casual reading and correspondence with learned gentlemen like Frederick Pollock. In this respect Holmes differed from all the other men I have been considering. His life with the professors was brief, and his respect for them was tempered by his fascination with battles and trials. He may have mellowed in later life, but at the height of his career Fortinbras held more attraction than Hamlet.

In spite of his dwindling interest in legal history for its own sake, a pursuit which he associated with the purest of science, Holmes would not admit that he was forsaking science. The approach to the law as an anthropological document may be that of the pure scientist, but then there are problems of practical science. He strains to prove that he is no legal philistine (hardly necessary when one realizes that he became and remained America's greatest legal historian on the basis of his *Common Law*). "I trust that I have shown that I appreciate what I thus far have spoken of as if it were the only form of the scientific study of law, but of course I think, as other people do, that the main ends of the subject are practical, and from a practical point of view, history . . . is only a means, and one of the least of the means, of mastering a tool. From a practical point of view . . . its use is mainly negative and skeptical . . . its chief good is to burst inflated explanations.[22] The main point of "Law in Science and Science in Law" is but a development of "Learning and Science" (1895). The positive science of law is what arises when a lawyer tries to justify a law. He cannot do this merely by showing that it has been followed, and therefore he must go beyond legal history. But in going beyond history he is not leaving science; on the contrary, he is entering science in a more profound way. We must approach the problem of justifying law systematically, and it is this concern with questions of justification that gives the practical lawyer the chance to be "truly" scientific. "The true science of the law does not consist mainly in a theological working out of dogma or a logical development as in mathematics, or only in a study of it as an anthropological document from the outside; an even more important part consists in the establishment of its postulates from within upon accurately measured social desires instead of tradition." [23] Particularly in this practical sphere is there a dependence on science, a science which will measure the "relative worth of our different social ends." He concluded "Law in Science and Science in Law" with a salute to science even more resounding than those delivered by its firmest devotees: "Very likely it may be that with all the help that statistics and every modern appliance can bring us there never will be a commonwealth in which science is everywhere supreme. But it is an ideal, and without ideals what is life worth?" [24] *"A Commonwealth in which science is everywhere supreme."* What could be more sympathetic to John Dewey?

Whatever the problems which arise in connection with the details of Holmes' view in the nineties, we must recognize the affinity which it bore to the views of Dewey, Beard, Robinson, and Tufts. He was anxious to distinguish between the law as it existed and ethical theories of what it ought to be; and yet he urged that an empirical, scientific evaluation of law could be made; he was impressed with the value of history as a means of explaining the law and revealing its antiquated aspects at any given moment. It should be clear, however, that at this date he was neither a radical nor a reformer. Nevertheless his intellectual outlook was permeated with a good many of the ideas that were stirring the liberals of his time, and his early writings helped to determine the intellectual climate of the first half of the twentieth century in America. He fortified the conviction of Dewey and Beard that the study of history was of vital importance in the solution of practical problems; he urged the need for a conception of law which would be closer to that entertained by the practicing lawyer; he insisted upon distinguishing what existed from what ought to have existed. In short, he shared a view of the relation between history, theory, and practice that dominated American liberalism in the opening years of the twentieth century.

CHAPTER VI

The Amoral Moralist

O NE OF the most obvious traits of the new outlook in social
thought which emerged at the turn of the century was the
tendency toward organicism as I have explained that term. The
new history, the new ethics, and the new jurisprudence were not
only interested in examining the past in an effort to understand and evaluate the present, but they were also parts of a
movement toward unification of the social sciences. Dewey,
Beard, Robinson, and Holmes were anxious to use whatever
materials they could find in their efforts to solve their own special problems. Consequently they were not hemmed in by any
academic barriers in their search for social truth. The historians
under the influence of Robinson called upon all the social sciences; the moralists under the influence of Dewey ranged widely
through them in the hope of finding material relevant to their
problems; Holmes' program for the law required a knowledge of
economics and anthropology; Beard's program for political science was equally demanding. But in their appeal to all the social sciences they saw fit to single out one of them as especially
useful—economics. The period which Beard called the American
Counter-Reformation was acutely conscious of the primacy of the
economic factor in modern life. Robinson traced the origins of
the new history to *The Holy Family* of Marx and Engels; Beard
made his reputation with his *Economic Interpretation of the*

Constitution of the United States; Dewey and Tufts located the most urgent ethical problems of 1908 in economics; Holmes looked to the lawyer trained in economics as the man of the future, anticipating in 1897 the emergence of Louis Brandeis's mode of legal thinking. This interest in the economic aspect of society cannot be underestimated as a component of the American ideology which began to form in the nineties.

If anyone were to be singled out as the patron saint of this outlook it would be Thorstein Veblen. It was Veblen who supplied this generation with a good deal of its economic theory and, more important, it was Veblen who gave it an idea of how economics might be used as a clue to the understanding of American culture. Robinson was the only one of the group who explicitly admitted Marx as his predecessor in emphasizing the economic factor; [1] Beard was inordinately concerned to trace his economism to Madison rather than to Marx; Dewey and Tufts had little occasion to deal directly with Marx or Engels in the first edition of their *Ethics;* Holmes persistently scoffed at Marx in his correspondence with Pollock. It was Veblen, however, who was cited by Beard as having given the "keenest analysis" of business enterprise; [2] and it was Veblen who supplied a good deal of information and viewpoint in economics to his erstwhile colleagues at Chicago, Dewey and Tufts. In fact Tufts explicitly admitted the influence of Veblen's *Theory of Business Enterprise* when he said: "I was groping from the outside for some angle at which I could view the ethics of business. Books on economic theory did not help much. Hadley's *Economics* took up ethical questions, but it seemed to find capitalism perfect in theory, even if defective in the case of some of its ramifications. Veblen's treatment, which was an effort to see business as actually conducted, especially in its newer phases, seemed to me to throw light that was much needed on the actual practices and theories of business in this century. It showed the inadequacy of the theories of the eighteenth century for the ethical as well as the economic problems of the twentieth." [3]

What are the chief characteristics of *The Theory of the Leisure Class* when it is looked upon as more than the source of the (now cliché) epithets "conspicuous consumption" and "conspicuous waste"? Viewed in the light of Veblen's other work at the time, it emerges as an attempt to apply the evolutionary method to economics, to divide modern economic society into two conflicting institutions—industry and business enterprise, to present an "objective" picture of the impact of the leisure class upon our society. Veblen's conception of social evolution as a blind impersonal process with no goal or purpose before it, and his conception of economics as a study of this evolution, led him to insist perpetually that he was not making evaluations, that his results came from a careful, impartial, scientific examination of the facts. Wherever a word with moral overtones creeps into his discussion he is quick to disclaim any ethical judgment. This anxiety to avoid explicit evaluation resulted in considerable speculation about his convictions; he was described as a great ironist, a teaser, a comic, and a coward. The grounds for this speculation become clearer when we compare it with attitudes toward Holmes, who also insisted on a sharp separation of legal science and ethics.

As we have seen, Holmes was just as interested in distinguishing between the law and ethics as Veblen was in freeing economics from ethical assumptions, concepts, and conclusions. But a difference in attitude toward them arose on the Left. Whereas Holmes did not reveal many "facts" about the law from which others claimed to infer ethical conclusions, Veblen supplied the liberals and radicals of his generation with what they took to be an arsenal of evidence in support of their moral convictions. From their point of view Veblen struck at the heart of modern culture and revealed its link with the most tawdry of institutions —money. Hence the feeling that Veblen in his "objectivity" lacked the courage of his convictions, the courage to make the moral inferences which any honest, humane person would have had to make about American society in 1899. Hence the feeling on the part of more delicate readers that these conclusions were so obvious that Veblen's failure to make them himself revealed only the deftness and brilliance of a great satirist. Holmes, on the other hand, was never put in this position, for he merely announced and tried sedately to observe in practice the distinction between what was and what ought to have been. He presented no propositions which might have been used as premises for a damning estimate of American law at the time. But Veblen's position in 1899 was very much like Beard's when the latter produced the *Economic Interpretation of the Constitution* in 1913, except that Beard's style never earned him the rewards of eccentricity. Most radical doctrines of the day were based upon the conviction that the American economy was responsible for the evils of society, and any professor who would contribute toward proving this was welcomed by the radical and reforming movement. When the movement was feeling charitable and amiable, it interpreted the professor's refusal to "draw conclusions" as evidence of his wit or his caution in the presence of trustees; when it was in other moods, it charged cowardice and moral corruption. Veblen received both kinds of treatment in the twentieth century.

Veblen's indifference to what he called moral questions was closely connected with his evolutionism. We have already discussed his anxiety to convert economics into an evolutionary science and his interest in the economic *process*. It was this which united him with the historical school of economics and with Hegelianism. But it is important to notice that, unlike some Hegelians, notably those of the Marxian wing, Veblen, in the earliest years of his writing, systematically avoided any moral commitments. Veblen's critique of classical political economy, for all its similarity to Marx's, is distinguished from Marx's through its lack of political purpose. When Marx criticized Ricardo for viewing capitalist economy as eternal and everlasting, he made it clear that he had political matters in mind. The Marxian attack on the static conceptions of Ricardo and his followers had a revolutionary implication. The point was that society could change and would change again until the day of the classless society. Veblen harbored no such optimistic belief in a final point of evolution; instead he thought such a view was animistic and that it involved an indefensible belief in the inevitable progress of mankind.

But this difference from Marxism ought not to obscure the broad basis on which Veblen was united with Marx. He was united with Marx methodologically in emphasizing the changing character of social relations, in urging the study of what he called cumulative sequences, and in attacking taxonomy. Trying to find out what Veblen meant when he referred to this despised taxonomy is no easy job. There are very few clear statements of what the word meant to him. It would appear that he was influenced by the kind of discussion one finds in Karl Pearson's *Grammar of Science* on the role of classification in science. Pearson regarded classification as a necessary forerunner of the discovery of sequences or laws, and Veblen's language suggests some familiarity with Pearson's views. But it is doubtful whether Veblen could have found support for his own peculiar version of scientific economic sequences in Pearson. It is doubtful whether Veblen's distinction between taxonomy and evolutionary economics could have been grafted on the relatively neutral discussions of classifications and sequences in the methodological treatises of the nineteenth century. As far as I can make out he regarded Darwin's work as a paradigm, arguing somewhat as follows: Prior to having hit on the theory of natural selection, Darwin tells us, he classified facts "on true Baconian principles"; this was the part which Veblen might have called "taxonomy." For example, Darwin spoke of having discovered in the Pampean formation great fossil animals with armor like that on existing armadillos. But when Darwin said that such facts as these "could only be explained on the supposition that species gradually become modified," he was mounting the ladder of knowledge for Veblen. And when he said, "I soon perceived that selection was the keystone of man's success in making useful races of animals and plants," he had reached the top rung; he had achieved the kind of hypothesis that Veblen was looking for in economics. The theory of natural selection was a theory of "cumulative sequence" in Veblen's language, and therefore it went beyond taxonomy. To explain the *connection* between the armor on great fossil animals and that on existing armadillos was the accomplishment of a scientific genius.

When Veblen wrote *The Theory of the Leisure Class* he must have had these fossils and armadillos in mind. It required little effort to replace the fossils by barbarians and the armadillos by modern men. Veblen became the Darwin of the piece, making innumerable taxonomic observations but finally presenting a grand theory which would do for economics what Darwin had done for biology. When he wrote *The Theory of the Leisure Class* Veblen regarded himself as the champion of evolutionary, dynamic, scientific thought as against the collectors of social butterflies, the taxonomists, the defenders of static analysis, classification, and illegitimate abstraction in economics. Just as the new historians were turning to economics in search of an explanation of the historical scene, the new economics under Veblen's guidance was proclaiming the virtues of historical method and Darwinism.

Veblen's anthropology is based on the assumption that in the process of cultural evolution groups of men have passed from an initial peaceable stage to a stage at which "fighting is the avowed and characteristic employment of the group." In this later stage we find the "habitual bellicose frame of mind" and the emergence of force and fraud as cardinal virtues. The first or peaceful stage he called savage society and the second barbarian society. The third, modern society, inherited the predaceous outlook of the barbarian in what Veblen called a "transmuted form," so that we now see barbarian survivals in some of our own institutions.[4] Chief among these is the institution of the leisure class. The leisure class is defined by its failure to take part in industry, and this exemption is the economic expression of its superior rank. The basic feature of the modern world is a division between those who participate in industry—broadly speaking, the engineers—and the leisure class, or the businessmen. It begins with a savage division of labor between man and woman, according to which man is primarily engaged in the honorable activity of exploit while the woman engages in the drab and menial tasks—in drudgery. Exploit and drudgery are the central savage occupations, which give way respectively to warfare and industry in the barbarian world, which in turn give way to business and industry in the modern world. These categories become more complicated and subdivided but they underlie the system of social relations.

Like Marx and Engels in the revised edition of *The Communist Manifesto* (where they amend their statement that *all* previous history is the history of class struggle, and except a stage of primitive communism), Veblen agreed that there was a time when there was no leisure class. The reason for its absence was the fact that at this stage society was peaceable, poor, and lacking in any system of individual ownership. But then war became a social institution and prepared the way for the leisure class, which requires a society in which "the infliction of injury by force and stratagem" [5] is necessary, and in which subsistence is obtainable easily enough to permit the exemption of some people from labor. A leisure class can appear, therefore, only in a warlike society which is not poor. It should be evident that Veblen was not producing a very flattering genealogy for the leisure class of his day, and that no matter how much he protested his "objectivity" and his avoidance of moral evaluation, he was unearthing a rather unpleasant family tree for a class which prided itself on its origins. The American leisure class of 1899 could not construe Veblen's tale as allegorical proof of congenital robustness. The prevalent ideology still celebrated the capitalist class as one which had been poor but honest when it began its ride from rags to riches. It could not have seen any

humor in an account which located its origins in skill at predatory fraud.

Veblen was aware of the bizarre character of some of his anthropology, and confessed that the distinction between the
worthy, exploitative pursuits and the unworthy, non-exploiting
pursuits "has but little obvious significance in a modern industrial community." But the emphasis is on the word "obvious,"
because Veblen believed that a more probing analysis would reveal the profundity and basic character of the distinction. Veblen, like Marx and Freud, searched for the skull beneath the
skin, and so his discoveries, like theirs, were not calculated to
please. In the case of the distinction between exploit and industry, Veblen had an elaborate explanation which threw considerable light on his method. In earlier times, he said, a distinction of this kind was more likely to be kept in mind than it
is today. "In the earlier stages of culture, when the personal
force of the individual counted more immediately and obviously
in shaping the course of events, the element of exploit counted
for more in the everyday scheme of life. Interest centered about
this fact to a greater degree." [6] But now that interest no longer
centers about it, how can we continue to maintain it as an important and useful distinction for a study of modern society? In
answer to this question Veblen appealed to "pragmatic" considerations in the broadest sense of that word.

He pointed out that facts are usually classified with an interest or purpose in mind. The man who is anxious to sit down in
a room is apt to distinguish chairs from all other pieces of furniture, while the connoisseur is likely to distinguish antiques from
ordinary pieces. And so the connoisseur will regard the sitter's
distinction as "insubstantial," and the converse will also be true.
In the same way barbarians and savages have purposes which
lead them to bear the distinction between exploit and industry
in mind where we moderns do not, because our purposes have
changed and our classificatory schemes are different. Veblen is
not as contemptuous here of "taxonomy" or classification as he

is in other places. He says, "The habit of distinguishing and classifying the various purposes and directions of activity prevails of necessity always and everywhere; for it is indispensable in reaching a working theory or scheme of life." [7] Indeed it should be remembered that Veblen's chief contribution to economics and social sciences was his (taxonomic) distinction between the leisure *class* and other classes. Of course, it might be said that Veblen did not oppose taxonomy but merely wanted to go beyond it, and therefore he is not to be charged with inconsistency. Moreover, we must observe his insistence upon the fact that classificatory schemes which are the products of one set of circumstances cannot be applied to another if certain basic social purposes and needs should change. But, granting that classificatory schemes change with social purposes, why should the barbarian distinction between exploit and industry still be useful in the description and analysis of modern life? Veblen answers that "the change of standards and points of view is gradual only, and it seldom results in the subversion or entire suppression of a standpoint once accepted. A distinction is still habitually made between industrial and nonindustrial occupations; and this modern distinction is a transmuted form of the barbarian distinction between exploit and drudgery." [8] Here we see how Veblen, along with Dewey, Holmes, and Beard, justified his interest in the past. *The Theory of the Leisure Class* appealed to the past much as *The Common Law* did; both of them attempted to reveal the historical antecedents of contemporary ideas; both of them looked upon the present as a descendant of the past whose traits would be more clearly understood when compared with its ancestor's.

The distinction between exploit and industry was based on another barbarian distinction—that between the animate and the inert. For the barbarian an animate object is one that strives for some end,[9] and therefore animate objects, especially those whose behavior is notably formidable or baffling, have to be confronted with skills of a different kind from those needed in dealing with inert things. To deal successfully with animate objects is a work of exploit rather than of industry.[10] It comes about, therefore, that exploit operates by the use of prowess, while industry employs diligence. "Industry is effort that goes to create a new thing, with a new purpose given it by the fashioning hand of its maker out of passive ('brute') material; while exploit, so far as it results in an outcome useful to the agent, is the conversion to his own ends of energies previously directed to some other end by another agent." [11] In the earliest communities, where exploit is masculine and drudgery feminine, the latter becomes unworthy of man, as does everything which is not a product of prowess. The man must bend other animate things to his own purpose, whereas the woman devotes herself to the "assiduous and uneventful shaping of materials." [12] Dignity, worth, honor, and esteem come to characterize exploit, and industry is looked down upon.

Veblen subscribed to the "instinct-psychology" and postulated an original instinct, a theory—which was later adopted by his colleague Jacques Loeb. He called it "the instinct of workmanship." Because man is an agent who seeks the accomplishment of ends, he develops a taste for effective work and a distaste for futile effort.[13] This is a basic drive in Veblen's theory of culture, and he cites it frequently in his discussion of the leisure class. Sometimes it secures powerful and obvious expression, as in early peaceable stages of society, and sometimes its effects are less clear. Its concomitant is efficiency—the successful accomplishment of purposes—which can be esteemed very highly in a peaceful society. Visible success at accomplishing one's goals becomes the basis of invidious distinction and emulation, and people will try to outdo each other in being efficient. In peaceable times this instinct will work itself out in a manner wholly compatible with, indeed a manner which leads directly to, industrially useful ends, and then it can have great social value. But as society becomes more and more predatory, the demonstration of force itself is honored, and seizure and aggression become the most worthy activities of man. "Arms are honorable, and the use of them, even in seeking the life of the meanest creatures of the fields, becomes an honorific employment. At the same time, employment in industry becomes correspondingly odious, and, in the common-sense apprehension, the handling of the tools and implements of industry falls beneath the dignity of able-bodied men. Labor becomes irksome." [14]

Because of the low esteem in which he holds industry, the barbarian engages in a constant search for booty and trophies. These come to be the signs of predatory skill, of prowess. Since the leisure class comes into being with the advent of individual ownership and the institution of private property, the predominant struggle appears to be one for the possession of goods. Although conventional economic theory perpetuates the myth, it is apparent, Veblen says, that the aim is not the consumption of these goods. This may be so when society is in its early stages and the struggle for subsistence is the major economic activity, but it does not continue after a certain point has been reached in technological progress. "It is only when taken in a sense far removed from its naïve meaning that consumption of goods can be said to afford the incentive from which accumulation invariably proceeds. The motive that lies at the root of ownership is emulation; and the same motive of emulation continues active in the further development of the institution to which it has given rise and in the development of all those features of the social structure which this institution of ownership touches. The possession of wealth confers honor; it is an invidious distinction. Nothing equally cogent can be said for the consumption of goods, nor for any other conceivable incentive to acquisition, and especially not for any incentive to the accumulation of wealth." [15] The motive of pecuniary emulation is basic in the behavior of men in our society. The possession of wealth, which at one time was taken as an outward sign of efficiency, now becomes worthy in itself. "Prowess and exploit may still remain the basis of award of the *highest* popular esteem . . . but for the

purposes of a commonplace decent standing in the community
these means of repute have been replaced by the acquisition and
accumulation of goods." [16]

Veblen makes clear that there are other incentives to acquisition and accumulation. For example, he does not deny that the
desire for added comfort and security from want is constantly
present as a motive. But even here "pecuniary emulation" shapes
"the methods and selects the objects of expenditure for personal
comfort and decent livelihood." It must also be remembered
that pecuniary emulation is not in conflict with Veblen's instinct of workmanship, because the instinct of workmanship
does not express itself in industry alone. The instinct of workmanship is simply "that propensity for purposeful activity and
that repugnance to all futility of effort which belong to a man
by virtue of his character as an agent," and it does not disappear
when man enters the predatory stage. All it does is to change
the form of its expression and the proximate objects to which
it directs man's activity. "Under the régime of individual ownership the most available means of visibly achieving a purpose
is that afforded by the acquisition and accumulation of goods;
and as the self-regarding antithesis between man and man
reaches fuller consciousness, the propensity for achievement—
the instinct of workmanship—tends more and more to shape itself into a straining to excel others in pecuniary achievement." [17]
Purposeful effort then becomes identified with the accumulation
of wealth.

"If its working were not disturbed by other economic forces
or other features of the emulative process, the immediate effect
of such a pecuniary struggle as has just been described in outline
would be to make men industrious and frugal." [18] This, it
should be remembered, comes from the pen of the man who
constantly attacked the classical economists for their notion that
there were "disturbing factors" which interfered with the expected working out of certain fundamental drives in men. And
yet Veblen feels no great qualms in resorting to a similar device

in accounting for the seeming incompatibility between his
theory and the facts. It would appear that Veblen needed the
devices of "abstraction" quite as much as the despised classical
economists. How else could he account for the fact that the instinct of workmanship didn't make everyone industrious, frugal,
and diligent? He too has his epicycles, and so he says that although the incentive to diligence is not absent in the leisure
class, "its action is so greatly qualified by the secondary demands
of pecuniary emulation, that any inclination in this direction is
practically overborne and any incentive to diligence tends to be
of no effect. The most imperative of these secondary demands
of emulation, as well as the one of widest scope, is the require-
ment of abstention from productive work. This is true in an es-
pecial degree for the barbarian stage of culture. During the
predatory culture labor comes to be associated in men's habits of
thought with weakness and subjection to a master. It is therefore a mark of inferiority, and therefore comes to be accounted
unworthy of man in his best estate. By virtue of this tradition
labor is felt to be debasing, and this tradition has never died
out. On the contrary, with the advance of social differentiation
it has acquired the axiomatic force due to ancient and unques-
tioned prescription." [19] It seems that pecuniary emulation has
conflicting consequences, one in the direction of diligence and
frugality, the other in the direction of abstention from productive work. The second of these consequences appears to win out
in the case of the leisure class, and this explains the simultaneous
presence of pecuniary emulation and avoidance of work in one
class of the population. From this point on Veblen's theory rolls
rapidly, and we arrive at the notions which made him famous
from Chicago to Greenwich Village—conspicuous consumption
and conspicuous leisure. These are simply two devices for making obvious to all that the class which indulges in them is ex-
empt from productive labor. Leisure, it must be remembered,
does not involve indolence or quiescence; it simply requires non-
productive consumption of time, and this may be carried out by

exhibiting one's leisure in full view, or by exhibiting possessions which testify to one's leisurely activity on other occasions. We need not enter upon the penetrating and hilarious details which Veblen marshals in support of his theory—they are clearly expounded in chapter after chapter. Although primarily exhibited by the leisure class, conspicuous leisure and consumption trickle down to the poorest orders of society. Here leisure is quite impracticable, but conspicuous consumption is much in evidence. "There is no class and no country that has yielded so abjectly before the pressure of physical want as to deny themselves all gratification of this higher or spiritual need." [20]

From a philosophical point of view the most interesting aspect of Veblen's work is his curious ambivalence on the question of value. The first impression after putting down *The Theory of the Leisure Class* is that Veblen has tried to show that the leisure class is a survival of a barbarian culture, that it is a remnant of an earlier stage of society which has outlived its function. It lingers, we gather, as a worse than useless appendage in modern life; worse than useless because it not only does not aid, but hinders, the functioning of industry, the most creative and valuable institution in society. But having inferred this moral we leaf through the book again and come across the usual collection of disclaimers of moral interest. Throughout his discussion of the distinction between worthy and unworthy employments, Veblen presents himself merely as a natural historian, merely as a reporter of the barbarian's invidious distinctions. The savages and the barbarians, he would have us know, do the discriminating, the valuing, and the invidious comparing; he simply records their behavior. "In making use of the term 'invidious,' it may perhaps be unnecessary to remark, there is no intention to extol or depreciate, or to commend or deplore any of the phenomena which the word is used to characterize." [21] Now we are mildly confused, for our moralist has suddenly turned amoral on us. What does he think of conspicuous consumption and conspicuous waste? Does he admire them or hate them? Does he think they ought to continue? Now he will not answer, for he assures us that he is not interested in such questions. But then, to make our confusion complete, we turn back to the first sentence of the book, which shouts at us: "It is the purpose of this inquiry to discuss the place and *value* of the leisure class as an economic factor in modern life" (my italics).

"Veblen repudiates preaching," Wesley C. Mitchell then tells us. "As an evolutionist his office is to understand; not to praise, or blame, or lead us into righteousness. From his point of view, any notions he may entertain concerning what is right and wrong are vestiges of the cultural environment to which he has been exposed. They have no authority, and it would be a futile impertinence to try to impose them upon others. There is much of the satirist in him; but it is satire of an unfamiliar and a disconcerting kind." [22] There is much to be said for this point of view; certainly Veblen said a good deal to bear out that interpretation, but let us look a little further into the matter.

We have already seen that Veblen explicitly announced his intention to study the value of the leisure class. What could he have meant by this? How shall we estimate its relevance to what Mitchell says? Perhaps the best way to begin is to observe that the chief activities of the leisure class are described by Veblen as "wasteful." One is a waste of time and effort, the other is a waste of goods. But, he says: "The use of the term 'waste' is in one respect an unfortunate one. As used in the speech of everyday life the word carries an undertone of deprecation. It is here used for want of a better term that will adequately describe the same range of motives and of phenomena, and it is not to be taken in an odious sense, as implying an illegitimate expenditure of human products or of human life. In the view of economic theory the expenditure in question is no more and no less legitimate than any other expenditure. It is here called 'waste,' because this expenditure does not serve human life or human well-being on the whole, not because it is waste or misdirection of effort or expenditure as viewed from the standpoint of the individual consumer who chooses it. If he chooses it, that disposes of the question of its relative utility to him, as compared with other forms of consumption that would not be deprecated on account of their wastefulness. Whatever form of expenditure the consumer chooses, or whatever end he seeks in making his choice, has utility to him by virtue of his preference. As seen from the point of view of the individual consumer, the question of wastefulness does not arise within the scope of economic theory proper. The use of the word 'waste' as a technical term, therefore, implies no deprecation of the motives or of the ends sought by the consumer under this canon of conspicuous waste." [23]

Veblen's main point, so far as I can see, is that the leisure class does not serve human life or human well-being on the whole, although it may like what it does. Now it should be obvious that, whatever qualifications Veblen might have added to rub the curse off the leisure class, most of his readers construed the fundamental ethical good as precisely the service of human life and human well-being on the whole. To say that Veblen was not passing ethical judgment, or that he merely wanted to "understand" economic behavior, is not to deny the moral implications drawn by many of his readers in 1899. Think of a man proclaiming the human wastefulness of the leisure class during the movement for economic freedom which characterized the last decade of the nineteenth century, and then being construed as a mere observer of economic society whose office was not to praise or blame! Even if Veblen was as "impartial" and amoral as Mitchell (and Veblen) says he was, there can be no doubt as to why he was seized upon by liberals and radicals as a champion of their cause. To understand his role we may compare him to a man who comes into a Benthamite utilitarian gathering and declares publicly that the leisure class does not contribute to the greatest good of the greatest number; that, in fact, it contributes to the greatest evil of the greatest number, but that we must remember that the leisure class likes what it does, and that the speaker refrains from passing judgment on its failure to contribute to the greatest good of the greatest number. Clearly it would make little difference what the speaker felt about the moral significance of the facts he had adduced; the utilitarian audience would seize upon his evidence as indicating the evil of the leisure class, for the audience understands "evil" to mean precisely the characteristic which the speaker assigned to the leisure class. The situation is quite analogous to that in which Veblen and his audience found themselves; I say analogous only because he was not addressing a utilitarian audience, but a generation of liberals and radicals who also saw the social good as basic, and who would have called anything that did not serve human life or human well-being on the whole, morally bad. Veblen, then, in spite of his own protest to the contrary, was a moralist to many who chose to translate his language into their own.

Veblen was also an evolutionist, as we have seen. He maintained that the life of man in society is a struggle for existence, and therefore a process of selective adaptation. Social evolution is a process of natural selection of institutions, which are defined as "prevalent habits of thought with respect to particular relations and particular functions of the individual and of the community." [24] Institutions, because they are products of the past, are adapted to past circumstances, and are therefore never fully in accord with the requirements of the present. These institutions, therefore, in their link with the past, function as conservative factors in society. Since institutions must, if they are to be preserved, adjust to constantly developing circumstances, there must be a maximum of freedom and facility of readjustment if the evolutionary process is to continue without obstruction. It follows that capacity for growth in social structure depends on the "degree of exposure of the individual members to the constraining forces of the environment." If any part of the community lives a peculiarly sheltered life it "will adapt its views and its schemes of life more tardily to the altered general situation; it will . . . tend to retard the process of social transformation." Veblen was primarily concerned with one of these parts of the community—the wealthy leisure class—whom he found "in . . . a sheltered position with respect to the economic forces that make for change and readjustment." "And it may be said," he added, "that the forces which make for a readjustment of institutions, especially in the case of a modern industrial community, are, in the last analysis, almost entirely of an economic nature." [25] We see, therefore, why Beard in his economic interpretations of 1913 looked to Veblen as an ally.

Veblen's evolutionism was not only linked with the new political science of Beard in its emphasis upon economic factors; it was also closely related to the new outlook which was developing in the theory of education. Just as Veblen turned his attention to the leisure class as a sheltered institution, so Dewey came to examine the school critically and found it equally distant from the mainstream of social progress.

CHAPTER VII

Progressive Education and Progressive Law

IN 1899 John Dewey published *The School and Society,* his most widely read book and the earliest exposition of his theory of progressive education. In it he focused upon the American school as a part of the community which was living in such seclusion and remoteness from changing circumstances that it couldn't possibly perform its proper function in modern society. *The School and Society* in its first edition comprised three lectures which Dewey had delivered in Chicago in 1899, and each of them was on a theme which had extraordinarily close connections with the problems discussed in *The Theory of the Leisure Class*—the school and social progress, the school as a device for giving expression to the child's fundamental instincts, and waste in education. In effect these lectures presented a criticism of elementary education based on general principles like those used by Veblen in his attack on the higher learning. Veblen had not spared the university in the last chapter of *The Theory of the Leisure Class,* where he treated it as an expression of pecuniary culture and anticipated his more devastating analysis of it in *The Higher Learning in America* (1918).

Dewey began his study by trying to indicate in what ways the "new education," as he called it, was related to the larger changes in society. "Can we connect this 'New Education,'" he asked, "with the general march of events? If we can, it will lose its isolated character, and will cease to be an affair which proceeds only from the over-ingenious minds of pedagogues dealing with particular pupils. It will appear as part and parcel of the whole social evolution, and, in its more general features at least, as inevitable. Let us then ask after the main aspects of the social movement; and afterwards turn to the school to find what witness it gives of effort to put itself in line." [1]

The social transformation which Dewey noted is the one Beard depicted in *Contemporary American History*, and the aspect which Dewey emphasized was the great industrial advance—the application of science, the growth of a world market, large-scale manufacture, cheap and rapid means of communication and distribution. Earlier than this there had been the household and the neighborhood systems, in which the home was the center of industry, and the child was able to observe the entire industrial process and even participate in it. But by 1899 the household and the neighborhood had disappeared in large sections of the country. Dewey reminded his audience what these social changes had taken away from the life of the child: training in habits of order and industry, the idea of an obligation to produce something in the world, an acquaintance with natural materials and ways of making them into socially useful things.[2] Dewey celebrated what Veblen called industry and respected the training in industry which the children of earlier generations had received. The earlier child was described as if he had lived in the pre-predatory world of Veblen's earliest primitives, before the culture of the leisure class was introduced. But Dewey was not overwhelmed with nostalgia for "the good old days of children's modesty, reverence, and implicit obedience." He also reminded his audience of the compensations which the world of 1899 supplied, speaking of the increase in toleration and in knowledge of human nature, and the increase of commerce. Although he emphasized the value of these compensations for the city-bred child of 1899, he posed the following problem: "How shall we retain these advantages, and yet introduce into the school something representing the other side of life—occupations which exact personal responsibilities and which train the child in relation to the physical realities of life?" [3] One of the earliest problems for progressive education was how to preserve certain of the values of the earlier child's world in the urban society of the twentieth century. How could the school restore the direct contact with materials and the personal responsibility which the child had learned on the farm or in the course of participating in and watching domestic production? New social conditions had introduced a new situation, had destroyed an earlier balance, and the problem was one of restoring certain desirable elements of the previous situation.

The one tendency in the schools of the time which Dewey found encouraging was the introduction of manual training—shopwork—and the household arts—sewing and cooking. These he conceived as methods of living and learning, as instrumentalities through which the school itself was to be made a genuine form of active community life, instead of a place set apart in which to learn lessons. Dewey's description of the atmosphere in such a school is remarkably like Veblen's picture of the early form of society, in which activity was carried on in a peaceable, nonpredatory manner, and in which emulation, where it existed, served the ends of the community. Dewey's description is worth quoting at length:

The difference that appears when occupations are made the articulating centers of school life is not easy to describe in words; it is a difference in motive, of spirit and atmosphere. As one enters a busy kitchen in which a group of children are actively engaged in the preparation of food, the psychological difference, the change from the more or less passive and inert recipiency and restraint to one of buoyant outgoing energy, is so obvious as fairly to strike one in the face. Indeed, to those whose image of the school is rigidly set the change is sure to give a shock. But the change in the social attitude is equally marked. The mere absorption of facts and truths is so exclusively individual an affair that it tends very naturally to pass into selfishness. There is no obvious social motive for the acquirement of mere learning, there is no clear social gain in success thereat. Indeed, almost the only measure for success is a competitive one, in the bad sense of that term—a comparison of results in the recitation or in the examination to see which child has succeeded in getting ahead of others in storing up, in accumulating the maximum of information. So thoroughly is this the prevalent atmosphere that for one child to help another in his task has become a school crime. Where the school work consists in simply learning lessons, mutual assistance, instead of being the most natural form of cooperation and association, becomes a clandestine effort to relieve one's neighbor of his proper duties. Where active work is going on all this is changed. Helping others, instead of being a form of charity which impoverishes the recipient, is simply an aid in setting free the powers and furthering the impulse of the one helped. A spirit of free communication, of interchange of ideas, suggestions, results, both successes and failures of previous experiences, becomes the dominating note of the recitation. So far as emulation enters in, it is in the comparison of individuals, not with regard to the quantity of information personally absorbed, but with reference to the quality of work done— the genuine community standard of value. In an informal but all the more pervasive way, the school life organizes itself on a social basis.[4]

If the reader will go through *The Theory of the Leisure Class* and then turn immediately to *The School and Society* he will see for himself the affinity in outlook. Dewey's school was to be socially minded, imbued with the values of community life, rather than with the values of individual acquisitiveness; it was to reject the traditional school's concern with accumulation and invidious competition. And where emulation (a good Veblenian word) did enter, it would enter as a service to the community and not as an expression of socially useless struggle or as evidence of the mere possession of learning. Dewey's school was clearly trying, in Veblen's words, to salvage that aspect of modern culture which was dominated by industry and socially useful occupation, while it tried to escape the educational counterparts of pecuniary emulation—useless learning. I am not interested in proving any "influence" here, for I am not sure that one could show any one-way relation between the early Dewey and the early Veblen. Rather, I want to stress the intellectual and social link between early institutionalism and instrumentalism—two of the chief intellectual movements originating in Chicago at the time.

The purpose of the new education was to affiliate the school with life, to make it a "miniature community," "an embryonic society." But in one respect this education was not to be a replica of early domestic industry. There the child had participated and shared in the work "not for the sake of the sharing," but for the sake of the product. "But in the school the typical occupations followed are freed from all economic stress. The aim is not the economic value of the products, but the development of social power and insight. It is this liberation from narrow utilities, this openness to the possibilities of the human spirit that makes these practical activities in the school allies of art and centers of science and history." [5] Dewey was trying to introduce the industrial aspects of modern life while he eliminated those which stemmed from business. The school was to be a miniature of only one part of capitalist society at the time—that part which was free from the stifling effects of pecuniary emulation; the school was to be a miniature of capitalism without tears. In this way Dewey began his half-century campaign in defense of instrumentalism as a humane philosophy which did not worship the commercial values of American society. If pragmatism were to be construed as an expression of American capitalism, it would best be construed as an expression of its industry rather than of its business in Veblen's sense.

Just as history, theory, and practice were the three fundamental categories in Dewey's ethical views at the time, so history, science, and art were looked upon as the central themes of education. In manual training the child was to have an opportunity to see the development of human history represented in the different processes involved in sewing and weaving. He would also gain insight into the method of science, since all activity, to be successful, Dewey said, has to be directed somewhere and somehow by the scientific expert. As early as 1899 Dewey, as we have seen, battled against the view that his system of education was narrowing. "When occupations in the school are conceived in this broad and generous way, I can only stand lost in wonder at the objections so often heard, that such occupations are out of place in the school because they are materialistic, utilitarian, or even menial in tendency. It sometimes seems to me that those who make these objections must live in quite another world. The world in which most of us live is a world in which everyone has a calling and occupation, something to do. Some are managers and others are subordinates. But the great thing for one as for the other is that each shall have had the education which enables him to see within his daily work all there is in it of large and human significance. How many of the employed are today mere appendages to the machine which they operate! This may be due in part to the machine itself, or to the regime which lays so much stress upon the products of the machine; but it is certainly due in large part to the fact that the worker has had no opportunity to develop his imagination and his sympathetic insight as to the social and scientific values found in his work. At present, the impulses which lie at the basis of the industrial system are either practically neglected or positively distorted during the school period. Until the instincts of construction and production are systematically laid hold of in the years of childhood and youth, until they are trained in social directions, enriched by historical interpretation, controlled and illuminated by scientific method, we certainly are in no position even to locate the source of our economic evils, much less to deal with them effectively." [6]

The school became for Dewey one of the central institutions in modern society, one which would help locate the source of our "economic evils" and give us a start toward eliminating them. Learning must cease to be a class matter; it must no longer be "possessed." He neatly turned the tables on those who said that his type of education would produce narrow specialists; on the contrary, he replied, "It is our present education which is highly specialized, one-sided and narrow. It is an education dominated almost entirely by the medieval conception of learning. It is something which appeals for the most part simply to the intellectual aspect of our natures, our desire to learn, to accumulate information, and to get control of the symbols of learning; not to our impulses and tendencies to make, to do, to create, to produce, whether in the form of utility or of art." The division between the so-called liberal education and technical education he viewed as an expression of the division between cultured people and workers, and ultimately of the separation of theory and practice. Nothing could have been closer to Veblen's view at the time, for Veblen looked upon the teaching of classics as an expression of conspicuous waste, and regarded the sciences as more directly concerned with the community's industrial life. Veblen's interpretation of the study of classics, correct spelling, elegant diction, syntax, and prosody as conspicuous waste was intimately related to Dewey's views of the traditional school as uselessly formal and symbolic. It was even more obviously related to Dewey's attack on waste in education. "This question of waste," Dewey said, "is not one of the waste of money or the waste of things. These matters count; but the primary waste is that of human life, the life of the children while they are at school, and afterward because of inadequate and perverted preparation." [7]

So it was that Veblen's attack on waste—the failure to serve human life—had its educational counterpart in the first great work on progressive education. But Dewey was less indifferent and coy about the moral implications to be drawn. For Dewey the failure to serve human life as a whole was enough to demand action, enough to substantiate the conclusion that things were going wrong, for he concluded that "the obvious fact is that our social life has undergone a thorough and radical change. If our education is to have any meaning of life, it must pass through an equally complete transformation." [8]

The social transformation which Dewey, Veblen, Beard, and Robinson came to observe was primarily economic in character. They stressed this in all their writings. It led them to emphasize economic factors in each of their special fields and to impose practical obligations on each of their disciplines. We have already seen the effects of this movement in Veblen, in Dewey's theory of progressive education, in Robinson's new history, in Beard's economic interpretation of American politics. Perhaps the most philosophical expression of it came in the chief distinction of the second part of Dewey's and Tufts' *Ethics*—the distinction between "real" and "formal" freedom. Here again Dewey appeared as the most forthright critic of American society in the group we are considering. Holmes was immersing himself in the technicalities of the law (as distinct from morals); Veblen was "avoiding" any "moral" judgments in his economic analyses; and Beard was insisting in 1908 that it was not the function of the student of politics to praise or condemn institutions or theories, but to expound them. Meanwhile Dewey was accepting the responsibility of a moralist and looking critically at American society.

The distinction which Dewey drew between "real" and "formal" freedom was related to the distinction between economic and political democracy which was so fundamental in the literature of socialism and social reform of the nineteenth century. In Dewey's case it is formulated in Hegelian terms which add little, as far as I can see, to the importance of the point. Following the Hegelian habit of calling that which one condemned or found incomplete "formal" and "external," he said: "In its external aspect, freedom is negative and formal. It signifies freedom *from* subjection to the will and control of others; exemption from bondage; release from servitude; capacity to act without being exposed to direct obstructions or interferences from others. It means a clear road, cleared of impediments, for action. It contrasts with the limitations of prisoner, slave, and serf, who have to carry out the will of others." [9] Formal freedom is contrasted with real or "effective" freedom. To be effectively free one must be at least formally free, but there are other requirements for effective freedom. Among them are "positive control of the resources necessary to carry purposes into effect, possession of the means to satisfy desires; and . . . mental equipment with the trained powers of initiative and reflection" necessary for "free preference and for circumspect . . . far-seeing desires." "The freedom of an agent who is merely released from direct external obstructions is formal and empty. If he is without resources of personal skill, without control of the tools of achievement, he must inevitably lend himself to carrying out the directions and ideas of others. If he has not powers of deliberation and invention, he must pick up his ideas casually and superficially from the suggestions of his environment and appropriate the notions which the interests of some class insinuate into his mind. If he have not powers of intelligent self-control, he will be in bondage to appetite, enslaved to routine, imprisoned within the monotonous round of an imagery flowing from illiberal interests, broken only by wild forays into the illicit." [10]

Our discussion in the chapter on the revolt against formalism should make it easier to understand the terminology of this distinction. But the Hegelian machinery should not obscure the important point which Dewey was making. Those who value the point implicit in the distinction will be able to accept it on its own account, and perhaps, where they are charitable, credit Hegel with having furnished Dewey with a vocabulary in which the point might be made. But Dewey himself has told us of his having continued to use Hegelian terminology long after he had repudiated the key doctrines of Hegel's logic, and this distinction between formal and effective freedom is a testimony to the survival of Hegel's language in Dewey's ethical writings. It is the ethical expression of his early revolt against formalism which, when read formally and externally, links him with the fuzzy tradition of Hegel, but which is real and effective evidence of his connections with the progressive, liberal ideology of 1908.

Dewey and Tufts published their *Ethics* just three years after Holmes' famous dissent in the Lochner case, in which the individualistic doctrine of formal freedom had been dealt its most severe blow in the history of the Supreme Court. The Lochner dissent was Holmes' contribution in 1905 to the progressive era, to the muckrakers and the liberals who wanted to distinguish between formal and effective freedom. But Holmes up to then had not been a vocal leader of the progressive or liberal movement. *The Common Law* had marked him as a scholar and given him the right to speak to the various ghosts which jurisprudence had harbored in its chambers, but nothing had as yet singled him out as a politically enlightened jurist. At best he appeared as a cultivated lawyer whose interest in checkmating chicane was somehow softened and made delicate by learning and taste.

The Lochner case arose when the State of New York enacted legislation providing for a ten-hour day and a sixty-four-hour week in the baking industry. The Supreme Court was called upon to test its validity. It invalidated the law by a vote of five to four with Justice Peckham writing the majority opinion, an opinion in which he maintained that the law jeopardized the liberty of contract guaranteed by the Fourteenth Amendment. If the police power were used to validate the legislation, "no trade, no occupation," the Justice warned, "no mode of earning one's living, could escape this all-pervading power, and the acts of the legislature in limiting the hours of labor in all employments would be valid, although such limitation might seriously cripple the ability of the laborer to support himself and his family." [11] It was before this legal backdrop and on the social stage created during the earliest years of this century that Holmes' dissent was made. It was a dissent which instantly made him a serious (though somewhat aloof) comrade-in-arms of the liberal, progressive, and professorial movement for reform. Overnight he became the idol of labor lawyers and social workers. "This case is decided upon an economic theory which a large part of the country does not entertain," began Holmes. The economic theory, of course, was that of the classical school as it was advanced in Herbert Spencer's austere theory of noninterference with the so-called natural phenomena of capitalist economics. But, Holmes pointed out, "it is settled by various decisions of this court that state constitutions and state laws may regulate life in many ways which we as legislators might think as injudicious or, if you like, as tyrannical as this, and which equally with this interfere with the liberty to contract. Sunday laws and usury laws are ancient examples. A more modern one is the prohibition of lotteries. The liberty of the citizen to do as he likes so long as he does not interfere with the liberty of others to do the same, which has been a shibboleth for some well-known writers, is interfered with by school law, by the Post Office, by every state or municipal institution which takes his money for purposes thought desirable, whether he likes it or not." And then that climactic declaration which became a battle cry (though a negative one): "The Fourteenth Amendment does not enact Mr. Herbert Spencer's *Social Statics.*" In this Holmes struck out against the conservative social Darwinists, against the intellectual roots of the senatorial philosophy which Beard described in his *Contemporary American History.*

In this dissent Holmes provides another problem for those who would understand the intricacies of his philosophy of law. We have observed his emphasis in *The Common Law* upon the judge's introduction of considerations of "public policy" in making his decisions. That approach, of course, is directed against the view that the judge is merely a well-trained student of syllogistic logic supplied with the vocabulary of the law. It emphasizes the indisputable presence of extra-legal factors in the judicial process. But in the Lochner dissent Holmes cited a series of cases which, as he put it, "cut down the liberty to contract" and then added: "Some of these laws embody convictions or prejudices which judges are likely to share. Some may not. But a constitution is not intended to embody a particular economic theory, whether of paternalism and the organic relation of the citizen to the state or of laissez faire. It is made for people of fundamentally differing views, and the accident of our finding certain opinions natural and familiar or novel and even shocking ought not to conclude our judgment upon the question whether statutes embodying them conflict with the Constitution of the United States." The question arises: Is this view consistent with the view that considerations of public policy do and ought to enter into judicial decision? The answer to this question depends upon a serious analysis of the phrase "considerations of public policy." One way of assuring Holmes' consistency is to underline the word "public." If "public" is emphasized in the phrase from *The Common Law*, then the Lochner dissent must be interpreted as an attack upon judicial reference to considerations of personal, narrow policy which thwart public policy, rather than as an attack on all judicial reference to policy. But, then, is it the implication of the Lochner dissent to urge the court to keep its hand on the country's political pulse? To sound out public opinion on each question that comes before it? Did Holmes mean to convey this in urging that the judge's economic theory be excluded from his reflections on constitutionality? Or did he mean to revert to some more formalistic view according to which the judge was to hold the statute in one hand and the Constitution in the other and to see in some "objective" legal way whether they dovetailed? Did he really believe that matters of constitutionality could be separated from all economic and political theories? On this the Lochner dissent for all of its excellence is not continuously clear. Nevertheless it was "a flash of lightning [in] the dark heavens of juridical logic," to use Beard's phrase [12]—a succinct expression of the progressive legal mind.

By now it will be clear how our thinkers are linked with each other. Their community is not so much that of an agreement on one set of principles as that of the links in a chain. Veblen, who is in so many ways remote from Oliver Wendell Holmes, becomes united with him through the mediation of Dewey. Dewey's views on education emphasized the wasteful character of the sheltered school, the school that is remote from society, while Veblen analyzed the leisure class in just about the same terms. But then Dewey advocated a kind of freedom which was effective and real, and it was this which brought his political philosophy into direct contact with the liberalism of the Lochner dissent. The result was an indirect link between Veblen and Holmes. It would be fallacious, of course, to argue that because Veblen and Dewey joined on a certain issue and because Dewey and Holmes joined on another that therefore there must be some third issue on which Holmes and Veblen were linked. But the linkage between them all resembles that of a large chain made up of tightly connected parts; this epitomizes the sense in which they came to make up a single philosophy in American social thought.

CHAPTER VIII

High Ideals and Catchpenny Realities

BY 1912 the outline of what I have called "the liberal ideology"
had been drawn. It was anti-formalist, evolutionary, historically oriented; it was deeply concerned with the economic aspects
of society. Veblen had dissected the leisure class and had set up
his war between business and industry; Dewey gave philosophical
support to the distinction between formal and effective freedom; Holmes had defined the law in practical terms and had
lent a hand to the reformers; Robinson had started his propa-
gandizing for the new history; and his younger colleague Beard
was beginning his study of the economic basis of politics. Pragmatism was already a national password.

Beard's *Economic Interpretation of the Constitution* hardly
appears surprising as an American product of 1913, for it comes
in the middle of an age interested in just such interpretation,
interest which Beard found in "Professor Roscoe Pound and
Professor Goodnow, and in occasional opinions rendered by
Mr. Justice Holmes of the Supreme Court of the United
States."[1] His reference to Pound and Holmes is extremely illuminating, and it gives considerable support to the view that
Beard felt a deep kinship with Holmes' campaign against formalism in legal philosophy. Holmes did not return Beard's
compliment, as we shall see, but we should not allow this to

obscure the great similarity in their thinking or the admiration for Holmes which Beard felt. Beard was especially affected by Holmes' Lochner dissent and he enthusiastically greeted the famous remark on Herbert Spencer's *Social Statics* as well as the aphorism, "General propositions do not decide concrete cases. The decision will depend on a judgment or intuition more subtle than any articulate major premise." [2] No wonder it was a flash of lightning that illuminated the "dark heavens of juridical logic" for Beard! Beard complained about American historians of law in a manner reminiscent of Holmes in *The Common Law* and "The Path of the Law." He quoted a statement from a typical legal history of the period: "The law of England and America has been a pure development proceeding from a constant endeavor to apply to the civil conduct of men the ever advancing standard of justice," and he commented: "In other words, law is made out of some abstract stuff known as 'justice.' What set the standard in the beginning and why does it advance?" [3] He complained of the devotion which American lawyers showed to deductions from "principles" in a vein which revealed the influence of Holmes. He associated himself with Roscoe Pound, who had described the Lochner dissent in 1909 as "the best exposition we have" of "the sociological movement in jurisprudence, the movement for pragmatism as a philosophy of law, the movement for the adjustment of principles and doctrines to the human conditions they are to govern rather than to assumed first principles, the movement for putting the human factor in the central place and relegating logic to its true position as an instrument." [4]

In support of his general outlook Beard cited Arthur Bentley's *The Process of Government,* another expression of a pragmatic movement in political science at the time. He also made it plain that his point of view was similar to that of A. M. Simons, Gustavus Myers, and E. R. A. Seligman. In short, he allied himself with legal realism, sociological jurisprudence, pragmatic political theory, and Marxian history in an intellectual movement against the dominant political science and constitutional history of his day.

When he described the prevailing temper in historiography his connections with Robinson and the new history became evident, for he outlined an account of historical attitudes in America which closely paralleled the history of European history which Robinson had presented in 1908.[5] In America Beard found three schools of historical research and generalization. One was the school best identified by its association with Bancroft, which "explains the larger achievements in our national life by reference to the peculiar moral endowments of a people acting under divine guidance," a school "which sees in the course of our development the working out of a higher will than that of man." [6] A second was the "Teutonic" school of interpretation, which saw in the Federal Constitution the political genius of the Germanic tribes who invaded England and whose English descendants settled America. A third was the school which, in reaction to the first two, avoided interpretation and generalization, and satisfied itself with careful editions of the documents and materials of history.

Beard's treatment of his predecessors employed a scheme which Robinson had already used to advantage. The first two schools in Beard's account fall into Robinson's category of historians who want to amuse, edify, or comfort the reader. The first is theological, while the second is racist in outlook. Beard turned his back on both, for he rejected the demands of theology, morals, and patriotism in his scientific study of politics. Now the third school listed in the *Economic Interpretation of the Constitution* was also considered by Robinson. It is essentially the group that wants to report things "as they really are," to state the elementary atomic facts. Let these speak for themselves, they said; let the reader form his own generalizations and interpretations. Beard's reaction to the third group was different in principle from his reaction to the first two. He completely rejected the providential, the racist, and the patriotic outlook, whereas he too was obviously anxious to get at the "facts" of history. But he wanted more than the facts. Like Robinson, he was interested in how things came to be as they are, as well as in how things are. His attitude toward the fact-finders was very much like Veblen's attitude toward some of his own predecessors in economics. Veblen, it will be recalled, found the historical school of economics satisfactory in so far as it unearthed vast amounts of data, but he deplored its failure to supply a theory of the process of economic development. Beard's sympathy with this critique of chronicle and classification extended even to the use of a biological analogy similar to Veblen's. "Such historical writing," he said, "bears somewhat the same relation to scientific history which systematic botany bears to ecology; that is, it classifies and orders phenomena, but does not explain their proximate or remote causes and relations." [7] Veblen, we remember, was also anxious to go beyond classification, beyond taxonomy, and on to laws of "sequence," theories of process and cumulative change. Both Veblen and Beard shared this point of view with the Marxists. For instance, one of the most learned of American socialists, A. M. Simons, had said in a historical work: "I have tried to describe the dynamics of history rather than to record the accomplished facts, to answer the question, Why did it happen? as well as, What happened?" [8] In the same spirit Beard had insisted in 1908 that "a treatise on causation in politics would be the most welcome contribution which a scholar of scientific training and temper could make." [9] His book on the Constitution, then, was part of a reaction to "barren political history" dominated by the needs of race, nation, and religion, a reaction in which the new history of Robinson also participated. Beard's attempt to link economics with politics was closely related to the new jurisprudence of Holmes and Pound, to pragmatic tendencies in political theory, and to the Marxian search for causal connections and historical explanations.

The role of Marx in this period is not entirely clear, but I

want to repeat that Robinson, more than any of the economically oriented scholars, credited Marx with having been an intellectual forerunner of the outlook. Robinson insisted that history
had been unscientific for three thousand years. Where, then, did
he place the origin of scientific history? In an "unexpected
source," he replied. "Perhaps Buckle was right," he said, "when
he declared that the historians have on the whole been inferior
in point of intellect to thinkers in other fields. At any rate it
was a philosopher, economist and reformer, not a professional
student of history, who suggested a wholly new and wonderful
series of questions which the historian might properly ask about
the past, and moreover furnished him with a scientific explanation of many matters hitherto ill-understood. I mean Karl Marx."
"In a singular pamphlet called 'The Holy Family,' written in
1845," he continued, "Marx denounced those who discover the
birthplace of history in the shifting clouds of heaven instead
of in the hard, daily work on earth. He maintained that the
only sound and ever valid general explanation of the past was
economic." Interestingly enough, Robinson added: "We are not
concerned here with the complicated genesis of this idea, nor
with the precise degree of originality to be attributed to Marx's
presentation of it." [10] This is interesting because, as we shall
see, Beard was not at all inclined to assign the idea to Marx.
Instead he found it in the writing of James Madison. Robinson
said that few historians would agree that "everything can be explained economically." "But," he concluded, "in the sobered and
chastened form in which most economists now receive the doctrine, it serves to explain far more of the phenomena of the
past than any other single explanation ever offered." [11]

/ The *Economic Interpretation of the Constitution* was a manifestation of this prevalent interest in sobered and chastened
economic determinism./ First of all, it did not advance a general theory about the relation of the economic factor to all other
aspects of culture—like literature, art, philosophy—all of which
comprised the "superstructure" for Marx; it simply advanced a

theory of the formation of the Constitution of the United States. As such it was limited to the political part of Marx's super-structure, a part which only the most absurd would cut off from economic factors. Moreover, it did not even advance a general theory of the relation between politics and economics (although such a theory was implicit in it); it was simply an attempt to give an "economic interpretation" of one political instrument, and to document that interpretation with an array of facts outnumbering any that had been offered by an American economic determinist. Up to then, Beard said, economic interpretation had "been more or less discussed as a philosophic theory" in America, and not as a theory to be subjected to the facts. "The theory of economic determinism," he argued quite pragmatically, "has not been tried out in American history, and until it is tried out, it cannot be found wanting." [12] And so Beard advanced defensively upon exalted material, brandishing a blunt instrument but fortified by the fact that it was not the exlusive weapon of foreigners, for it had been used by the great Madison in the tenth Federalist paper.

The Constitution, Beard pointed out, was created by some men and opposed by others. If it were possible, he said, to have what he called economic biographies of all the men who participated in its framing and adoption (whose number he estimated at about 160,000), "the materials for scientific analysis and classification would be available." An economic biography must include "a list of the real and personal property owned by all of these men and their families: lands and houses, with incumbrances, money at interest, slaves, capital invested in shipping and manufacturing, and in state and continental securities." Once you have these biographies you line up both sets of men—those for and those opposed to adoption—and you see whether they exhibit a marked division according to the amount and kind of property they own. If you were to find that "men owning substantially the same amounts of the same kinds of property were equally divided on the matter of adoption or rejection—it would then become apparent that the Constitution had no ascertainable relation to economic groups or classes, but was the product of some abstract causes remote from the chief business of life—gaining a livelihood." [13] *But,* if you found "that substantially all of the merchants, money lenders, security holders, manufacturers, shippers, capitalists, and financiers and their professional associates are to be found on one side in support of the Constitution and that substantially all or the major portion of the opposition came from the non-slaveholding farmers and the debtors—would it not be pretty conclusively demonstrated," Beard asks, "that our fundamental law was not the product of an abstraction known as 'the whole people,' but of a group of economic interests which must have expected beneficial results from its adoption?" [14]

This is a statement of what Beard thought he had to show in order to establish his thesis conclusively. He candidly admitted that "all the facts here desired cannot be discovered," referring, no doubt, to the 160,000 biographies. His study, however, tried to present enough evidence to render his view of the situation plausible. To this end he piled fact upon fact in a series of economic biographies of the framers of the Constitution, and came to the conclusion that the vague thing known as "the advancement of general welfare" or some abstraction known as "justice" was not the immediate guiding purpose of the leaders. Rather, the impelling motives were the economic advantages which the beneficiaries expected would accrue from their action. Moreover, he concluded, "the Constitution was not created by 'the whole people' as the jurists have said; neither was it created by 'the states' as Southern nullifiers long contended; but it was the work of a consolidated group whose interests knew no state boundaries and were truly national in their scope." [15]

Because of the character of the period in which this book appeared, later historians, as well as those present at its appearance, linked it with the tumultuous political scene. So, for example, Parrington described Beard's work and J. Allen Smith's

Spirit of American Government (1907) as summaries of "the democratic case against the Constitution as it was formulated by the liberalism of the pre-war days, and they go far to explain the temper of the Progressive movement in its labors to democratize the instrument through the direct primary, the initiative, the referendum, the recall and the like." [16] In the same way Joseph Freeman reports the glee with which socialists cited Beard's work as professional evidence in favor of their cause.[17] Beard, like Veblen, became the scholarly idol of all those who were engaged in reformist and radical activity. But we have seen that Beard himself regarded the task of a political scientist as different from that of a moralist.[18] Yet even his own disclaimer cannot erase the fact that his "objective" discoveries, like Veblen's at the time, were more useful to one political party than to another. To this extent they had great moral consequences, in spite of Beard's reluctance to draw any. We must remember that Beard explicitly denied that certain famous Americans had acted in the interest of the "advancement of general welfare" and "justice." To be sure, he did not pass judgment on this failure, but his readers had certain values which must have led *them* to make the necessary judgments. To some Beard appeared like a man who was reporting objectively a series of murders and tortures, but who left it to his reader to judge their morality. Justice Holmes' attitude toward the book is revealing in this connection. Beard reports that Holmes once remarked "that he had not got excited about the book, like some of his colleagues, but had supposed that it was intended to throw light on the nature of the Constitution, and, in his opinion, did so in fact." [19] But a slightly different reaction is recorded in Holmes' letters to Pollock (published *after* Beard's report of his conversation with Holmes). Writing in 1928, Holmes says: "I am reading an able book: Parrington, *Main Currents in American Thought,* which gives a very interesting picture, or rather analysis, of the elements at work from the beginning. But I shall not easily believe the thesis running through it and started by earlier works of Beard (*An Economic Interpretation of the Constitution*, etc.) to the effect that the Constitution primarily represents the triumph of the money power over democratic agrarianism and individualism. Beard I thought years ago when I read him went into rather ignoble though most painstaking investigation of the investments of the leaders, with an innuendo even if disclaimed. I shall believe until compelled to think otherwise that they wanted to make a nation and invested (bet) on the belief that they would make one, not that they wanted a powerful government because they had invested. Belittling arguments always have a force of their own, but you and I believe that high-mindedness is not impossible to man." [20]

Holmes' feeling that Beard was discrediting the framers was shared by many, and although Beard did not discredit them explicitly he assigned motives to them which, if he were right, would have denied them that "high-mindedness" which so many of their worshipers valued. There can be no doubt that Beard was effectively "belittling" the founding fathers in the eyes of some, no matter how much he disclaimed any moral interest. In 1916 Holmes had been even more disturbed at this. "I have taken up *An Economic Interpretation of the Constitution of the U.S.* S. Patten set an example years ago in seeking the origins of new philosophies in economic changes and to that end studied the biographies from Hobbes to Darwin to find the original *aperçu* that started them, by which they broke in, subsequent system-making being immaterial. This cove in like manner studies the account of the members of the Const. Convention. To find out what? He mentions the amount of U.S. or state scrip held by them. Why? It doesn't need evidence that the men who drew the Constitution belonged to the well-to-do classes and had the views of their class. The writer disclaims the imputation of self-seeking motives yet deems it important to constate all the facts. Except for a covert sneer I can't see anything in it so far." [21]

Beard's conception of economic interpretation was, in part,

responsible for the reactions of his readers, particularly those who shared Holmes' attitudes. It is primarily concerned with motives, and motives are the stock in trade of moralists. Indeed Holmes identified ethics with a concern with motives. He was prepared to believe that laws are not mere deductions from ethical principles, and to this extent Beard had reason to expect his sympathy. Hadn't he proclaimed that the life of the law was not logic, and that the felt necessities of the time and matters of social policy entered in? But that would have directed him against merely one doctrine which Beard was opposing, and need not have entailed his support of so "ignoble" a research as Beard's. Although Holmes felt that the judges made the law, as a judge he could hardly have agreed that legislators were generally motivated by such base considerations. As a descendant of the class which had participated in the framing of the Constitution he was not in sympathy with Beard's forthrightness on the matter. And yet in so far as Beard's study is an expression of what I have called organicism, it is part of the same movement which included Holmes' philosophy of the law. Although differences crop up, they ought not to blur the broad alliance of Beard and Holmes against other intellectual traditions in America.

We must make allowances for the discrepancy in tone between Holmes' noncommittal remark to Beard and his more candid letter to Pollock about the *Economic Interpretation of the Constitution.* In a sense the remark is not strictly inconsistent with the disparagement intended by the letter. But Beard did have reason to expect more emotional sympathy than the letter expressed. He might have expected it not only because of the affinity between himself and Holmes associated with their common opposition to formalism, but also on the basis of Holmes' published reflections on class interest in legislation. Indeed Mr. Justice Frankfurter, one of Holmes' most distinguished successors (it is difficult to say "followers" any longer), has associated Holmes with James Madison on this question. In the tenth Federalist paper Madison dealt with the subject of faction in government. A faction for Madison is a group of people actuated by a common interest which runs counter to the interest of the community as a whole. Factions are caused, he says, by the unequal distribution of property; the unequal distribution of property is caused by "the diversity in the faculties of men." The direct source of faction is liberty, and so if you wish to remove faction you have two alternatives: either to remove liberty as the source of faction or to control the effects of faction. Madison speedily rejects the first alternative. It would be like destroying the atmosphere in order to prevent fire. He chooses the second, and so he takes the position that "the regulation of these various and interfering interests forms the principal task of modern legislation, and involves the spirit of party and faction in the necessary and ordinary operations of government."

Frankfurter has justly made Holmes out as a supporter of the Madisonian view to which Beard subscribed throughout his life. For this reason Holmes' dismissal of Beard's work may seem even more surprising. Even if his letter to Pollock did not express a logical disagreement, it revealed an animus against Beard's "ignoble" research and his "innuendo" that the founders were governed exclusively by self-seeking motives. The passage which Frankfurter cites in order to justify assigning a Madisonian view of society to Holmes is also interesting because of its political implications. Frankfurter presents the following excerpt from "The Gas-Stokers' Strike" (1873) as evidence of Holmes' agreement with Madison and as an expression of Madison's view in Holmes' "own way":

This tacit assumption of the solidarity of the interests of society is very common, but seems to us to be false . . . in the last resort a man rightly prefers his own interest to that of his neighbors. And this is as true in legislation as in any other form of corporate action. All that can be expected from modern improvements is that legislation should easily and quickly, yet not too quickly, modify itself in accordance with the will of the *de facto* supreme power in the community, and that the spread of an educated sympathy should reduce the sacrifice of minorities to a minimum. . . . The objection to class legislation is not that it favors a class, but either that it fails to benefit the legislators, or that it is dangerous to them because a competing class has gained in power, or that it transcends the limits of self-preference which are imposed by sympathy. . . . But it is no sufficient condemnation of legislation that it favors one class at the expense of another; for much or all legislation does that, and none the less when the *bona fide* object is the greatest good of the greatest number. . . . If the welfare of all future ages is to be considered, legislation may as well be abandoned for the present. . . . The fact is that legislation in this country, as well as elsewhere, is empirical. It is necessarily made a means by which a body, having the power, puts burdens which are disagreeable to them on the shoulders of somebody else.[22]

It must be remembered that this was published in 1873, forty years before the appearance of the *Economic Interpretation of the Constitution*. It was written by a young lawyer whose generation, as Max Lerner has reminded us, sat at the feet of Darwin, Spencer, and Bagehot. In 1873 Holmes not only admitted the existence of class interests in legislation, but he saw no moral objection to legislating in their behalf. The relation between the Beard of the *Economic Interpretation of the Constitution* and the Holmes of "The Gas-Stokers' Strike" on this question may be formulated as follows: they agreed that class interest functioned in legislation but, while Holmes was not morally repelled by this, Beard gave the impression that *he* was (even though he avoided any explicit moral comment). Holmes' attitude on this question is made more explicit in the passages which Frankfurter omits in his quotation. For example, after Holmes refers to the greatest good of the greatest number, he asks: "Why should the greatest number be preferred? Why not the greatest good of the most intelligent and most highly developed? The greatest good of a minority of our generation may be the greatest good of the greatest number in the long run." And two lines further on he says: "If the welfare of the living majority is paramount, it can only be on the ground that the majority have the power in their hands." Passages like these have led some to associate Holmes, not with Madison, but rather with Pareto and theories of the elite.

Beard outlined the history of various doctrines about the relations between class interest and legislation in his *Economic Basis of Politics* (1916). In it he pointed out that the recognition of the existence of class interest in politics was not peculiar to radical or revolutionary thinkers, and that not all those who admitted the fact of class interest in legislation deplored it. He made clear that legislation in the interest of one's own class was not regarded by all economic determinists as morally contemptible. Hence his reminder that Madison, Webster, and Calhoun shared this kind of view. From Beard's account of their ideas it would seem that Holmes in "The Gas-Stokers' Strike" followed them even more faithfully than Beard did. Perhaps this explains Holmes' feeling that "it doesn't need evidence that the men who drew the Constitution belonged to the well-to-do classes" and his annoyance at the suggestion that this was inconsistent with high-mindedness in legislating for their fellow men. There were other indications that Holmes was closer to Madison than Beard was. In another passage from "The Gas-Stokers' Strike" Holmes added to his statement that legislation is a means of transferring disagreeable burdens from one class to another his conviction that "communism would no more get rid of the difficulty than any other system, unless it limited or put a stop to the propagation of the species." [23] Frankfurter, we may say, was right. Holmes' position was very close to Madison's, even to the point of accepting biological rooting of class differences in human nature, and this biologism about classes was the one important difference between Marx and Madison which Beard failed to emphasize.

While Holmes plainly stood with Madison as against Marx, Beard's position on this matter is somewhat clouded. Beard constantly claimed Madison as his predecessor, of course. But Beard's collaborator, Robinson, was quite forthright in establishing Marx as the originator of the new history and in *The Development of Modern Europe* they both celebrated Marx as one of the most important intellectual forces of the nineteenth century. Furthermore, Beard said in 1913 that his more general views were closely related to those of his Columbia colleague, E. R. A. Seligman, whose *Economic Interpretation of History* (1902) was the most forthright academic defense of Marx's theory of history available in America at the time. Beard said: "The theory of the economic interpretation as stated by Professor Seligman seems as nearly axiomatic as any proposition in social science can be: 'The existence of man depends upon his ability to sustain himself; the economic life is therefore the fundamental condition of all life. Since human life, however, is the life of man in society, individual existence moves within the framework of the social structure and is modified by it. What the conditions of maintenance are to the individual, the similar relations of production and consumption are to the community. To economic causes, therefore, must be traced in the last instance those transformations in the structure of society which themselves condition the relations of social classes and the various manifestations of social life." [24] It should be pointed out that the passage from Seligman was in turn almost a verbatim transcription of a paragraph in Engels, so that, even if Beard had not been familiar with Marx and Engels at first hand, he did acknowledge the influence of a reasonably accurate second-hand version of their ideas.

Beard was, of course, in a peculiar position in his work on the Constitution. He was dealing with an extremely sacred thing, and he was not treating it with awe, but rather as an earthly affair subject to the economic forces of modern society. He was also writing at a time when such an approach to the Constitution might have elicited the well-known conditional request: "If you don't like it here why don't you go back where you came from?" Now this street-corner question was also being asked in the academic and legal corridors of 1913, and Beard was anxious to show that his position was authentically American. This he did quite well, for he found an eminently respectable grandfather for the child in James Madison. But not without self-consciousness. As if in anticipation of the theory's being told to go back where it came from he said (in 1913): "Those who are inclined to repudiate the hypothesis of economic determinism as a European importation must, therefore, revise their views, on learning that one of the earliest, and certainly one of the clearest, statements of it came from a profound student of politics who sat in the Convention that framed our fundamental law." [25]

Although there is something irrelevant about Beard's protest, there is justice in his urging the Madisonian origin of his views, because in at least one way Beard was closer to Madison than he was to Marx. There are two important respects in which Marx's economic determinism differs radically from that which Beard assigned to Madison: First of all, they assigned different roles to economic motives. Marx did not maintain that all human beings selfishly devote themselves to maximizing their wealth and that they have no capacity for "high-minded" action in which they sacrifice their economic interests. It may be said with assurance that Marx's view was not so bald and direct as this. On the other hand Beard's view came close to it and could easily be construed in this way by someone like Holmes. Second, Marx differs from Madison in his conception of the basis of class differences and in his view as to how long class differences will continue in society. In this respect Beard tends to side with Marx in maintaining that class societies are transient and not rooted, as Madison thought, in human nature. Let us elaborate.

1. The concern with economic motive which antagonized Holmes while he read Beard is a distinctive component of Beard's version of economic interpretation, a version which is closely connected with Beard's admiration of Madison. This was the side of Beard which led to his dismissing the hypothesis that the framers had acted out of interest in that vague thing "the advancement of general welfare" or that abstraction "known as

'justice.' " But, ironically enough, in spite of Beard's declared sympathy with the thesis of Seligman's *Economic Interpretation of History,* he was not obviously affected by the chapter on "The Spiritual Factors in History," in which Seligman dealt with what he thought was a misdirected objection to Marx's point of view—the objection that it "neglects the ethical and spiritual forces in history." Seligman said: "It would . . . be absurd to deny that individual men, like masses of men, are moved by ethical considerations. On the contrary, all progress consists in the attempt to realize the unattainable—the ideal, the morally perfect. History is full of examples where nations, like individuals, have acted unselfishly and have followed the generous promptings of the higher life. The ethical and religious teachers have not worked in vain. To trace the influence of the spiritual life in individual and social development would be as easy as it is unnecessary. What is generally forgotten, however, and what it is needful to emphasize again and again, is not only that the content of the conception of morality is a social product, but also that amid the complex social influences that cooperated to produce it, the economic factors have often been of chief significance—that pure ethical or religious idealism has made itself felt only within the limitations of existing economic conditions." [26]

Although Beard may have been empirically justified in his ascription of predominantly economic motives to the founding fathers and quite right in denying that they sought "justice" in quotation marks, this conclusion was not implied by the theory which he quoted from Seligman. Because he was interested in a peculiarly narrow problem, Beard's "application" of the economic interpretation of history gave a peculiar twist to the theory. It suggested that his method was intrinsically psychological, individual, and atomistic in character. Indeed it almost suggested that Beard had surrendered the formalists' political man only to adopt an equally formalistic economic man, whereas only five years earlier he had himself insisted on avoid-

ing both of these abstractions. That Beard should have been
the object of criticisms which Seligman had already parried in
a general way does not mean that Beard was wrong in the particular conclusion which he drew concerning the Constitution,
nor does it justify Holmes' somewhat pompous claim that "it
does not need evidence" to show that the founders were well-
to-do. Nevertheless, it does reveal the need for distinguishing
Beard's version of economic interpretation from those which
were current at the time—in fact those which he cited as allies
of his own. Beard could not have intended that his box-score
method of tallying up incomes on two sides of a controversy
should be the only legitimate application of the theory of
economic interpretation, nor could he have intended to convey
by his somewhat sneering references to "justice" that high-
mindedness was impossible to man. Seligman might well have
added in his defense of Marx that the latter had once said that
the working class valued its dignity more than its bread, and
that he had attacked Bentham repeatedly for his "shopkeeper"
conception of morality. Readers of Beard should have realized
that an economic interpretation of philosophy could not explain
philosophical controversies simply by adding up the total incomes of warring epistemologists. Economic interpretation must
be made more subtly, and one of the unfortunate effects of
Beard's book was its fostering of a peculiarly rigid and lifeless
conception of the general theory. Imitators, anxious to produce
startling conclusions, paid no attention to the specific features
of Beard's research and applied themselves to day-by-day corre-
lations of cultural attitudes with stock-market prices.

2. In his attempt to show the Madisonian origin of his own
views Beard constantly urged the priority of Madison and others
over Marx on the subject of recognizing the existence of classes.
As to this point there should be no question, but we must not
overlook two important historical facts: a. Marx himself did
not claim priority on this point; b. the rooting of classes and
their origin in human nature is a keynote of Madison's "eco-

nomic determinism" but not of Marx's.[27] Madison, although he did believe, as did Marx, that economic classes played a tremendous role in society, also believed, in opposition to Marx, that they were permanent institutions, rooted as they were in the "diversity of human faculties." The same is true of Aristotle, of course, who is also cited by Beard as a precursor.[28] Although liberty, according to Madison, was the avenue whereby property differences led to factions, he could not as a democrat eliminate factions by destroying liberty. Hence he urged their "regulation." The difference between Marx and Madison on this point could hardly have been unknown to Beard. Indeed he mentions the difference in his *Economic Basis of Politics* without explicitly mentioning Marx and Madison. After stating the views of Aristotle, Machiavelli, Locke, Madison, Webster, and Calhoun, Beard says that from their economic views we may derive one of two conclusions. "We may, upon reflection, decide that the distribution of property is the result of changeless forces inherent in the nature of man, and that the statesman is not a maker but an observer of destiny. Or we may hold that once the forces of social evolution are widely understood man may subdue them to his purposes. He may so control the distribution of wealth as to establish an ideal form of society and prevent the eternal struggle of classes that has shaken so many nations to their foundations." [29]

In urging that his idea had an American source Beard was obviously not adding to the theory's probability, and from a scientific point of view it was quite superfluous to have protested so much concerning its American origin. There was nothing attractive about this appeal to the flag. Nevertheless it should be recognized that there was some point to Beard's distinguishing himself from Marx. For, although he undoubtedly was familiar with Marx's writing and although people as close to him as Robinson and Seligman did fix upon Marx as the source of their viewpoints, Beard did not fully agree with Marx. His view of personal economic gain as the motive force in history was not intrinsic to Marx's outlook, and Beard's apparent endorse-ment of *all* of Madison's tenth Federalist paper brought out sharply a fundamental difference between Marx and Beard. For Madison classes were rooted in human nature, but for Marx they were associated only with specific transitory phases in the development of production.

Although Beard insisted upon his own scientific neutrality in his work on the Constitution and emphasized (at least in one place) the historian's need for "coldness" in the face of the facts, his work, like that of Veblen, was the center of a storm. Par-rington may have been wrong, as Beard suggests, in regarding Beard's work along with J. Allen Smith's as prompted by the needs of political liberalism, but there can be no doubt that the viewpoint was used by the progressives of the day. It was seized upon by leftists and liberals. Furthermore, many who defended similar theories of the Constitution and with whom Beard might be associated ideologically were quite outspoken in their political intentions. Smith, for example, was very ex-plicit in linking his position on the "Constitution as a reaction-ary document" with a general point of view in politics. The last chapter of his *Spirit of American Government* is a vigorous attack on laissez-faire doctrine. It is not surprising, therefore, that Beard's book should have been associated with Marxism, socialism, and the progressive movement in spite of his own protestations of scientific coldness and Madisonian intentions. At the time anyone who unearthed an economic reason for a document surrounded with awe and reverence was digging deep into the prevailing ideology. To unmask such a source (as the Marxists would have said) was to reveal the economic bases of political instruments. To construe them as economic instruments obviously made them less sacrosanct. If they were products of one age they might easily be scrapped in another, especially where the other was obviously different from the first. In 1913 any work like this was bound to be construed as a weapon in the hands of those critical of the Constitution. They did not know that its Madisonian philosophy predicted the perpetuation of factional struggles in all future constitutional conventions. For them it was a weapon in the struggle for political change in the interest of their class, and they needed little more than that to idolize its author. And just as they idolized Beard, their opponents vilified him. As an index of the alarm which Beard's ideas caused outside intellectual circles, consider the editorial which appeared in the *New York Times* on October 10, 1917, the day after Beard had resigned from Columbia University. Its title was "Columbia's Deliverance": "Columbia . . . is better for Professor Beard's resignation. Some years ago Professor Beard published a book in which he sought to show that the founders of this Republic and the authors of its Constitution were a ring of land speculators who bestowed upon the country a body of organic law drawn up chiefly in the interests of their own pockets. It was pointed out to him at the time, with due kindness but frankly, that his book was bad, that it was a book no professor should have written, since it was grossly unscientific. . . . It was the fruit of that school of thought and teaching . . . borrowed from Germany, which denies to man in his larger actions the capacity of noble striving and self-sacrifice for ideals, that seeks always as the prompting motive either the animal desire to get more to eat or the hope of filling his pockets. If this sort of teaching were allowed to go unchecked by public sentiment and the strong hands of University Trustees, we should presently find educated American youth applying the doctrine of economic determinism to everything from the Lord's Prayer to the binomial theorem."

Van Wyck Brooks in *America's Coming-of-Age* urged that the antithesis between "highbrow" and "lowbrow" was the most central, explanatory, and illuminating factor in American life. "In everything," he said, "one finds this frank acceptance of twin values which are not expected to have anything in common: on the one hand a quite unclouded, quite unhypocritical assumption of transcendent theory ('high ideals'); on the other a simultaneous acceptance of catchpenny realities." [30] Charles Beard in 1913 was a disturbing scholar who tried to show that certain high ideals had their lines of communication with these catchpenny realities. He was one of the Americans of the early twentieth century who did most to link these two worlds, a pioneer in the century that was to worship and despise Marx and Freud. In his own fashion he was acting out the implications of the revolt against formalism and dualism. Politics and economics were merely aspects of the seamless web of culture, and Beard was carefully following their connecting strands. In the same period John Dewey was doing the same thing for all thought and action.

CHAPTER IX

Creative Intelligence

I N THE first decades of this century American liberal thought was haunted by a fear of being remote. This was one of the sources of the revolt against formalism. Our scholars, though reluctant to propagandize or take part in political action, seemed anxious to maintain some contact with pressing social problems. Veblen was personally aloof, but his doctrine bore vitally on social affairs; Holmes was an urbane defender of legal pragmatism; and Beard was a cool observer who supplied socialists with arguments. Dewey, like James before him, wanted to drag the loftiest of all disciplines down to earth, and in 1916 he called for a recovery in philosophy to free man and society. "Philosophy recovers itself when it ceases to be a device for dealing with the problems of philosophers and becomes a method, cultivated by philosophers, for dealing with the problems of men." [1]

By 1916 Dewey had consolidated his position. In *Democracy and Education* (1916) he had outlined his entire philosophy of education and related it to other aspects of his thought. In *Essays in Experimental Logic* (1916) he republished his 1903 papers on logic (which had previously appeared in the *Studies in Logical Theory*) and added some essays of the intervening years—controversial defenses of pragmatism as he understood it, considerations of the new realistic tendencies in epistemology.

America's entry into the First World War, therefore, found Dewey a philosopher of first importance. Later years saw the appearance of a metaphysics in *Experience and Nature,* an esthetics in *Art as Experience,* and a theory of scientific method in the *Logic,* but these were the fruits of a long, industrious life. Dewey's basic ideas had appeared before World War I and were developed and applied later in an attempt to round out a system, a view of all the serious problems of philosophy.

For Dewey in 1916 the most important general characteristic of philosophy was its conservative attachment to certain problems. This conservatism, he felt, was reinforced by overdependence upon the academic tradition. Hence philosophers bickered over traditional problems stemming from traditional texts and avoided contemporary difficulties, which were left to literature and politics. Because Dewey wanted to bring philosophy into a more practical arena and to rescue it from its exclusive attachment to traditional problems, he began his program of persuasion by emphasizing the differences between the classical tradition and the revolutionary outlook he proposed. In this way he became a renegade philosopher, an academic agitator along with Beard, Robinson, and Veblen. He began by criticizing the notion of experience he found at the base of traditional philosophy. And in order to dramatize what he thought original in his own view he pointed out that the conception of experience he wanted to dislodge was accepted by both empiricism and its traditional opponents. If he could successfully discredit it, therefore, he would go far in his attempt to destroy the philosophical rags which all his predecessors had been chewing for centuries. Then he would construct a theory which would overarch traditional differences, and he would rise above the idle controversy of his contemporaries to a philosophical position which could give "meaning" to the "newer industrial, political, and scientific movements." [2]

According to the orthodox view, experience is "primarily a knowledge-affair." But Dewey denied this and held rather that experience is "an affair of the intercourse of a living being with its physical and social environment." [3] This became a momentous proposition for Dewey, and he hammered at it again and again for the rest of his career. It was said to have the most extreme importance for technical philosophy, and it became a premise with which Dewey attacked the whole realistic epistemology of the day.[4] The assertion that experience is not primarily a knowledge-affair seems to mean simply that human beings do other things or engage in other activities besides knowing. Sometimes we hit baseballs, we listen to symphonies, we buy clothes. This may appear as an enormous triviality to us today, but evidently it meant a great deal to Dewey and to the entire movement called "anti-intellectualism." It should be realized that while engaged in other activities we may concurrently engage in knowing, i.e., we may think rapidly as we face the pitcher who throws us the ball we're about to hit, and we may reason about the price of a suit of clothes, but batting is not thinking, nor is buying, even though both may involve thinking. Having distinguished knowledge from other experiences, Dewey advances to a more specific proposition: "Inquiry occupies an intermediate and mediating place in the development of an experience." [5] In other words, knowledge is a kind of experience; the process of knowing, or inquiry, is a kind of behavior which is usually sandwiched in between other kinds of behavior. In particular, inquiry begins because a human being is engaged in some other kind of activity which creates a problem, and inquiry ends when the problem is solved. This tendency to view thought in a biological and social context has very close affiliations with Beard's economic interpretation. Just as Beard felt that political instruments are devoted to the accomplishment of certain ends that are not political in character, so Dewey urged that thought is always stimulated and initiated by things and activities which are not intellectual in character.

The theory that political action takes place in an economic context and the theory that thought issues from other types of situations share the organicism which has already been discussed. Both of them appeal to factors normally omitted by political science and epistemology. They send the political scientist and the philosopher in search of extra-political and extra-philosophical facts. Just as Beard's theory led him to an economic interpretation of the Constitution, so Dewey's analysis of any particular bit of human thought led him to a study of its motives and consequences. Why did thought begin in this way? Dewey asked, and at once he entered into a field commonly excluded as irrelevant by the traditional logician and methodologist. Beard regarded those who dealt in a purely juridical way with a political document like the Constitution just as Dewey regarded those who approached scientific theory in a purely logical way—as formalists who failed to see the contextual and instrumental character of politics and thought. At the time Beard's view was more specific than Dewey's, for he focused on one type of thinking—politics—and sought one type of extra-political context as a basis for explanation—economics. Dewey was not committed to anything so specific in his epistemology, for when he spoke of extra-intellectual types of behavior or experience, he referred to them as "social, affectional, technological, esthetic." [6] Beard and Dewey shared the theory that politics and thought don't go on in a vacuum, but whereas Beard replaced the vacuum by an economic situation, Dewey held that any number of "social, affectional, technological, esthetic" factors envelop the process of thought. According to Dewey the common denominator of all these extra-intellectual factors was their problem-presenting character.

One of the other objectionable aspects of the traditional view of experience, according to Dewey, was its claim that the past counts exclusively. "Registration of what has taken place, reference to precedent, is believed to be the essence of experience. . . . But experience in its vital form is experimental, an effort to change the given; it is characterized by projection, by reaching forward into the unknown; connection with a future is a salient trait." [7] This cannot be understood without a reference to David Hume.

Hume had insisted that the connection of cause and effect was based on past experience. When we say that a flame will cause a sensation of heat if touched, we say something which can be supported only by reference to past cases of flame-touching constantly conjoined with heat-feeling. But, Hume argued, those who assert a casual connection go beyond constant conjunction and claim that there is a *necessary connection* between the two, which he found hopelessly vague as they explained it. He began by observing that the idea of necessary connection was not based on sensory impressions; he could not see, feel, hear, smell, or taste anything in the long series of flame-heat sequences which corresponded to the idea of necessary connection. Moreover, he would have none of the mumbo-jumbo surrounding the unanalyzed idea of power, according to which the flame had a power to produce heat, because this simply begged the question. Hume was anxious to clear up the idea of cause (and hence necessary connection) while he made peace with his empirical conscience. And so he concluded that the idea of necessary connection did not correspond to any sensible impression of anything in or about the flame-heat sequence, but that it did correspond to a feeling of determination which the mind felt in the presence of flame to pass to the idea of heat. This feeling of determination was an "impression of reflection" (as distinct from an impression of sensation), and it was this which provided the impressional counterpart of the idea of necessary connection. The necessary connection, he said, depended on the causal inference and not the other way around.

Now if it was Hume Dewey was attacking when he invidiously compared the old view of experience with his own, it is hard to know how Dewey could have represented Hume as denying that experience is experimental and projective in character. For Hume maintained in one clear sense precisely that; he insisted that we do project our past experience with flame-heat sequences, for we do predict that the next flame touched *will* be followed by a sensation of heat. What Hume tried to do was to analyze the process whereby this projection could be justifiably carried out, and although Dewey might have been suggesting that Hume dealt with a pseudo-problem, Dewey did not argue his point clearly. It must be remembered that in 1916 Dewey retained a good deal of his Hegelian antagonism to traditional British empiricism. It was "deductive empiricism" rather than "empirical empiricism," [8] and he said, "British empiricism, with its appeal to what has been in the past, is, after all, only a kind of apriorism. For it lays down a fixed rule for future intelligence to follow; and only the immersion of philosophy in technical learning prevents our seeing that this is the essence of apriorism." [9] Here we have confirmation of our theory that Dewey's opposition to formalism included opposition to the tradition of Locke, Berkeley, and Hume. The dependence of this tradition on past experience smacked of conservatism and passivity; its search for "fixed rules" was an expression of its rigidity. One cannot help feeling that Dewey's attack on the empiricists for their concern with what happened in the past is ideologically related to Robinson's attack on the "old history" for its preoccupation with the past. Instrumentalism was plainly associated with the new history and the new political science in its stress on the organic connections of different aspects of experience and its concern with the present and the future. And although instrumentalism strove to show that it was quite different from idealism, it did believe "that faith in the constructive, the creative, competency of intelligence was the redeeming element in historic idealisms." [10]

There were two other important complaints about the orthodox philosophy of experience. It made the mistake, Dewey said, of claiming that experience is primarily psychical and subjective, something which goes on in our heads, a process in an internal world. It also believed that experience could be divided into distinct particulars—this sensation here and now is different from each one preceding and following it, and so on into the future. Hume had held that all our distinct perceptions (ideas and impressions) are distinct existences; what he meant, for example, was that the visual impression of this flame with which I light my pipe is different from the impression of heat I get when I touch the flame. This committed the Humean tradition to what Dewey called "particularism," for, according to Dewey, it followed that Hume could discover no "connections or continuities" in experience. "But the doctrine that sensations and ideas are so many separate existences," Dewey said, in an effort to challenge the empiricism of the empiricists, "was not derived from observation nor from experiment. It was a logical deduction from a prior unexamined concept of the nature of experience. From the same concept it followed that the appearance of stable objects and of general principles of connection was but an appearance." [11]

Kant, according to Dewey, tried to restore connection by postulating a reason which transcends experience. But Kant's great mistake was to accept Hume's particularism and then to try to supplement it from non-empirical sources. Bergson, Dewey thought, made some advance by substituting a doctrine of flux and interpenetration of psychical states, for this removed rigid discontinuity. But this still violated the other misconception of experience as inner and psychical. Dewey believed that Kant's attempt ought to have suggested, though it did not present, a correct account of experience. "For we have only to forget the apparatus by which the net outcome is arrived at, to have before us the experience of the plain man—a diversity of ceaseless changes connected in all kinds of ways, static and dynamic. This conclusion would deal a deathblow to both empiricism and rationalism. For, making clear the non-empirical character of the alleged manifold of unconnected particulars, it would render unnecessary the appeal to functions of the understanding in order to connect them. With the downfall of the traditional notion of experience, the appeal to reason to supplement its defects becomes superfluous." [12] Dewey's proposed solution simply called for a rejection of the problem. The original Humean set of distinct perceptions which demands Kant's external reason as a cementing device is simply an unwarranted fiction, an unfounded abstraction. There are no distinct and separate perceptions, Dewey says, and in this way he thinks that he removes Hume's greatest worry, and *dis*solves the problem. If there are no distinct perceptions which make up experience, then why try to put together things which have never been truly separate?

In stating his attitudes toward traditional schools, Dewey is much more sympathetic to objective idealism than he is to rationalism and empiricism. In a way that reveals his own past affiliations with Hegelianism he speaks of objective idealism with all its short-comings as more positively instructive than its predecessors. Although his break with Hegel was sharp and explicit, he did not react from the doctrines of his youth with contempt and loathing. "Idealism," he said, "is much less formal than historic rational-ism." Because it treats thought as "constitutive of experience," it is a philosophy according to which "thought . . . loses its abstractness and remoteness. But, fortunately, in thus gaining the whole world it loses its own self. A world already, in its intrinsic structure, dominated by thought is not a world in which, save by contradic-tion of premises, thinking has anything to do." [13] This discussion gave him an opportunity, however, to resign his membership in the idealist party, and to say that he deplored a doctrine which appeared to emphasize the importance of thought and yet really deprived it of any efficacy. Those who wanted to use intelligence to improve the world, he said, could hardly regard it as fixed and completely rational.

It should be remembered that *Creative Intelligence* appeared in January 1917, shortly before we entered the First World War. This gives a peculiar significance to Dewey's rejection of both empiri-cism and idealism, for empiricism was British and idealism pre-dominantly German in origin. Hence he was neutral in philosophy at the time when he was neutral in international politics, for in 1916 Dewey was all for keeping out of the war between England and Germany. And so he says: "A practical crisis may throw the relationship of ideas to life into an exaggerated Brocken-like spec-tral relief, where exaggeration renders perceptible features not or-dinarily noted. The use of force to secure narrow because exclusive aims is no novelty in human affairs. The deploying of all the intelligence at command in order to increase the effectiveness of the force used is not so common, yet presents nothing intrinsically remarkable. The identification of force—military, economic, and administrative—with moral necessity and moral culture is, however, a phenomenon not likely to exhibit itself on a wide scale except where intelligence has already been suborned by an idealism which identifies 'the actual with the rational,' and thus finds the measure of reason in the brute event determined by superior force." [14] Here was a jibe at military Hegelianism. It was quickly followed by a statement of how a philosopher could steer a neutral course between this and the equally defective British empirical tradition. "If we are to have a philosophy which will intervene between attachment to rule of thumb muddling [England?] and devotion to a systematized subordination of intelligence to pre-existent ends [Germany?], it can be found only in a philosophy which finds the ultimate measure of intelligence in consideration of a desirable future and in search for the means of bringing it progressively into existence. When professed idealism turns out to be a narrow pragmatism—narrow because taking for granted the finality of ends determined by historic conditions—the time has arrived for a pragmatism which shall be empirically idealistic, proclaiming the essential connection of intelligence with the unachieved future—with possibilities involving a transfiguraton." [15] And so instrumentalism was "empirically idealistic" in the war of knowledge, a superior philosophy which took the best that England and Germany had to offer while they were both struggling for the world. Presumably American epistemology was to sit by with the American Army, secure in the effectiveness of its intelligence, while the narrowly pragmatic Germans and the rule-of-thumb muddling British killed each other. That was the "spectral relief" into which the war had thrown the relationship of ideas in 1916, but Dewey's practical outlook (if not his instrumentalism) was to change in one year.

Dewey's lingering attachment to some of the doctrines of idealism led him to stress the intrinsic connection between thought and its object. At the same time he vigorously denied, as we have seen, that he was an idealist. He also had the greatest difficulty in steering a clear course between the realists, who held that there are objects distinct from the minds which could adequately know them or something about them, and Bergson's view that scientific analysis always falsifies. Philosophers were, as usual, splitting into a scientific and an anti-scientific party. Without going into the obscure and technical details here, we may say that Dewey tried to maintain that "in a sense" there was something "out there," but that in another sense the object of scientific thought was not out there. The scientific object he described as an "objective"—something to be attained or constructed by science itself. The most extensive attempt at clarifying these "senses" was made in Dewey's *Logic,* which appeared in 1938. In 1916 Dewey's emphasis upon the scientific process as the center of the knowledge-situation led him to walk out of the fruitless conventions of American realists and their epistemological enemies. Instead he urged philosophers to turn to a statement of the conditions of success and failure in scientific inquiry. This was logic for Dewey, and it differed radically from what Russell and Whitehead meant by logic. When Charles Peirce saw its first fruits, he called it not logic but "the natural history of thought," and for the Platonic Russell it was, at best, psychology. But in Dewey's eyes it was the only way to escape formalism in logic, a discipline which had been the refuge of the formalist and rationalist tradition. On some occasions he seemed willing to abandon the whole discipline of formal logic; on others he hinted (somewhat obscurely) that "an empirical empiricism, in contrast with orthodox deductive empiricism, has no difficulty in establishing its jurisdiction as to deductive functions." [16] What that meant and whether it is true was more extensively explained and argued in a less oracular manner in the 1938 *Logic.* In 1916 it was the hypothesis of an instrumentalist who was shooting arrows at the mighty fortress of formalism, classical mathematics, and its outer philosophical defense, mathematical logic. Those who claimed that logic demonstrated a radical difference between a knower and a realm of Platonic classes, numbers, relations, and propositions were simply the agents of the most pernicious theory of the day, the spectator theory of knowledge, a theory which Dewey criticized even more severely in *The Quest for Certainty* (1929).

The rejection of the spectator theory of knowledge—according to which there is a true Reality (with a capital R) and a separate knower—leads to the view that knowledge (Dewey came to prefer the word "inquiry") involves active use of the environment. *"Knowledge is always a matter of the use that is made of experienced natural events,* a use in which given things are treated as indications of what will be experienced under different conditions." [17] Now what does this mean concretely? Dewey tried to explain by means of an illustration. Suppose, he begins, "it is a question of knowledge of water"; and what he means, I take it, is, suppose we want to analyze what is involved in knowing that a volume of water has a certain property. "The thing to be known," he goes on, "does not present itself primarily as a matter of knowledge-and-ignorance at all. It occurs as a stimulus to action and as the source of certain undergoings." When he says that it is "a stimulus to action," he means that it leads us to drink, to use it in washing, to use it in extinguishing fire. When he says it is a source of "certain undergoings," he means, for example, that it "makes us undergo disease, suffocation, drowning." A given volume of water, therefore, "enters into experience," or our intercourse with the physical environment, in two ways: (1) we can have intercourse with water by using it to wash our clothes, and (2) the water can have intercourse with us by drowning us. So much is fairly clear, and thus far water is entering experience without being a "matter of knowledge-and-ignorance." Most of us grant that we have used water in washing and that ocean waves have hit us while we were oblivious of the chemical properties of water. Such illustrations help us understand the following: "Such presence [of water] in experience has of itself nothing to do with knowledge or consciousness; nothing, that is, in the sense of depending upon them, though it has everything to do with knowledge and consciousness in the sense that the latter depends upon prior experience of this non-cognitive sort." [18] The first part is relatively clear. But when Dewey says in the second part of his discussion that consciousness and knowledge of water "depend" on experiences like washing and being hit by breakers, he is going on to a new point. He means here that we could not have begun an inquiry into water without first having used it or encountered it in these untheoretical ways. In other words, the scientific inquiry which will terminate in our knowing that water is H_2O does not or cannot start without our having first washed with water, for example, or without water's having "done" something to us.

"When water is an adequate stimulus to action or when its reactions oppress us or overwhelm us, it remains outside the scope of knowledge," Dewey says. "When, however," he continues, "the bare presence of the thing (say, as optical stimulus) ceases to operate directly as stimulus to response [as the water we use to wash with operates], and begins to operate in connection with a forecast of the consequences it will effect when responded to, it begins to acquire meaning—to be known, to be an object. It is noted as something which is wet, fluid, satisfies thirst, allays uneasiness, etc." [19] Now here we have a very instructive passage, one that helps us understand a good deal of Dewey's confusing language about "thought constructing its own object." Clearly the water we used to wash with in our untheoretical moods was in some sense an *object*, for certainly an anthropologist who was watching our washing might have said, "Why, look at that man using that object, i.e., that tub of water, to wash with." But in Dewey's philosophy the volume of water is not an object for us, the washers, while we are simply washing with it and not noting that it is wet, fluid, and so forth. The water does not begin "to be an object" in this curious language until it is known to be wet, fluid, and so on. Needless to add, the original ignorant bather must also be careful not to know that the water is something he is washing with, I imagine, in order to allow Dewey's illustration to keep the volume of water denuded of "objectivity" in his sense.

In amplification of his position Dewey continues: "The conception that we begin with a known visual quality which is thereafter enlarged by adding on qualities apprehended by the other senses does not rest upon experience [i.e., there is no evidence for it]." According to Dewey the whole philosophical tradition from the time of Socrates erred by making all experience a form of knowledge, and "if not good knowledge, then a low-grade or confused or implicit knowledge." Although Dewey does not document this, no doubt he could have pointed to some examples. The reader who has fully grasped his distinction, however, finds it hard to believe that he was the first philosopher to distinguish between bathing in water and noting that water is wet. It is difficult to believe that many philosophers (much less the entire European tradition) had been "hypnotized . . . into thinking that all experiencing is a mode of knowing." Nevertheless this appears to be his charge, and we have duly recorded it here.

When we act in a cognitive way, that is, "in the attitude of suspended response in which consequences are anticipated, the direct stimulus becomes a sign or index of something else—and thus matter of noting or apprehension or acquaintance, or whatever term may be employed. This difference (together, of course, with the consequences which go with it) is the difference which the natural event of knowing makes to the natural event of direct organic stimulation." Right here we have reached one of the most important statements of all of Dewey's philosophy—his theory that knowing makes a difference to that which is known, and that knowing ushers in the object of knowing. It allows him to admit that there are "brute" pre-cognitive existences, which are the direct organic stimuli of the inquiring process; but it also permits him to say that these organic stimuli are changed by coming to be known as the signs of future experiences. And when they become known as signs of future experiences, i.e., signs that future experiences will be had by the knower, they become objects of knowledge. He adds a word to the doubtful: "It is no change of a reality into an unreality, of an object into something subjective;

it is no secret, illicit, or epistemological transformation; it is a genuine acquisition of new and distinctive features through entering into relations with things with which it was not formerly connected—namely, possible and future things." In this way knowledge involves the *use* of things, for we use given things by treating them "as indications of what will be experienced under different conditions." [20]

Dewey tried to apply this conception of knowledge to philosophy itself and he concluded that on his view philosophy "becomes not a contemplative survey of existence nor an analysis of what is past and done with, but an outlook upon future possibilities with reference to attaining the better and averting worse." [21] In drawing this conclusion at least one premise is not made explicit. It is one thing to say that the process of inquiry or knowing "uses" given things because it treats them as indications of what will come; this is implicit in the notion of prediction. Hume might have said that he "used" his impression of a flame when he treated it as an indication of the fact that the flame would burn him if he touched it. This premise would have committed the Deweyan philosopher to prediction, but the sense in which prediction is pragmatic in using something as an index of something else must be distinguished from the sense in which control is pragmatic. Dewey holds, and plausibly, that most of us engage in scientific prediction (and therefore knowing) because we wish to control or direct our environment. We try to predict on the basis of the cloud-stimulus that it will rain, presumably because we wish to do other things in anticipation of the expected rain—we want to close our barn, call in our animals, close our car. And presumably we want to do these things in the light of certain things we value; we wish to avert worse. But the important point is that the act of prediction can be distinguished from the act of controlling the environment, even though (in fact, precisely because) the first is directed toward the second as an aim. For, even though this is not true of most farmers, there are certain "spectator" amateur meteorologists who predict the advent of rain with little desire to do anything about it. They predict without any obvious aim at controlling in the Deweyan sense. In the same way it would appear that Dewey's philosopher might be a pragmatic forecaster without being thereby personally committed to "attaining the better and averting the worse." Dewey wished to impose this second obligation on the philosopher, of course, but it seems necessary to regard it as a *second* obligation and not one which is entailed by the fact that he must predict, as all knowers must on Dewey's view. However, it makes little difference to us here whether the moral search for the better was a simple consequence of the pragmatic view of knowing. The important point for a historian of ideas (and we are being mainly historical at the moment) is the fact that Dewey did want the philosopher to analyze critically the environment in which he lived. Beard and Veblen might have excused the economist, the historian, and the political scientist from this job, but Dewey did not excuse the philosopher. Later Dewey very explicitly defined philosophy as criticism in a sense that went beyond that of Kant, for Dewey urged the philosopher to survey his society and judge it good or bad. And if he found it bad, he was to change it or at least persuade others to change it.

As early as 1916 Dewey was anxious to distinguish his own version of pragmatism from the interpretations which had been put upon the pragmatism of William James. Since James had generously cited Dewey in his *Pragmatism* (1907) as one of the chief exponents of this new idea, and since James (rightly or wrongly) had been labeled as someone who reduced truth to personal caprice and vulgar "cash value," Dewey was obliged to distinguish his own position. He tried to do this somewhat technically in a review of James' book in 1908, which was reprinted as the twelfth of his *Essays in Experimental Logic,* and he continued in *Creative Intelligence.* He denied that his own test of validity by reference to consequences meant that "apprehensions and conceptions are true if the modifications effected by them were of an emotionally desirable tone." [22] He also denied that "consciousness or mind in the mere act of looking at things modifies them." And, like a good anti-formalist, he insisted that these are misunderstandings based on a neglect of temporal considerations. "The change made in things by the self in knowing is not immediate and, so to say, cross-sectional. It is longitudinal—in the redirection given to changes already going on. Its analogue is found in the changes which take place in the development of, say, iron ore into a watch-spring, not in those of the miracle of transubstantiation. For the static, cross-sectional, non-temporal relation of subject and object, the pragmatic hypothesis substitutes apprehension of a thing in terms of the results in other things which it is tending to effect. For the unique epistemological relation, it substitutes a practical relation of a familiar type:—responsive behavior which changes in time the subject-matter to which it applies. The unique thing about the responsive behavior which constitutes knowing is the specific difference which marks it off from other modes of response, namely, the part played in it by anticipation and prediction." [23]

Although "noting" was said earlier to make a difference to what is noted, this is evident only when noting is construed as a process which takes time. To find out whether someone knows that clouds indicate rain you must observe his behavior. The whole process, beginning with the organic stimulus of clouds, and ending with his search for and success-or-failure in seeking shelter, will constitute his inquiry for the behaviorist observer, and it is this process which modifies its stimulus and converts it into an object. If you view knowing in this way you are supposed to see that something is modified. With the cogency of this argument I am not concerned here, but I cannot overlook the opportunity to say how clearly this reveals that instrumentalism was an anti-formalist theory of knowledge—one that insisted upon the fact that knowing is a temporal process which can only be described genetically.

"Many critics have jumped at the obvious association of the word pragmatic with practical. They have assumed that the intent is to limit all knowledge, philosophic included, to promoting 'action,' understanding by action either just any bodily movement, or those bodily movements which conduce to the preservation and grosser well-being of the body." [24] And of course James' critics thought that he held that a true belief was one which satisfied us, so that we might believe anything we liked. The whole controversy is now obscure, but several things seem to emerge with some clarity. When Dewey spoke of "consequences" he seems to have meant experiences which the knower will have after he has been led to perform certain experiments. What these experiences are depends on what is under investigation. James' critics understood him to say that his belief in the presence of lightning could be established by examining the consequences this belief had upon James, independently of the objective facts so-called. The most unfair critics assigned to James the view that if believing that there were dark clouds in the heavens would increase his income, James would believe there were, even if there were no clouds to be seen. Now Dewey did not answer this second group of critics directly. In fact, he confused the issue somewhat. He took the critics to mean what *he* meant by "consequences" rather than what they understood James to have meant by "consequences," and went on to say that pragmatism put no restrictions on the kinds of consequences which could figure in the test of knowledge. Dewey said: " 'Cashing in' to James meant that a general idea must always be capable of verification in specific existential cases. The notion of 'cashing in' says nothing about the breadth or depth of the specific consequences. As an empirical doctrine, it could not say anything about them in general; the specific cases must speak for themselves. If one conception is verified in terms of eating beefsteak, and another in terms of a favorable credit balance in the bank, that is not because of anything in the theory, but because of the specific nature of the conceptions in question, and because there exist particular events like hunger and trade. If there are also existences in which the most liberal esthetic ideas and the most generous moral conceptions can be verified by specific embodiment, assuredly so much the better." [25]

Dewey's last remark may be taken as implying two propositions:

(1) if we say "this beefsteak is rare" we can verify that "pragmatically" by eating the beefsteak; (2) if we say "this is a beautiful picture" we can verify that in the pragmatic manner by looking at the picture. But James' critics attacked him for maintaining that testing any belief always boiled down to testing whether it produced "satisfaction" or gain in some personal sense. Dewey was quite sensitive about charges of coarseness and concern with narrow utilities and so he added a peroration:

> The pragmatic theory of intelligence means that the function of mind is to project new and more complex ends—to free experience from routine and from caprice. Not the use of thought to accomplish purposes already given either in the mechanism of the body or in that of the existent state of society, but the use of intelligence to liberate and liberalize action, is the pragmatic lesson. Action restricted to given and fixed ends may attain great technical efficiency; but efficiency is the only quality to which it can lay claim. Such action is mechanical (or becomes so), no matter what the scope of the performed end, be it the Will of God or *Kultur*. But the doctrine that intelligence develops within the sphere of action for the sake of possibilities not yet given is the opposite of a doctrine of mechanical efficiency. Intelligence *as* intelligence is inherently forward-looking; only by ignoring its primary function does it become a mere means for an end already given. The latter *is* servile, even when the end is labeled moral, religious, or esthetic. But action directed to ends to which the agent has not previously been attached inevitably carries with it a quickened and enlarged spirit. A pragmatic intelligence is a creative intelligence, not a routine mechanic.[26]

Dewey and his followers continued for years to protest that pragmatism, or at least his own version, was radically different from utilitarianism. Utilitarianism, according to Dewey, celebrated habit and routine while pragmatism meant freedom from the past and the right to be creatively intelligent about the future. Nevertheless, pragmatism in 1916 and for years to come had to establish its good character, to disassociate itself from the coarse, the narrowly useful, and the philistine. Dewey's protests went unheard in some quarters, and even Veblen identified pragmatism with the spirit of business.[27] Yet it would appear that Dewey regarded traditional philosophy as a leisure-class occupation and strenuously urged philosophers to leave the business of metaphysics for the industrial science of social engineering.

CHAPTER X

German Philosophy, Politics, and Economics

B Y THE year 1914 pragmatism, institutionalism, legal realism, the new history, and economic determinism had almost become popular doctrines. Their chief spokesmen were already public fig-ures who carried weight beyond the reaches of the classroom and the law court. Since they all shared to some degree a strenuously practical outlook, the First World War provided an occasion for testing their doctrines on a vast scale. For almost twenty-five years they had been labeling other theories remote and abstract in the face of events of lesser magnitude; then suddenly they were con-fronted by an opportunity to demonstrate the immediate social relevance of their ideas. In 1915 Dewey published a volume called *German Philosophy and Politics,* and in the same year Veblen brought out his *Imperial Germany and the Industrial Revolution.* Both of them were well versed in German thought, and the state of the world made it possible to present those insights into "the German mind" which periodically engage the American mind. Both Veblen and Dewey had been trained in German philosophy and both of them were products of a generation which had looked with scorn on British empiricism. For this reason their critical comments on German thought in 1915 and their growing respect for British thought and culture mark an important turn in twentieth-century American thought.

The publication of Dewey's *German Philosophy and Politics* shows that interest in the relation between ideas and society had penetrated even academic philosophy. *How* general ideas influence practical affairs is of course a central question for any pragmatist. Dewey strongly opposed all views claiming that thought does not influence action. He criticized evolutionists who held that intelligence is a "deposit from history," rather than "a force in its making." Even Bergson, he said, confined the intellect to the task of conserving a life already achieved, and trusted to instinct as a guide to the future. Moreover, he added, "I do not see that the school of history which finds Bergson mystic and romantic, which prides itself upon its hard-headed and scientific character, comes out at a different place. I refer to the doctrine of the economic interpretation of history in its extreme form—which, so its adherents tell us, is its only logical form." [1] Dewey also understood the economic determinists, or at least the extreme ones, to deny the efficacy of thought, to hold that it is simply a by-product of vast economic movement, incapable of affecting that movement itself. This question had been discussed in America as far back as 1902 when Seligman in his *Economic Interpretation of History* pointed to letters in which Engels had insisted that the relation between the economic factor and so-called "superstructural" elements was not one-way—that thought might very well revise and influence material circumstances. Indeed this was a point strongly emphasized later by some of Dewey's Marxian disciples, in an effort to unite instrumentalism and Marxism. Dewey himself noted the Marxist belief that general recognition of the truth of economic determinism would help "us out of our present troubles and indicate a path for future effort." The Marxian recognition of this amount of human control over the course of history led Dewey to "take heart." "These writers do not seem to mean just what they say. Like the rest of us, they are human, and infected with a belief that ideas, even highly abstract theories, are of efficacy in the conduct of human affairs, influencing the history which is yet to be." [2]

Dewey's study of German philosophy and its relation to politics was an exercise in describing the effect of ideas on social affairs and, although it was directed against an "extreme form" of the economic interpretation of history, the difference between Dewey and some of the economic determinists was not very great. Dewey certainly believed in the tremendous importance of technological and economic factors in history, but in *German Philosophy and Politics* he appealed to confused historical materialists against themselves, and urged them to surrender some of the absurdly fatalistic implications of their interpretations of Marx.

Why did Dewey write on this problem at this time? Before 1915 he had broken with the classical tradition in philosophy precisely because he believed it was ineffective. He came to the conclusion that all his philosophical predecessors had been mere spectators. How, in that case, could German philosophy have had any impact on German society? How could Dewey have treated one of the more metaphysical and hence one of the more "otiose" philosophical systems as an effective political force? Dewey dealt with this question only in passing. He insisted upon the esthetic character of a good deal of philosophy, upon the fact "that very much of what has been presented as philosophic reflection is in effect simply an idealization, for the sake of emotional satisfaction, of the brutely given state of affairs." ³ But for Dewey there are no *pure* ideas. "Every living thought represents a gesture made toward the world, an attitude taken to some practical situation in which we are implicated. Most of these gestures are ephemeral; they reveal the state of him who makes them rather than effect a significant alteration of conditions. But at some times they are congenial to a situation in which men in masses are acting and suffering. They supply a model for the attitudes of others; they condense into a dramatic type of action. They then form what we call the 'great' systems of thought. . . . Even emotional and esthetic systems may breed a disposition toward the world and take overt effect." ⁴

Dewey's attitude may be easily justified in the language of contemporary philosophers who distinguish between the cognitive and emotive use of words. Science is dominated primarily by cognitive purposes, by the desire to supply knowledge, and therefore Dewey took science as the voice of intelligence in action. But unscientific and "cognitively meaningless" metaphysics may very well achieve dramatic and emotive effect, and the most obscure speculative systems and theologies may play active roles in human life. The most nightmarish mumbo-jumbo may cause social action, but it takes a philosophy formulated with the techniques of intelligence to *guide* action in a successful way. When Dewey selected German metaphysics for study ("somewhat arbitrarily," as he said in 1915) he was in part determined by a desire to prove that even with "its highly technical, professorial, and predominantly a priori character" it had close connections with the tendencies of collective life.[5] Furthermore, the German university system placed an unusually high value on its philosophy of law and religion, and the universities trained the German bureaucracy. Thus German metaphysical ideas slid rapidly along a well-greased chute from the universities into the affairs of political life.

It is not surprising that Dewey should have started his critique of German philosophy with a criticism of Kant's dualism, since it was an old and familiar stalking horse. The doctrine upon which he seized first was one he named "Kant's Two Worlds." "Kant's decisive contribution is the idea of a dual legislation of reason by which are marked off two distinct realms—that of science and that of morals. Each of these two realms has its own final and authoritative constitution: On one hand, there is the world of sense, the world of phenomena in space and time in which science is at home; on the other hand, is the supersensible, the noumenal world, the world of moral duty and moral freedom." [6] This idea in German philosophy is of prime importance for Dewey's understanding of German life. Kant's doctrine of two realms—one outer, physical, and necessary; the other inner, ideal, and free—served Dewey as an explanation of the chief feature of German civilization—"its combination of self-conscious idealism with unsurpassed technical efficiency and organization in the various fields of action." Given their high-powered mechanization and efficiency, one might have expected the Germans to run to materialism and utilitarianism more than they did. But they didn't, because Kant revealed the limited sphere of mechanism. He put it in its place, so that Germany might end the paralysis of action arising from the conflict between science and spirit. "Each feeds and reinforces the other. Freedom of soul and subordination of action dwell in harmony. Obedience, definite subjection and control, detailed organization is the lesson enforced by the rule of causal necessity in the outer world of space and time in which action takes place. Unlimited freedom, the heightening of consciousness for its own sake, sheer reveling in noble ideals, the law of the inner world. What more can mortal man ask?" [7]

In this way Dewey tried to explain the "paradoxical" assertion that Germany first recognized the principle of freedom and that the German people were incompetent for political self-direction. In the same way he explained the use of the *Critique of Pure Reason* as a justification of German militarism. Kant separated science from morals, but he also maintained that the moral world can influence or intrude upon the world of physical necessity. "It is the very nature of moral legislation that it is meant to influence the world of sense; its object is to realize the purposes of free rational action within the sense world." [8] It followed from Kant's view that man as a personality was free and that it was he who imposed duties upon himself. His higher, supranatural self imposed duties upon his lower, empirical self; the rational self imposed obligations upon the self of passions and inclinations, but the duties it imposed were not specifically enumerated. Kant would do no more than present a general formal rule, the Supreme Categorical Imperative, with which men were to test particular moral rules. If, upon application of the Supreme Categorical Imperative, proposed obligations were found formally satisfactory, they were to be accepted as duties. To determine whether it is wrong to break promises, we must find out whether we could will that this be done by anyone in similar circumstances. By questionable dialectic, it must be said, Kant concluded that such a rule, if acted upon, would lead to a formal contradiction, and therefore concluded further that the rule against breaking one's promise was shown to be *formally* incapable of meeting the requirements of the Supreme Categorical Imperative. But this is the only technique he presented, and each individual was to go about testing proposed duties by means of this formal device, much as Aristotle expected people to test their syllogistic inferences by using his moods and figures.

Dewey made much of this in order to link Kant and German militarism. He quoted Bernhardi in a passage in which Bernhardi advanced Kant's "gospel of moral duty" in defense of the idea of military service. "I do not mean," Dewey quickly added, "that Kant's teaching was the cause of Prussia's adoption of universal military service and of the thoroughgoing subordination of individual happiness and liberty of action to that capitalized entity, the state. But I do mean that when the practical political situation called for universal military service in order to support and expand the existing state, the gospel of a duty devoid of content naturally lent itself to the consecration and idealization of such specific duties as the existing national order might prescribe. The sense of duty must get its subject matter somewhere, and unless subjectivism was to revert to anarchic or romantic individualism . . . its appropriate subject matter lies in the commands of a superior. Concretely what the state commands is the congenial outer filling of a purely inner sense of duty." [9]

By this time Dewey had come to see certain virtues in English ethical theory. He was prepared to fight instantly if called a utilitarian, and he was constantly calling utilitarianism the ethics of routine and habit. But here, with the text of Kant before him, he confesses to a preference for British insistence on "intelligent self-interest." This is rather intriguing in the light of his later choice of Kant and idealistic epistemology against Hume's view of experience, in *Creative Intelligence*. Although he deplored both German idealism and British empiricism, he was to give the first the advantage in the theory of knowledge (in *Creative Intelligence*), while he started to lean toward the second in ethical outlook (*German Philosophy and Politics*). I think his attitude is rather significant in 1915 and 1916, up to one year before he came to support the war against Germany. For clearly an affinity in ethics meant more than epistemological agreement when it came to fighting in the same trenches. Intelligent self-interest, he admitted in 1915, was "hardly an ultimate idea. But at least it evokes a picture of merchants bargaining, while the categorical imperative calls up the drill sergeant. Trafficking ethics, in which each gives up something he wants to get something which he wants more, is not the noblest kind of morals, but at least it is socially responsible as far as it goes. 'Give so that it may be given to you in return' has at least some tendency to bring men together; it promotes agreement. It requires deliberation and discussion. This is just what the authoritative voice of a superior will not tolerate; it is the one unforgivable sin." [10] "The morals of bargaining, exchange, the mutual satisfaction of wants may be outlived in some remote future, but up to the present they play an important part in life. To me there is something uncanny in the scorn which German ethics, in behalf of an unsullied moral idealism, pours upon a theory which takes cognizance of practical motives. In a highly esthetic people one might understand the display of contempt. But when an aggressive and commercial nation carries on commerce and war simply from the motive of obedience to duty, there is awakened an unpleasant suspicion of a suppressed 'psychic complex.' When Nietzsche says, 'Man does not desire happiness; only the Englishman does that,' we laugh at the fair hit. But persons who profess no regard for happiness as a test of action have an unfortunate way of living up to their principle by making others *un*happy. I should entertain some suspicion of the complete sincerity of those who profess disregard for their own happiness, but I should be quite certain of their sincerity when it comes to a question of my happiness." [11]

In 1915, then, Dewey had come to identify German ethics with the drill sergeant and British ethics with the merchant, and he leaned to the second in a choice between two admitted evils. But this granting of an advantage to British ethics, slight as it was, represented a shift in Dewey's outlook. Dewey's thought, as we have seen, began under the domination of German idealism. But by 1908, when he wrote his *Ethics* with Tufts, his own independent position had emerged. He was no longer an idealist, and he could no longer support idealistic ethics. The part of the *Ethics* for which Dewey was mainly responsible was offered as an improvement on British empirical ethics and Kantian intuitive ethics. Indeed the pattern in almost all his chapters is the same —a statement of the theories of a utilitarian like Bentham, a statement of those of Kant, a recitation of their respective defects and virtues, and finally an indication of the advantages of a somewhat neutral improvement which would absorb all the good in previous theories and none of the shortcomings. But *German Philosophy and Politics,* written in the middle of a war which would ultimately lead America to struggle against Germany, is a sign of the times. It is to Dewey's credit that he was not drawn into absurd, jingoistic denunciations of the "German mind," but circumstances did draw him into an increasing respect for British utilitarianism and the ethics of the "merchant." This invidious comparison was wholly absent from the *Ethics,* where he had charged Kant with the same errors without adding dubious generalizations about their connection with German militarism, and without assigning any special virtues to British ethics. Furthermore, the war atmosphere made Dewey stress the peculiar need for an American philosophy suitable to the conditions of this country.

The situation which Dewey found so paradoxical was confronted more objectively by Veblen. He regarded idealistic ethics in a commercial nation simply as a barbaric survival, an expression of Germany's failure to adjust its entire culture and civilization to its new economic status. Unlike the British, who developed utilitarianism and a scientific philosophy along with a predominance in industry and business, Germany revealed an uneven development. This was a special case of a more general theory about Germany which emerged in Veblen's work. Like Dewey, Veblen was struck by the industrial efficiency of modern Germany during the First World War. He offered an account of its causes "without drawing on the logic of manifest destiny, Providential nepotism, national genius, and the like"— an opening statement which was spiritually linked with that of Beard in the *Economic Interpretation of the Constitution*. He also demonstrated his affinity with Beard by describing his study as "the first attempt yet made at an explanation, as distinct from description or eulogy, of this episode in modern economic history." His "immediate, explicit objective," according to his biographer, was "to explain why and how Germany with its dynastic political organization made such rapid strides in the machine technology as to outstrip the democratic English-speaking peoples from whom emanated the modern industrial process." [12] Veblen's answer is formulated in terms of his distinction between industry and business enterprise, between technology and the price system. He presented his explanation by way of a comparison between England and Germany.

Veblen regarded England as the model of mechanistic culture —the culture of matters of fact, science, and technology. As the original home of scientific industry, it was also the first country to suffer industry's greatest curse—domination by business enterprise. It was also the first to accept democratic processes, utilitarian ethics, and scientifically oriented philosophy. All of these formed a cultural *Gestalt* for Veblen; they were factors which were historically linked with predominance in industry. But, as we have seen, Veblen regarded business as a drag on industry, a point he had developed at length in *The Theory of Business Enterprise* (1904). Business rulers of the industrial mechanism forced the retention of obsolescent methods and equipment, and so England paid "the penalty for having been thrown into the lead," a penalty which Germany was able to escape as a latecomer to industrial methods. It was because of this freedom from the impediments of business that German industry was able to forge ahead as rapidly as it did. Domination by business enterprise was replaced in Germany by a modern counterpart of feudalism—the dynastic state—and the result was an efficient use of the technical methods which industry had made available as well as a subservient people ruled by "a government of constitutionally mitigated absolutism." "Germany offers what is by contrast with England an anomaly, in that it shows the working of the modern state of the industrial arts as worked out by the English, but without the characteristic range of institutions and convictions that have grown up among English-speaking peoples concomitantly with the growth of this modern state of the industrial arts. . . . The case of Germany is unexampled among Western nations both as regards the abruptness, thoroughness and amplitude of its appropriation of this technology, and as regards the archaism of its cultural furniture at the date of this appropriation." [13]

Perhaps one of the most antique pieces which Veblen found in German culture was its philosophy. Although he had been a close student of Kant in his youth, here—unlike Dewey—he paid no attention to Kant's philosophy of science. He simply labeled the entire German tradition as an expression of the romantic and unscientific spirit. As such

it is viable only within the spiritual frontiers of romanticism; that is to say, since and in so far as the German people have made the transition from romanticism to the matter-of-fact logic and insight characteristic of modern technology and applied science, the characteristic philosophy of Germany's past is also a phenomenon of the past age. It can live and continue to guide and inspire the life and thought of the community only on condition that the community return to the condition of life that gave rise and force to this philosophy; that is to say, only on condition that the German nation retreat from its advance into the modern state of industrial arts and discard such elements of the modern scheme of institutions as it has hitherto accepted. But with such a retirement in the direction of the medieval and feudalistic scheme of life, if such a retreat were conceivable, the question in hand would also lapse; since such a retreat would involve a return to the small and incompetent conditions of Germany's pre-capitalistic and pre-imperial age.

The peculiarly German philosophy is peculiarly ineffectual for the purposes of modern science, and peculiarly incapable of articulating with or illuminating any of the questions with which modern scientific inquiry is occupied. It is an idealistic philosophy; that is to say, at its nearest approach to the domain of fact it is a theoretical construction in terms of sufficient reason rather than of efficient cause, in terms of luminous personal valuation rather than of opaque matter of fact.

Its high qualities and great esthetic value may not be questioned; it is a monument of what was best in German life in the days before the technological deluge; but it finds no application in the scheme of thought within which the modern science and technology live and move. Remnants of it are still afloat in the atmosphere of the German scholarly world, and it is even true that, under the shadow of the feudalizing Prussian State, well-intended endeavors, whether well-advised or not, have also latterly been made to rehabilitate it. But this is to be taken as indicating the degree of reversion embodied in the imperial policies and the degree of revulsion induced by the discipline of life under its institutional scheme, rather than as evidence of the viability of this philosophical scheme under modern conditions of life, properly speaking. Similar anachronistic remnants of the ancient regime are, of course, also to be met with in some degree of vigor elsewhere, and a correspondingly atavistic revulsion of taste in philosophical speculation is also to be found elsewhere; although, apart from the frankly medieval aspirations of the theologically-minded sons of the Church, such recidivism is greatly more in evidence in Imperial Germany, perhaps particularly in Prussian Germany, than among the scholars of Christendom at large.[14]

Veblen's approach to German philosophy is obviously less technical than Dewey's, but they complement each other. Dewey was struck by the combination of idealism and efficiency, and so was Veblen. Veblen maintained that they presented an unstable mixture, and suggested that they could not hold together much longer, for he believed in the stability only of certain cultural compounds. For Veblen the combination of industrial efficiency and German idealism was unnatural in some sense, and he thought that industry (which was as fundamental and controlling for him as the mode of production was for Marx) would sweep aside all cultural impediments. But the question still remained: how could these culturally anomalous idealisms exist and even help the trend of German efficiency for any length of time? Here Dewey entered with his explanation, his contention that Kant successfully compartmentalized the spiritual and the efficient so that Germany might attend its philosophical churches on Sunday in an atmosphere of moral purity, while it operated its belt lines and battleships during the week.

Both Veblen and Dewey shared a common evolutionism, we have seen, and it was this which led them to regard certain cultural combinations as defective. Democracy supposedly went with science, whereas the dynastic state couldn't—or at least not for very long. Democracy represented a more perfect adjustment to modern industry. Now Dewey insisted that adjustment didn't mean total acceptance of the environment but that it could also involve, indeed necessarily did involve, a transformation of the environment as well as of the human being or group. But on the whole Dewey's attitudes were favorably oriented toward the results of the evolutionary process. For this reason pragmatism was construed as a more successful philosophical adjustment to modern American life than idealism or Aristotelianism. Because it was, it was necessarily better in some sense. Moreover, Dewey's historicism required him always to ask of a given philosophy whether it was better *for a certain period or problem*. Hence Aristotle was better for Greece and William James better for America. Veblen indulged in similar judgments, as we have seen, but always with a qualification. And after he had delivered himself of his estimate of German philosophy's connection with German culture, he added characteristically: "The tedious caution may again be pardoned, that all this implies nothing in the way of praise or disparise of the philosophical predilections so handed down from the pre-mechanistic past, and aimed to be rehabilitated in the mechanistic present by men schooled in the institutional methods carried over into this present under the aegis of the dynastic state. It is not even intended to imply that such endeavor to rehabilitate a logic and outlook that once articulated with the discipline of workday life in that institutional past need be a bootless endeavor. What is implied is that a competent rehabilitation of the romantic philosophy is conditioned on the rehabilitation of the romantic institutional and technological scheme—perhaps somewhat after the fashion of things in the days when the Holy Roman Empire was in the hands of a receiver. It is at least extremely doubtful whether the dynastic system of the Empire and its institutional scheme will avail to effect a retention of or reversion to the romantic philosophy, even as it stood in the immediately pre-Darwinistic days of German scholarship. One might go farther and say that unless the discipline of the imperial system should have some such effect upon the prevalent attitude of its subjects, it will itself fall into decay under the impact of the same forces of habituation that go to make the romantic philosophy futile in the eyes of modern men." [15]

Dewey and Veblen were part of that generation which had been brought up on German university methods of the nineteenth century. Their earliest work had been done in an atmosphere dominated by Hegel and Kant. They were the most distinguished products of an American university system which had looked to Germany for ideas, graduate seminars, and doctors' degrees. For this reason their 1915 books represent a significant shift in outlook; they decisively marked the end of what an early English critic of Dewey called "germanizing," or, at any rate, of explicit germanizing. Later historians and critics who could not resist the easy polemical virtues of national labeling continued to point to survivals of Hegel and *Historismus* in Dewey and Veblen. But Dewey, who has lived long enough to see his philosophy amalgamated with the strangest ideas, constantly protested his disagreements with Hegel, and Veblen openly attacked Hegel. On some later occasions Dewey recalled his attachment to Hegel and gave Hegel credit for the seeds of his own ideas, but always with enough qualifications to discourage any imputation of continued Hegelianism. In spite of this Dewey has had to keep up a perpetual struggle against at least one alleged misinterpretation; he has been forced to show that he is no idealist or "teutonic holist." Veblen and his disciples too have been pressed to prove that institutionalism is not simply an American variant of German historical economics. There can be no doubt, however, that Dewey and Veblen ceased very early to regard themselves as conscious spokesmen of German ideas, and Germany's peculiarly obnoxious position in the world of 1915 gave them an opportunity to reveal this change in attitude. Their expression of their attitude marked the end of American academic nostalgia for German seminars. German thought entered America once more in the twenties and thirties, but this time without a visa, for it came by way of Russia with admirers of Karl Marx and Friedrich Engels. In this same postwar period America proceeded to atone for its hysteria and to revive its feeling for international culture until the appearance of Hitler. Then the accounts of concentration camps and gas chambers made it feasible to reissue *German Philosophy and Politics* and *Imperial Germany and the Industrial Revolution*.

CHAPTER XI

Destructive Intelligence

G ERMAN philosophy and the German economy were subjects
on which abstract speculation was possible in 1915, but
very soon our liberal scholars were called upon to deal with
more specific questions. Dewey had been the apostle of intelligence since the turn of the century, but soon he came to find
entry into World War I compatible with, indeed prescribed by,
the canons of scientific procedure. Holmes was now one of the
most distinguished judges of the Supreme Court, and his liberalism was about to meet its greatest test in the famous series of
civil liberties cases on which the court had to decide. Beard was
about to become an academic rebel and to resign courageously
from Columbia over an issue involving academic freedom.

Dewey's celebration of intelligence had led many of his friends,
among them Randolph Bourne and Jane Addams, to expect that
he would not support the First World War. His entire philosophy had constantly emphasized the virtues of peaceful and
intelligent solution of problems. Although a Darwinist, he rejected the militarist and racist conclusions which some of the
more bloodthirsty readers of *The Origin of Species* had drawn
from it. In 1908 he had written with Tufts: "The argument for
the necessity (short of the attainment of a federated international
state with universal authority and policing of the seas) of pre-

paring in peace by enlarged armies and navies for the possibility of war, must be offset at least by the recognition that the possession of irresponsible power is always a direct temptation to its irresponsible use. The argument that war is necessary to prevent moral degeneration of individuals may, under present conditions, where every day brings its fresh challenge to civic initiative, courage, and vigor, be dismissed as unmitigated nonsense." [1] When the First World War came, he certainly did not reverse himself on these broad issues, for he continued to reject the more absurd and extreme versions of social Darwinism. But he did feel compelled to show that the method of intelligence did not exclude the use of force in international relations. The result was a series of articles in which he tried to show the compatibility of pragmatism and war.

The most philosophical justifications of Dewey's attitude toward the war appear in his effort to distinguish force and violence.[2] Force per se is presented as morally neutral. It becomes violence only when put to wasteful or unintelligent use. On this view law cannot be sharply distinguished from force, for it ultimately involves the use of force. Law and violence are respectively the intelligent and unintelligent uses of force. It follows that we cannot condemn any act merely because of its use of force. It also follows, of course, that an intelligent man may support the war, provided he can show that the shooting of his fellow men is neither wasteful nor unintelligent, i.e., not violent. Dewey had not yet committed himself as to the intelligence of the First World War, but he was providing himself with a reason for not instantly ruling it out as incompatible with the spirit of creative intelligence. In short, creative intelligence countenanced destruction and force, provided that they could be shown to be reasonable, provided that in the last analysis they weren't "wasteful." The point is most clearly expressed in the following passages:

Common sense still clings to a *via media* between the Tolstoian, to whom all force is violence and all violence evil, and that glorification of force which is so easy when war arouses turbulent emotion, and so persistent (in disguised forms) whenever competition rules industry. I should be glad to make the voice of common sense more articulate. As an initial aid, I would call to mind the fact that force figures in different roles. Sometimes it is energy; sometimes it is coercion or constraint; sometimes it is violence. Energy is power used with a eulogistic meaning; it is power of doing work, harnessed to accomplishment of ends. But it is force none the less—brute force if you please, and rationalized only by its results. Exactly the same force running wild is called violence. The objection to violence is not that it involves the use of force, but that it is a waste of force; that it uses force idly or destructively. And what is called law may always, I suggest, be looked at as describing a method for employing force economically, efficiently, so as to get results with the least waste.[3]

No ends are accomplished without the use of force. It is consequently no presumption against a measure, political, international, jural, economic, that it involves a use of force. Squeamishness about force is the mark not of idealistic but of moonstruck morals. But antecedent and abstract principles can not be assigned to justify the use of force. The criterion of value lies in relative efficiency and economy of the expenditure of force as a means to an end. With advance of knowledge, refined, subtle and indirect use of force is always displacing coarse, obvious and direct methods of applying it. This is the explanation to the ordinary feeling against the use of force. What is thought of as brutal, violent, immoral, is a use of physical agencies which are gross, sensational and evident on their own account, in cases where it is possible to employ with greater economy and less waste means which are comparatively imperceptible and refined.[4]

In this period Dewey's writings contain admiring references to the tough-mindedness of seventeenth- and eighteenth-century political theorists, to their frank recognition of the importance of force and power in politics. By comparison, Dewey thought, some political theorists of his own age were "moonstruck." A hardness and down-to-earth quality enters Dewey's writings which contrasts sharply with the sweet, light, and uplifting quality of his *Ethics*. In many ways his war writings are spiritually related to Beard's celebrations of the early rough-and-tumble political philosophers for their "realistic" recognition of the importance of material economic interests in society; they are also related to Holmes' definition of the law. Holmes, it will be recalled, charged the lawyer with "predicting the incidence of the public *force* through the instrumentality of the courts," [5] and this implied that the law was itself a study of how the court would use force. Holmes reached the peak of this variety of realism, for he frankly denied that the courts always used this force intelligently, or for the moral good.

Dewey's 1916 statement on force is hardly more than a commonplace when freed of certain verbal tricks. He simply maintained that even when we persuade a man gently to do something we use the force of our breath. Even when we walk we use force. But clearly some of those whom he opposed understood the word "force" differently. They did not understand it as applying to international discussion. Discussion for them did not involve force, while war did. Dewey simply urged a terminological shift. Regard every human act as an act of force, he seemed to argue, and then call violent those which result in waste and inefficiency. It is clear that no intelligent pacifist could have refused to proceed on Dewey's definitions; but if he did, he would have to revise the language of his argument against war. Wherever the pacifist had formerly written "force" he would now have to write "violence." Certainly if he decided with Dewey to use the word "force" so that peaceful means of settling international disputes were "forceful" in a Pickwickian sense, he would now have to shift his verbal ground. The pacifist believed in using steamshovels but not in using guns, to be sure. The first was forceful but not violent; the second forceful *and* violent. But such a terminological shift would be hard to maintain in the face of the ordinary political use of the word "force," and this was illustrated by Dewey himself. In 1917, after he had come to support the war, he tried, heroically, to stem what he called the conscription of thought, and in trying to save opponents of the war from brutality he denied "the efficacy of force to remove disunion of thought and feeling." [6] But clearly a philosopher who held that force was the only thing in the world which could effect anything could not consistently deny that force could remove disunion of thought and feeling. His lapse is more than a slip of the tongue, for it reveals the folly of trying to change the usage of words which have well-fixed political meanings. "Force" and "violence" have been traditionally equated in political language, and it seems idle to try to reject this equation. This is not to deny that there are occasions when violence (or force) is intelligent or right and occasions when it is wrong, but it seems useless arbitrarily to call the right ones cases of non-violent force.

Dewey has faced the issue of force and violence in two ways. As a supporter of World War I he refused to oppose force "per se." Later, as a peaceful socialist, he had to defend his position against Communists, who urged the use of force (violence) in bringing about the socialist society. Dewey has consistently opposed revolution (in our times at least) as a political means. In such polemics he has rarely introduced his distinction between force and violence, but on the contrary he has identified them. So, for example, he wrote in 1939: "To take as far as possible every conflict which arises—and they are bound to arise—out of the atmosphere and medium of force, of violence as a means of settlement, into that of discussion and of intelligence, is to treat those who disagree—even profoundly—with us as those from whom we may learn, and in so far, as friends." [7] Here it is plain that Dewey identifies force and violence, and urges that we avoid both of them in the spirit of intelligence. Nothing could more plainly indicate the departure from the verbal distinctions of 1916. The 1939 essay was, of course, written before our entrance into World War II, when the discussion of force and violence was still carried on as part of a polemic against the philosophies of communism and fascism. In general, as we shall see, Dewey has opposed force as an instrument for the achievement of a socialist society (an ideal which he came more and more to espouse) although he rallied to its support quite vocally in World War I. It would not be unfair to say that Dewey has disliked civil war more than he has disliked international war, no doubt because he believes the first less intelligent and more wasteful in our time. But he has never consistently tried to perpetuate his 1916 distinction between force and violence as a basis for this choice, nor has he ever advanced a clear and consistent philosophy of the relative merits of both kinds of war as instruments of social policy. In this respect the practical implications of his position are hardly less varied or more uniform in tendency than those of hundreds of philosophers, political theorists, and journalists who have never even heard of the virtues of creative intelligence in politics.

Dewey seems to have had the misfortune of attracting disciples with one mode of analysis, usually in peacetime, and then disappointing them with another, usually in wartime. Perhaps the most dramatic case of disappointment was that of Randolph Bourne. The immediate background for Bourne's attack was a series of articles which Dewey had published in the *New Republic* in 1917. They represented his reflections on our entry into the war, and appeared just after he had published a little essay, "In a Time of National Hesitation," in *The Seven Arts* for May 1917. This essay had been written before America's declaration of war against Germany, although it was published after the formal beginning of hostilities. Its theme is national (and presumably Dewey's) hesitation about support of the war, hesitation which would not end, Dewey said, "until the almost impossible happens," that is, "until the Allies are fighting on our terms for our democracy and civilization." The "gallant fight" for democracy and civilization which was being fought on French soil was not our fight, he reported sadly, for it was not being fought for "our" conception of democracy and civilization.[8] The nature of this conception was not clear in this article, but we may assume that "our" conception was Dewey's, since by that time he had come to identify his own social libertarianism with the American spirit. This article represented the "one moment of hesitation" to which Bourne referred in his attack.[9] It was the moment of hesitation which preceded Dewey's fall in the eyes of Bourne and some of his friends. For beginning with its issue of July 14, 1917, the *New Republic* issued Dewey's short articles: "Conscience and Compulsion," "The Future of Pacifism," "What America Will Fight For," and "Conscription of Thought." [10]

The shift from Dewey's hesitation in the May article to "Conscience and Compulsion" in July is remarkable. For the second is not sad or brooding or dirgelike in tone. By this time Hamlet had conquered his indecision and in his newly won confidence he turned to those who still had "doubts, qualms, clouds of bewilderment" about America's entry into the war. He turned to their gnawing question, "How could wrong so suddenly become right?" to this "crisis in moral experience," and finally to the moral education which had produced this American aversion to war. He felt that most pacifists were "victims of a moral innocency and an inexpertness . . . engendered by the moral training which they have undergone." What was the defect of this moral education? Dewey thought it emphasized the emotions rather than intelligence, ideals rather than specific purposes, the nurture of personal motives rather than the creation of social agencies and environments. "The tendency to dispose of war by bringing it under the commandment against murder, the belief that by *not* doing something, by keeping out of a declaration of war, our responsibilities could be met, a somewhat mushy belief in the existence of disembodied moral forces which require only an atmosphere of feelings to operate so as to bring about what is right, the denial of the efficacy of force, no matter how controlled, to modify disposition; in short, the inveterate habit of separating ends from means and then identifying morals with ends thus emasculated, such things as these are the source of much of the perplexity of conscience from which idealistic youth has suffered. The evangelical Protestant tradition has fostered the tendency to locate morals in personal feelings instead of in the control of social situations, and our legal tradition has bred the habit of attaching feelings to fixed rules and injunctions instead of to social conditions and consequences of action as these are revealed to the scrutiny of intelligence." [11]

In "The Future of Pacifism" Dewey held that pacifists wasted their energies in opposing our entrance into "a war which was already all but universal, instead of using their energies to form, at a plastic juncture, the conditions and objects of our entrance." He called upon "those who still think of themselves as fundamentally pacifists in spite of the fact that they believed our entrance into the war a needed thing" and urged them to try to convert the aims of the war to accord with Wilson's ideals.[12] In "What America Will Fight For" he could describe our aim in no more concrete terms than these: to create "a world somehow made permanently different by our participation in a task which taken by itself is intensely disliked." He spoke of "a world organization and the beginnings of a public control which crosses nationalistic boundaries and interests." [13] And finally, after so thoroughly deprecating the moral philosophy from which pacifists opposed the war, he called upon the country to avoid conscription of thought, to be less harsh with these wrong-minded pacifists, because of "the historically demonstrated inefficiency of the conscription of mind as a means of promoting social solidarity, and the gratuitous stupidity of measures that defeat their own ends." [14] In "Conscription of Thought" Dewey completed the circle and implored the brass hats to be kinder to these misguided opponents of the war in the interests of social efficiency. Dewey was alternately patronizing toward and angry at those with whom he had marched just a few months earlier. He also revealed his own uncertainty and defensiveness in his philosophical justification of his own reversal, for he hauled up his heaviest technical apparatus to show that pragmatism was no ally of pacifism, indeed to prove that pacifism was the product of schooling which had failed to take seriously the chief tenets of progressive education. Here was the doctrine of *The School and Society* and *Democracy and Education* placed at the service of the country at war.

Bourne reacted bitterly. Here, he felt, was the evidence of the poverty of Dewey's philosophy. Bourne was no technical philosopher. He was never especially interested in logic or epistemology, or any of the traditional disciplines in which Dewey had been thoroughly versed. But he was sensitive and acute in his political insights. His criticism of Dewey's philosophy, therefore, was not technical or built upon minutiae. It was a pragmatic evaluation of Dewey's pragmatism, and it came to the conclusion that pragmatism was not geared for emergencies. Dewey called for the conversion of the war to a socially useful instrument. Bourne replied: "If the war is too strong for you to prevent, how is it going to be weak enough for you to control and mold to your liberal purposes?" Dewey called for intelligence and democracy. Bourne replied: "I search Professor Dewey's articles in vain for clews as to the specific working out of our democratic desires, either nationally or internationally, either in the present or in the reconstruction after the war." Bourne asked:

What is the matter with the philosophy? One has a sense of having come to a sudden, short stop at the end of an intellectual era. In the crisis, this philosophy of intelligent control just does not measure up to our needs. What is the root of this inadequacy that is felt so keenly by our restless minds? Van Wyck Brooks has pointed out searchingly the lack of poetic vision in our pragmatist "awakeners." Is there something in these realistic attitudes that works actually against poetic vision, against concern for the quality of life as above machinery of life? Apparently there is. The war has revealed a younger intelligentsia, trained up in the pragmatic dispensation, immensely ready for the executive ordering of events, pitifully unprepared for the intellectual interpretation or the idealistic focusing of ends. The young men in Belgium, the officers' training corps, the young men being sucked into the councils at Washington and into war organization everywhere, have among them a definite element, upon whom Dewey, as veteran philosopher, might well bestow a papal blessing. They have absorbed the secret of scientific method as applied to political administration. They are liberal, enlightened, aware. They are touched with creative intelligence toward the solution of political and industrial problems. They are a wholly new force in American life, the product of the swing in the colleges from a training that emphasized classical studies to one that emphasized political and economic values. Practically all this element, one would say, is lined up in service of the war technique. There seems to have been a peculiar congeniality between the war and these men. It is as if the war and they had been waiting for each other. One wonders what scope they would have had for their intelligence without it. Probably most of them would have gone into industry and devoted themselves to sane reorganization schemes. What is significant is that it is the technical side of the war that appeals to them, not the interpretive or political side. The formulation of values and ideals, the production of articulate and suggestive thinking, had not, in their education, kept pace, to any extent whatever, with their technical aptitude. The result is that the field of intellectual formulation is very poorly manned by this younger intelligentsia. While they organize the war, formulation of opinion is in the hands of professional patriots, sensational editors, archaic radicals. The intellectual work of this younger intelligentsia is done by the sedition-hunting Vigilantes, and by the saving remnant of older liberals. It is true, Dewey calls for a more attentive formulation of war purposes and ideas, but he calls largely to deaf ears. His disciples have learned all too literally the instrumental attitude toward life, and, being immensely intelligent and energetic, they are making themselves efficient instruments of the war technique, accepting with little question the ends announced from above.[15]

Bourne thought of pragmatism as a philosophy of technique, a philosophy which tells you how to accomplish your ends once the ends have been established. And although he admitted that Dewey hoped to develop his technique along with vision—a capacity for framing ideals and ends—he felt that Dewey's disciples had become completely technique-conscious and morally blind. In their win-the-war rush the *New Republic* liberals ceased to play for wider political goals. Bourne was quite piercing in his description of one inconsistency which instrumentalism had engendered in some its disciples. It demanded relevance and it attacked "moonstruck" morals, and even though it protested against customary morality as the morality of routine and habit, it found itself supporting the most routine and habitual institution of 1917—the war. Although Bourne did not emphasize the point, it would appear that Dewey's observations on Kant were being turned against him. For just as Kant had presented a formal doctrine of duty, which German militarism had filled in with the specific obligation of patriotism, so Dewey's abstract doctrine of intelligence was made concrete in the limited demands of American militarism. Dewey's philosophy of creative intelligence with its emphasis upon adjustment and the accomplishment of specific goals in a scientific way was converted into a justification of the smooth accomplishment of the fixed goals of selfish, narrow interests.

Bourne's philosophical aim was partly obscure. It was not clear whether he was urging a surrender of the methods of intelligence when he urged the development of poetic vision. His language was vague, but his emotional demands were clear. He wanted to rise above the conventional humdrum morality which he associated with blind, opportunistic pragmatism. "If your ideal is to be adjustment to your situation, in radiant cooperation with reality, then your success is likely to be just that and no more. You never transcend anything. You grow, but your spirit never jumps out of your skin to go on wild adventures." [16]

This was probably the first time that Dewey's pragmatism had been attacked so vigorously by someone on the liberal left in America. Pragmatism seemed inadequate in a world of struggle in spite of its Darwinian associations. It seemed too conventional for the generation whose history Bourne predicted, the generation which joined the Communist party in the twenties or became lost in Paris. "They will be harsh and often bad-tempered, and they will feel that the breakup of things is no time for mellowness. They will have a taste for spiritual adventure, and for sinister imaginative excursions. It will not be puritanism so much as complacency that they will fight. A tang, a bitterness, an intellectual fiber, a verve, they will look for in literature, and their most virulent enemies will be those unaccountable radicals who are still morally servile, and are now trying to suppress all free speculation in the interests of nationalism. Something more mocking, more irreverent, they will constantly want. They will take institutions very lightly, indeed will never fail to be surprised at the seriousness with which good radicals take the stated offices and systems." [17]

Bourne's outlook and his attitude toward Dewey's pragmatism impressed itself on the literary left in the twenties, when Dewey was viewed as safe and professorial. The thirties witnessed a change. For by that time Dewey had taken on a good deal of the cynicism which Bourne had urged. The depression had driven Dewey to socialism, and the same forces which sent men to social science and Marxism during the depression made instrumentalism a respectable philosophy on the left once again. Writers and intellectuals came out of their Village basements and onto the streets; they came home from Paris willing to listen to the virtues of scientific method, at least until the Second World War began to breed a new boredom with the canned slogans of intelligence.

Bourne's attack on Dewey in 1917 was based on disappointment. Dewey had served as a symbol of intelligent humanitarianism, of a desire to mold society in the interests of peace, economic security, and freedom. His support of the war, therefore, came as a shock to those who saw it as a direct contradiction of all these values. Dewey ceased to be the gentle, sage spokesman of creative liberalism in certain quarters. Like the German Social Democrats, he was described as the philosophical representative of a selling-out movement, a failure to face the crisis which the war presented to liberals.

In contrast, curiously enough, Holmes gained stature as a consequence of his response to the war. With his Civil War experiences, his defense of the military life, and his celebration of the military virtues, he was well prepared for battle. He had no pacifist past or brooding conscience to block him or torment him. The war called forth his immediate and unquestioning support even before we entered it, a fact at which liberal pacifists could not possibly be surprised. There was no question of treachery to prewar ideals. Max Lerner has observed the consistency which spared Holmes the kind of attack that Bourne leveled against Dewey. "It is characteristic of him," Lerner said of Holmes, "that while with the outbreak of the war he had far fewer words to eat and fewer attitudes to erase than anyone else, he did not go as far as others in uncritical glorifications of the war. . . . It was . . . characteristic of Holmes that one who all his life had had a fighting faith should now be so moderate in trumpeting it and so wary of its abuse." [18]

Holmes' so-called fighting faith is neither profound nor interesting, and it was wisely soft-pedaled by his liberal admirers during the twenties and the thirties, fortified as they were by his own statement after the First World War: "I loathe war." [19] Unfortunately the Second World War led some followers to see virtues in even Holmes' more absurd theoretical professions. Holmes was then hailed on the very issues which were thought to reveal his worst side in the "naive" twenties and thirties. So it is that in 1943 Lerner approached Holmes' conviction that the war experience gave the individual a sense of being part of "an unimaginable whole" with solemn applause: "If this is mysticism it is the sort that the recent experiences of Britain, Russia, and America tend to validate." [20] We need not enter the vexed problem of what it means to validate mysticism, and we may leave it to Lerner to suggest methods whereby mysticism will help relations between these same countries in 1949. Wars may bring visions of unimaginable wholes, but postwar periods mean hangovers and delirium. Holmes was a soldier and an aristocrat, and some of his reflections embodied the outlook which Veblen had attacked in *The Theory of the Leisure Class*. For example, Holmes said on one military occasion: "In this snug, over-safe corner of the world we need it [war], that we may realize that our comfortable routine is no eternal necessity of things, but merely a little space of calm in the midst of the tempestuous untamed streaming of the world, and in order that we may be ready for danger. We need it in this time of individualist negations, with its literature of French and American humor, revolt-

ing at discipline, loving fleshpots, and denying that anything is
worthy of reverence—in order that we may remember all that
buffoons forget. We need it everywhere and at all times. For
high and dangerous action teaches us to believe as right beyond
dispute things for which our doubting minds are slow to find
words of proof. Out of heroism grows faith in the worth of heroism. The proof comes later, and even may never come. Therefore I rejoice at every dangerous sport which I see pursued. The
students of Heidelberg, with their sword-slashed faces, inspire
me with sincere respect. I gaze with delight upon our polo
players. If once in a while in our rough riding a neck is broken,
I regard it not as a waste, but as a price well paid for the breed-
ing of a race fit for headship and command." [21] Nothing could
have been more revolting to the Veblen who wrote on the "Modern Survivals of Prowess" in *The Theory of the Leisure Class,*
the chapter in which he argues that war, government, and sports
are modern expressions of barbarian traits—force and fraud. In
spite of sharing a good deal with Veblen in matters of methodology, Holmes was almost his exact opposite in manners and
morals. He differed in temperament from Dewey, too, and it is
not surprising that William James should have resented Holmes'
repeated celebrations of manly duty, war, and life. When Holmes
produced one of them in 1900, James wrote: "I must say I'm disappointed in O. W. H. for being unable to make any other than
that one set speech which comes out on every occasion. It's all
right for once, in the exuberance of youth, to celebrate mere
vital excitement, *la joie de vivre,* as a protest against humdrum
solemnity. But to make it systematic, and oppose it, as an ideal
and a duty, to the ordinarily recognized duties, is to pervert it
altogether." [22] Holmes was a soldier and a lawyer, and his characteristic attitudes on matters like war, action, and danger were
very different from those of his professorial contemporaries in
the liberal movement. His responses were less Hamlet-like, less
sicklied o'er with the pale cast of intelligence. For this reason he
suffered less than Dewey during the war. He could never have

written in hesitation about our entering the war, and he could never have drawn as vigorous an attack from a disciple as Bourne's "Twilight of the Idols." And in the assurance that went with his unquestioning support of the war he wrote some of his greatest decisions. These decisions were born of honesty and integrity and were made with enormous confidence in the rightness of the war. For this reason he could be sparing and kind toward those whose ideas he could hardly conceive as "a clear and present danger" to a cause he found so just.

The decisions for which Holmes was hailed throughout the liberal world dealt mainly with questions concerning free speech in wartime. The war had led to hysteria, fanaticism, and prejudice, just as Bourne had predicted it would and as Dewey had hoped it wouldn't. The Espionage Acts of 1917 and 1918 were passed,[23] and as a result a series of problems came before the Supreme Court, arising out of the prosecution of opponents of the war. Usually the defendants were socialists or pacifists, and so Holmes was put in a most delicate position. His liberalism was to meet its greatest test. It should be remembered, however, that Holmes' decisions were not made during the heat of battle, for the Espionage Acts, as Chafee points out, "did not come before the Supreme Court until 1919, after the fighting was ended and almost all the District Court cases had been tried. It was too late for anything our highest court said to lessen the restrictive effect of the act upon the discussion of public affairs during the war. Thus we cannot rely on the Supreme Court as a safeguard against the excesses of war legislation. . . . The nine justices in the Supreme Court can only lock the doors after the Liberty Bell is stolen."[24]

The two most important decisions on the question of civil liberties during the First World War were *Schenck* v. *United States*,[25] and *Abrams* v. *United States*.[26] In the first case Holmes wrote the court's opinion; in the second he produced his most moving and most philosophical dissent. The first was one of a series of disappointing decisions for those who had hoped the

Supreme Court would invalidate the Espionage Acts, for in it Holmes upheld the conviction of Schenck, then general secretary of the Socialist party. But its great accomplishment was the formulation of a principle that could be used in the defense of free speech in later cases—the so-called doctrine of "clear and present danger." The previous history of the debate over free speech had raised a fundamental issue: "Whether the state can punish all words which have some tendency, however remote, to bring about acts in violation of law, or only words which directly incite to acts in violation of law." [27] The first alternative was held by the traditional opponents of free speech, by the defenders of sedition laws and of the curtailing of freedom during "emergencies." The second has received at least two interpretations, depending upon the construal of the word "direct." In one construal a direct incitation is one which *explicitly* urges the violation of law. This was the so-called "objective" test set forth by Justice Learned Hand in the *Masses* case.[28] In another interpretation a direct incitation is understood more broadly as one which creates a clear and present danger that the words will cause some behavior which Congress has a right to prevent. This was Holmes' view of the matter in the Schenck case:

The question in every case is whether the words used are used in such circumstances and are of such a nature as to create a clear and present danger that they will bring about the substantial evils that Congress has a right to prevent. It is a question of proximity and degree. When a nation is at war many things that might be said in time of peace are such a hindrance to its effort that their utterance will not be endured so long as men fight and that no court could regard them as protected by any constitutional right.[29]

Holmes emphasized that whether such acts are criminal depends upon the circumstances in which they are done. "The most stringent protection of free speech would not protect a man in falsely shouting fire in a theater and causing a panic." [30]

The Schenck decision was one of three which were rendered in the earliest considerations of the Espionage Acts, and in them

Holmes did not appear as the great protector of the downtrodden. For the Schenck decision was quickly followed by two others, particularly that in the case of Eugene Debs, in which Holmes sided with colleagues whom he and Brandeis would soon abandon to hopeless conservatism. "These three decisions in March 1919 came as a great shock to forward-looking men and women, who had consoled themselves through the wartime trials with the hope that the Espionage Act would be invalidated when it reached the Supreme Court. They were especially grieved that the opinions which dashed this hope were written by the Justice who for their eyes had long taken on heroic dimensions." [31] In the Debs case Holmes again wrote the majority opinion and sustained the conviction without even applying his own clear-and-present-danger principle, a course which caused some of his liberal admirers great concern. Some, like Chafee, are inclined to endow it, retrospectively, with great wisdom; for, "looking backward," Chafee added, after having remarked on the misgivings which the decision had caused "forward-looking men and women," "we see that Justice Holmes was biding his time until the court should have before it a conviction so clearly wrong as to let him speak out his deepest thoughts about the First Amendment." We may pause here simply to note the godlike wisdom which some of Holmes' lawyer followers have assigned to him. It seems rather striking that a scholar as courageous and as forthright as Professor Chafee should have been willing to sacrifice Debs in the interest of saving Holmes' reputation as a wise and just man. Holmes had accepted the jury's verdict that Debs had intended actual interference with the war and that this was the actual proximate effect of the words he had used in a speech. For this failure to investigate the clarity and presence of danger Chafee chides Holmes rather gently: "It is regrettable that he felt unable to go behind the verdict."

It was the Abrams conviction which was so "clearly wrong as to let him speak out his deepest thoughts on the First Amendment," and it was the Abrams case which vindicated Holmes in

the eyes of those who were "forward-looking." In it he produced
the document which was to stand to free speech as the Lochner
decision stood to social justice in the history of twentieth-century
liberal law. In addition to applying the doctrine of clear and
present danger and urging that it was necessary to prove that the
defendants had an actual intent to obstruct the war effort,
Holmes announced a semi-philosophical conviction which en-
deared him to the generation that had learned its philosophy
from Dewey. For in the Abrams dissent he described the Constitution as an experiment, indeed he described life as an experiment. He also associated himself with the doctrine which the
pragmatists called "fallibilism" when he said that "time has
upset many fighting faiths." In his plea for "free trade in ideas"
he contributed another commercial metaphor to American liberal prose, a metaphor which expressed his attitude toward free
speech as James' search for the "cash value" of ideas delineated
his pragmatism. It is worth observing the centrality of these two
businesslike expressions in the key doctrines of American liberalism, for they provided ammunition for those delicate Europeans
who had already marked America as the home of greed and
avarice. Ironically enough, two of our more refined Americans
were responsible for this market language, and it remained for
their more practical follower Dewey to argue with those who regarded the pragmatic spirit as the unavoidable philosophy of an
acquisitive society.

All of our liberal scholars supported America's entrance into
the war, but with varying degrees of enthusiasm. Their attitudes
ranged from Dewey's conscience-ridden hesitation to Holmes'
admission that "even my detachment and would-be impartiality
are shaken somewhat and whatever I may think privately I
would do what I could to cherish in my countrymen an unphilo-
sophic hatred of Germany and German ways." [32] Ironically
enough their efforts were not always regarded as the maximum
which they might have put forth. Holmes was attacked in patriotic terms by his legal brother Wigmore for his Abrams deci-

sion,[33] and Veblen's *Imperial Germany and the Industrial Revolution,* although recommended by Creel's Committee on Public Information as containing damaging information on Germany, was excluded from the mails by that self-appointed censor, Postmaster General Burleson.[34] But the most interesting case of supporting the war insufficiently for those who imposed more stringent patriotic requirements was that of Charles Beard. In October of 1917 he resigned from Columbia University in protest against the expulsion of some of his colleagues because of their views on the war. Although he had supported the war and indeed had urged our early entry into it, he said: "I have merely held that teachers should not be expelled without a full and fair hearing by their peers, surrounded by all of the safeguards of judicial process. Professors in Columbia University have been subjected to humiliating doctrinal inquisitions by the trustees, they have been expelled without notice or hearing, and their appointment and promotion depend upon securing, in advance, the favor of certain trustees. Without that favor scholarship and learning avail nothing." [35]

CHAPTER XII

The Twenties

THE twenties began with an intense revulsion against the war,[1] against the forces which had brought it on and perpetuated themselves in a disastrous peace, a peace whose effects were then foreseen by few but which later became frightening and real with the rise of Hitler. The twenties began with criticism and proposals for reconstruction in which America's liberals turned back to the social problems they had discussed in the days before 1914. But this time they approached their problems with more irony, with more of the spirit that Randolph Bourne had predicted, with more outspoken contempt for the world which they had only prodded or satirized in prewar days. The ingenious publishers of the first crossword-puzzle book presented the annals of one side of the early twenties in an advertisement:

1921—Coué
1922—Mah Jong
1923—[Yes, we have no] Bananas
1924—THE CROSS-WORD-PUZZLE BOOK [2]

For our purposes the following list is more revealing:

1919—*The Vested Interests and the State of the Industrial Arts* (Veblen)
1919—*The Place of Science in Modern Civilisation* (Veblen)

1920—*Reconstruction in Philosophy* (Dewey)
1920—*Collected Legal Papers* (Holmes)
1921—*The Engineers and the Price System* (Veblen)
1921—*The Mind in the Making* (Robinson)
1922—*Human Nature and Conduct* (Dewey)
1923—*Absentee Ownership* (Veblen)

The war had a double effect on the postwar writings of our scholars. It strengthened their fears of the most depressing aspects of capitalism and it led them to propose schemes for avoiding the catastrophes which they saw ahead. When they spoke of nationalism and the profit system, they gave no quarter. They looked upon these phenomena as the central scourges of their day, the two chief causes behind the war, which some of them now recalled with disgust and embarrassment. But they looked ahead too, some of them more incapable of pessimism than others. As might have been expected, Veblen was more bitter about nations and captains of industry than ever, and teasingly ironic about some of his practical proposals for freeing mankind of the incubus of absentee ownership. As might have been expected, Dewey was seriously worried about the problems which faced society, but still confident in the powers of intelligence— a confidence which he communicated to Robinson. The early twenties were dominated by disillusion with the past and plans for reconstructing the future. The general ideas which they produced were not essentially new but they were given more poignancy and influence by the world as it lay in ruins, economically and morally depressed. Veblen and Dewey became active critics of American culture whose warnings were taken more seriously than ever and whose social views reached the height of their popularity among those who took the *New Republic*. After the twenties ended in economic collapse, Veblen, who had died a few months before the market's crash, was made a saint in the technocratic church, and Dewey was driven to his most outspoken defense of socialism. In the early twenties these men came to see their agreements more clearly than ever and they formed a group comparable to the French *philosophes* in their plea for sanity and intelligence.[3]

They wavered between hope and despair like so many postwar intellectuals, and their feelings were given expression by H. G. Wells when he said: "I know that I believe so firmly in this great World at Peace that lies so close to our own, ready to come into being as our wills turn toward it, that I must needs go about this present world of disorder and darkness like an exile doing such feeble things as I can towards the world of my desire, now hopefully, now bitterly, as the moods may happen before I die." [4] The writings of Dewey in those days represented hope even as Veblen's registered despair. Together with Robinson they recorded the faults of the past they were so anxious to forget and presented a negative of the future which they seemed incapable of developing. Today some of us occasionally look at the negative, less glossy than it was, and slightly worn, in dusty copies of *Reconstruction in Philosophy* or *Absentee Ownership*.

Western civilization, Veblen and Dewey began to insist more loudly than ever, was dominated by values and ideals which were outmoded. Veblen harped on the inapplicability of eighteenth-century economics to the modern world, and Dewey shifted his guns from British empiricism to what he thought was an even more pernicious tradition—the spectatorial indifference of philosophers under the spell of the Greeks. Both of them dramatically described science and technology in chains, frustrated and curbed by business and bigotry. Robinson became their popular spokesman, and America was presented with a strikingly unpedantic statement of professorial ideas in *The Mind in the Making*—a statement emasculated somewhat by Robinson's oversimplification but strengthened by his courageously concrete picture of America under the well-oiled machine of Warren Gamaliel Harding.

Robinson was a historian, and so it fell to him to supply the detail which made vivid the complaints and proposals of Dewey and Veblen. He outlined the circumstances leading to "the philosophy of safety and sanity" that dominated those who frantically pursued "normalcy" after the war was over:

The war brought with it a burst of unwonted and varied animation. Those who had never extended their activities beyond the usual routine of domestic and professional life suddenly found themselves participating in a vast enterprise in which they seemed to be broadening their knowledge and displaying undreamed of capacity for cooperation with their fellows. Expressions of high idealism exalted us above the petty cares of our previous existence, roused new ambitions, and opened up an exhilarating perspective of possibility and endeavor. It was common talk that when the foe, whose criminal lust for power had precipitated the mighty tragedy, should be vanquished, things would "no longer be the same." All would then agree that war was the abomination of abominations, the world would be made safe for right-minded democracy, and the nations would unite in smiling emulation. Never did bitterer disappointment follow high hopes. All the old habits of nationalistic policy reasserted themselves at Versailles. A frightened and bankrupt world could indeed hardly be expected to exhibit greater intelligence than the relatively happy and orderly one which had five years earlier allowed its sanctified traditions to drag it over the edge of the abyss. Then there emerged from the autocracy of the Tsars the dictatorship of the proletariat, and in Hungary and Germany various startling attempts to revolutionize hastily and excessively that ancient order which the Hapsburg and Hohenzollern rulers had managed to perpetuate in spite of all modern novelties. The real character of these movements was ill understood in our country, but it was inevitable that with man's deep-seated animistic tendencies they should appear as a sort of wicked demon or a deadly contagion which might attack even our own land unless prevented by timely measures. War had naturally produced its machinery for dealing with dissenters, sympathizers with the enemy, and those who deprecated or opposed war altogether; and it was the easiest thing in the world to extend the repression to those who held exceptional or unpopular views, like the Socialists and members of the I.W.W. It was plausible to charge these associations with being under the guidance of foreigners, with "pacifism" and a general tendency to disloyalty. But suspicion went further so as to embrace members of a rather small, thoughtful class who, while rarely socialistic, were confessedly skeptical in regard to the general beneficence of existing institutions, and who failed to applaud at just the right points to suit the taste of the majority of their fellow-citizens. So the general impression grew up that there was a sort of widespread conspiracy to overthrow the government by violence or, at least, a dangerous tendency to prepare the way for such a disaster, or at any rate a culpable indifference to its possibility.

Business depression reinforced a natural reaction which had set in with the sudden and somewhat unexpected close of the war. The unwonted excitement brought on a national headache, and a sedative in the form of normalcy was proffered by the Republican party and thankfully accepted by the country at large. Under these circumstances the philosophy of safety and sanity was formulated. It is familiar and reassuring and puts no disagreeable task of mental and emotional readjustment on those who accept it. Hence its inevitable popularity and obvious soundness.[5]

This came from the very same historian who had written in the 1918 edition of his *Medieval and Modern Europe: An Introduction to the History of Western Europe:* "Our country has rightly been summoned to take up its part of the burden of conflict which the Allies have borne for four bitter years, and it is facing its obligations bravely and cheerfully and will make all the great sacrifices necessary to bring the struggle to a victorious end." [6] No other juxtaposition of two passages from one author could express more clearly the feelings of pro-war liberals in the post-Versailles world.

The philosophy of safety and sanity as Robinson understood it in 1921 was a popular counterpart of the ideology which both Veblen and Dewey attacked at its intellectual roots. He formulated it for popular consumption in language that dispensed with Veblen's ponderous wit and Dewey's slow-moving obscurity. Nevertheless, to understand more thoroughly the attitudes which liberals of the early twenties opposed we must turn to the writings of Dewey and Veblen, difficult as they are in comparison with the sunny clarity of *The Mind in the Making.*

Veblen came to stress more than ever the changing character of standards and principles of "right, equity, propriety, duty, . . . knowledge, belief, and taste." It seemed evident to him that those standards would vary from age to age in response to changing conditions of life. Acceptance of a given set of standards and principles he viewed as simply a habitual response to circumstances, although he recognized certain limits which were set upon the variety of response by "human nature," the "changeless native proclivities of the race." Veblen recognized no absolutes, no principles which might be called "fundamentally and eternally right and good," since all of them were tied up with institutions and institutions were notoriously creatures of habit, capable of disappearing with the forces that had created them. Hence what he called "the modern point of view" was simply a product of that vast and cataclysmic process that had broken down medieval habits and instituted the familiar elements of modern culture.[7]

When Veblen discussed what Marx would have called the "superstructure"—the intellectual and cultural expression of these pervasive shifts in material circumstance—he distinguished between two kinds of principles and standards. On the one hand there were the standards of knowledge and belief; on the other those of morals and custom. While both of them were dependent upon the basic and pervasive forces of society, the first set, he felt, responded with less torpor to the demands of human and social life. "The canons of knowledge and belief," as he called them, "the principles governing what is fact and what is credible," are more intimately and intrinsically involved in the habitual behavior of the human spirit than any other determinants of social habit. Conceptions of scientific adequacy are the prime ingredients of a "point of view"; change the social foundation and they respond first. "Such is necessarily the case, because the principles which guide and limit knowledge and belief are the ways and means by which men take stock of what is to be done and by which they take thought of how it is to be done." "The principles governing knowledge and belief at any given time are primary and pervasive, beyond any others," he said, "in that they underlie all human deliberation and comprise the necessary elements of all human logic." [8] Once witch-craft was able to satisfy the demands of credibility, but today it no longer does. The canons which permitted men to accept and believe in witchcraft began to crumble first, because they came to appear futile, misleading, and meaningless. Experience brought home the futility of such modes of thought, and they were replaced by new standards of knowledge which have thus far been restricted to science in the conventional sense. But soon, Veblen predicted in a way that Dewey would have applauded, the new outlook will extend itself to "those imponderable rela-tions, conventions, claims and perquisites, that make up the time-worn system of law and custom," and they too "will un-avoidably . . . be brought under review and will be revised and reorganized in the light of the same new principles of validity that are found to be sufficient in dealing with material facts." [9]

Veblen visualized some basic process producing a change in the standards of scientific procedure which would then filter into the system of morals. This was a root idea which tightly joined Dewey, Robinson, and Veblen—the idea that there would come a day when the scientific outlook dictated by the great industrial transformation of modern times would be commu-nicated to politics and law. And if the industrial locomotive did not succeed in communicating its speed to morality—the cul-tural caboose—Dewey and Robinson were prepared to help haul the lazy cars of morality and social philosophy, to give them some of the velocity of economics and industry, to grease the wheels of progress.

Veblen saw modern society under the domination of an eighteenth-century world view, a legal, moral, and political phi-losophy which was enshrined in the Declaration of the Rights of Man, the Declaration of Independence, and the American Con-stitution (he made no subtle distinctions between the second and the third). He saw this same outlook in the writings of John Locke, Montesquieu, Adam Smith, and Blackstone. They ac-cepted the outlook as axiomatic, indeed as "self-evident," he remarked with some contempt. But he had no doubt about its uselessness in 1919. He felt that it did not meet the requirements of what he called "the new order," for it "specifically makes provision for certain untoward rights, perquisites and disabilities which have, in the course of time and shifting circumstance, become incompatible with continued peace on earth and good will among men." [10] Few commentaries on the Constitution have been more outspoken. In 1913 Beard was content with unearthing the economic interests behind the Constitution; in 1919 Veblen called it bad—a document whose spirit ran counter to the Christian values of peace and good will.

Veblen continued to hold that the fundamental forces of society are material or economic in character. But the modern era, he went on to say, has witnessed a vast change in material circumstances, a change which can best be seen by examining the writings of Adam Smith, who, according to Veblen, formulated the eighteenth-century credo just as the Industrial Revolution was making it obsolete. "What he [Smith] has to say on the mechanics of industry is conceived in terms derived from an older order of things than that machine industry which was beginning to get under way in his own lifetime; and all his illustrative instances and arguments on trade and industry are also such as would apply to the state of things that was passing, but they are not drawn with any view to that new order which was then coming on in the world of business enterprise." [11]

Veblen represented Smith's picture of the economic world with a few vivid strokes. Smith conceived industry as handicraft and not as a matter of mechanical engineering; he thought of capital stock as savings accumulated out of the past industry of its owner, and he regarded business as petty trade. In this scheme of things trade is subsidiary to industry, and money is simply a vehicle to facilitate the distribution of goods to consumers. "Credit is an expedient of the needy; a dubious expedient. Profits (including interest) are justified as a reasonable remuneration for productive work done, and for the labor-saving use of property derived from the owner's past labor. The efforts of masters and workmen alike are conceived to be bent on turning out the largest and most serviceable output of goods; and prices are competitively determined by the labor-cost of the goods." [12]

The chief cause of the inadequacy of this picture of economic society, according to Veblen, was the growth of investment and financial enterprise. It was only beginning to get under way in Adam Smith's time, but it really sounded the death knell of the whole economics of which Smith was the acknowledged founder. Only because he did not know or clearly foresee this development could Smith have viewed business as subsidiary to industry. But this was the detail which made Smith's picture ghostly, the picture of an economy which no longer existed in 1919. It was this which led Veblen to label Smith's theories "make-believe." But there were powerful forces interested in perpetuating this make-believe, and therefore Veblen did not expect that it would be quickly surrendered. Smith's theories were so many fixed ideas in a world that had changed beyond recognition. He concluded characteristically: "It should be a case of break or bend." [13] This was his prognosis for the world of 1919 as it labored under what Robinson called "the philosophy of safety and sanity" and what Veblen called "the modern point of view," the view whose two chief elements were national ambition and the vested rights of ownership.

Just as Veblen tried to discredit the entire classical tradition in economics as inadequate to the twentieth century, so Dewey attacked his own classical predecessors in philosophy. In Dewey's case the attack was shifted from the empiricists whom he had so vigorously questioned in his early Hegelian days to the Greeks. In *Reconstruction in Philosophy* he explicitly avowed a genetic approach to the nature of philosophy. He began by asking for the sources or roots of philosophical speculation and concluded that philosophy does not simply arise as an intellectual response to a purely intellectual problem, but rather as an attempt to justify certain social, moral, and emotional convictions of a disappearing age. Dewey's attitude toward classical philosophy was similar to Veblen's attitude toward Adam Smith, since Dewey regarded the entire classical tradition as a conservative apologetic for the standards of a bygone day. Just as Veblen felt that classical economics was incapable of appreciating the "matter-of-fact" character of scientific method, so Dewey found classical philosophy guilty of a similar opposition to what he too called the matter-of-fact outlook of positive science. The outward logical scheme of classical philosophy was only that—outward. "Since it aimed at a rational justification of things that had been previously accepted because of their emotional congeniality and social prestige, it had to make much of the apparatus of reason and proof. Because of the lack of intrinsic rationality in the matters with which it dealt, it leaned over backward, so to speak, in a parade of logical form. In dealing with matters of fact, simpler and rougher ways of demonstration may be resorted to. It is enough, so to say, to produce the fact in question and point to it—the fundamental form of all demonstration. But when it comes to convincing men of the truth of doctrines which are no longer to be accepted on the say-so of custom and social authority, but which also are not capable of empirical verification, there is no recourse save to magnify the signs of rigorous thought and rigid demonstration. Thus arises that appearance of abstract definition and ultra-scientific argumentation which repels so many from philosophy but which has been one of its chief attractions to its devotees." In one instant Dewey discredited the entire two thousand years that preceded him in philosophy, meanwhile expressing the temperamental aversion to formal, "rigid" logic and "hair-splitting" which has been part of his philosophical personality for almost seventy years.[14]

Because of its aloofness toward matters of fact, and because of its need to justify pre-existing social values, philosophy, he said, "arrogated to itself the office of demonstrating the existence of a transcendent, absolute or inner reality and of revealing to man the nature and features of this ultimate and higher reality.

It has therefore claimed that it was in possession of a higher organ of knowledge than is employed by positive science and ordinary practical experience, and that it is marked by a superior dignity and importance—a claim which is undeniable *if* philosophy leads man to proof and intuition of a reality beyond that open to day-by-day life and the special sciences." [15]

Dewey's sociological approach to the history of philosophy appears in *Reconstruction in Philosophy* in its most blatant form. Marx couldn't have been more forthright in his attempts at "exposing" the ideological commitments of bourgeois thought. Dewey concluded his indictment with an aside: "This account of the origin of philosophies claiming to deal with absolute Being in a systematic way has been given with malice prepense. It seems to me that this genetic method of approach is a more effective way of undermining this type of philosophic theorizing than any attempt at logical refutation could be." [16] So, of course, would be the application of a crowbar to the skulls of the classic philosophers. Dewey was quite explicit in his aims. He wanted to "undermine" this tradition and he found it easier to do so by revealing its alleged roots and motives than by "logical refutation." And of course logical refutation would have involved him in a hair-splitting crusade against hair-splitting, and this he firmly resisted. Having ruthlessly condemned the entire philosophical tradition, Dewey added an observation which was to rub the curse off his charge, and, indeed, to justify his own perpetual preoccupation with these people of whom he thought so little. He urged his readers to study the history of philosophy "not as an isolated thing but as a chapter in the development of civilization and culture." "If one will connect the story of philosophy," he continued, "with a study of anthropology, primitive life, the history of religion, literature and social institutions, it is confidently asserted that he will reach his own independent judgment as to the worth of the account which has been presented. . . . Considered in this way, the history of philosophy will take on a new significance. What is lost from the standpoint of would-be science is regained from the standpoint of humanity. Instead of the disputes of rivals about the nature of reality, we have the scene of human clash of social purpose and aspirations. Instead of impossible attempts to transcend experience, we have the significant record of the efforts of men to formulate the things of experience to which they are most deeply and passionately attached. Instead of impersonal and purely speculative endeavors to contemplate as remote beholders the nature of absolute things-in-themselves, we have a living picture of the choice of thoughtful men about what they would have life to be, and to what ends they would have men shape their intelligent activities." [17] No longer would anyone convinced of the absurdity of Hume's arguing for skepticism really take Hume's argument seriously in its own terms; instead he would sweep Hume's technical concern aside as mere froth, as a mere hair-splitting subterfuge, and look for a more basic moral and social commitment. And this commitment he would then study simply as a part of culture. Once we become convinced of the insanity or absurdity of an idea we look for its social background and "role" and then devote ourselves to the sociological task of relating the idea to its culture. The history of philosophy was no longer to be read as an account of a series of men wrestling with soluble problems, but rather as a history of social and moral aspiration, of unconscious apologetics.

One might have supposed that Dewey merely regarded this basic moral interest as a characteristic of past philosophy, and that he was hoping to eliminate it from his own thinking. In other words, one might have supposed that serious philosophical reflection, stripped of the emotional, moral prejudices of the past, was to begin with Dewey. But no, this is not the moral or the claim. This is not the lesson of philosophy's past tragedy. Rather it is that philosophers must come to see that their chief task (one gets the impression that their *only* task) is to moralize. For he who has really learned his lesson from Dewey "will inevitably be committed to the notion that what philosophy has been unconsciously, without knowing or intending it, and, so to speak, under cover, it must henceforth be openly and deliberately. When it is acknowledged that under disguise of dealing with ultimate reality, philosophy has been occupied with the precious values imbedded in social traditions, that it has sprung from a clash of social ends and from a conflict of inherited institutions with incompatible contemporary tendencies, it will be seen that the task of future philosophy is to clarify men's ideas as to the social and moral strifes of their own day. Its aim is to become so far as is humanly possible an organ for dealing with these conflicts. That which may be pretentiously unreal when it is formulated in metaphysical distinctions becomes intensely significant when connected with the drama of the struggle of social beliefs and ideals. Philosophy which surrenders its somewhat barren monopoly of dealings with Ultimate and Absolute Reality will find a compensation in enlightening the moral forces which move mankind and in contributing to the aspirations of men to attain a more ordered and intelligent happiness." [18]

There is an interesting analogy between this view of the task of philosophy and the theory of the law which Holmes advanced in the nineties. Holmes' version of the law as scientific when it consciously judges the relative worth of the social ends involved in any given legal problem is a counterpart of Dewey's view as set forth in *Reconstruction in Philosophy*. Dewey's view that value propositions are scientific, when added to his view that philosophy is essentially a value discipline, yields a conclusion analogous to Holmes' on the law—that philosophy will become scientific when it systematically pursues the task of moral criticism. Philosophy will become a science when it devotes itself to the problems of scientific ethics, when it devotes itself to the problems of men. Dewey might very well have accepted a statement of Holmes if "philosophy" were substituted for "the law": "The true science of philosophy does not consist mainly in a theological working out of dogma or a logical development as in mathematics, or only in a study of it as an anthropological document from the outside; an even more important part consists in the establishment of its postulates from within upon accurately measured social desires instead of tradition." [19] Dewey might have said that the life of philosophy has not been logic, but experience. And there is even something to match Holmes' innuendo that some lawyers pretend that the life of the law is logic in order to mask the policy-making and evaluation that actually goes on.

It is not difficult to see how closely united these scholars were in the twenties—confirmed opponents of the ideas which had dominated the past in economics, philosophy, and history. Veblen needled Adam Smith and the philosophy of vested interests and national ambition; Dewey was battling the Greeks and the English on all philosophical fronts; Robinson was poking fun at the philosophy of safety and sanity and urging historians and scholars to "humanize" their knowledge, that is, to popularize their knowledge without compromise, the better to stem irrational manifestations like Bryanism in biology.[20] These were days in which scholars were still active, when, in Veblen's phrase, academics did more than indulge in "truculent quietism."

Thus far we have focused on the complaints of the early twenties, but there were two aspects of the movement. One was the product of disillusion and disgust; the other was more positive. What were the positive ideas which appeared in the twenties? What were the recommendations? What were the programs? No one can help us more than James Harvey Robinson in approaching the answers to these questions. His work not only reveals the negative attitude toward the past which I have already discussed, but it also gives us some glimpse of the positive outlook of the new liberalism. *The Mind in the Making* (1921) was written while Robinson was teaching at the New School for Social Research, the shrine of academic liberalism in the twenties. It communicates not only the liberal critique of the past but also liberal optimism, the forward glance to the bravest of all possible worlds; it is also the sigh of an intellectual who survived a horrible war, the critical and cynical reaction of a believer in the new social science. Instrumentalism, progressive education, Veblenism, and Freudianism—all of them are drawn upon and marshaled in defense of intelligence. A Baconian contempt for scholastic metaphysics, a patronizing attitude toward the Greeks, a hatred of superstition, and a firm attachment to the scientific method turn up on every page. Dewey and Veblen are glowingly cited for their attacks on classical philosophy and economics; Keynes, Russell, Tawney, Hobson, Laski, and the inevitable Graham Wallas are imported from England, forever to take their places in the footnotes of the twenties.

The book was mainly historical, of course, and a good deal of it was devoted to damning the past, but some of it was offered as a positive solution to what Dewey called the problems of men. The main theme was simple. Up to then the method of science —intelligence—had been used in connection with physical problems, but it had never been systematically turned on the problems of human morals and politics. Every reader of Dewey is (and was then) familiar with this contention, and Robinson in no way improved upon Dewey in the matter. He had "no reforms to recommend, except the liberation of intelligence, which is the first and most essential one." [21] What is most striking, however, is Robinson's ambivalent attitude toward the social sciences. On the one hand he thought they were the key sciences, those to which we must turn for a solution of all our troubles, and yet he believed that "the progress of mankind in the scientific knowledge and regulation of human affairs has remained almost stationary for over two thousand years." [22] Now it is to be remembered that Robinson was not saying that our social knowledge had been neither distributed nor applied, but rather that we hadn't had any new knowledge. But then he looked at the feverish speculation on social matters and concluded that the two thousand years of scarcity were over. Long live the New School and (in anticipation) the *Encyclopedia of the Social Sciences*! It is very important to bear in mind this combination of contempt and optimism about the social sciences in Dewey and Robinson because of its political implications. Clearly, if our political action is to be a function of our social knowledge, and if the latter is meager or rudimentary, we are hardly in a position to act with assurance. We can make very general proposals, and outline programs, but we must be ever so tentative. Perhaps it is this which has determined the programmatic character of Dewey's political thought; perhaps it is this which explains his excessive concern with *method* in politics—his celebration of intelligence in the abstract, and his admitted failure to build what he calls a "political technology." Surely it is a partial explanation of Robinson's unwillingness or incapacity to offer any "specific reforms." Robinson seemed content with being a latter-day Bacon for the social sciences, a cheerleader rather than a playing captain. But cheerleaders are notoriously handicapped by poor teams, and even more so when there is no team on the field.

The refusal or inability to offer specific reforms in the case of so concrete and practical a professor is rather ironical, and the irony comes out in the extraordinary similarity between Robinson's own vagueness about specific solutions and the vagueness of President Harding, of whom he had no high opinion. After protesting his own inability to offer specific reforms, Robinson quotes with obvious despair the following gem from the apostle of normalcy: "With a Senate advising as the Constitution contemplates, I would hopefully approach the nations of Europe and of the earth, proposing that understanding which makes us a willng participant in the consecration of nations to a new relationship, to commit the moral forces of the world, America included, to peace and international justice, still leaving America free, independent, self-reliant, but offering friendship to all the world. If men call for more specific details, I remind them that moral committals are broad and all-inclusive, and we are contemplating peoples in the concord of humanity's advancement." [23] But surely Robinson, who offered no specific reforms and who would urge nothing beyond the liberation of intelligence, was in no position to laugh at Harding for being broad and vague. For beyond urging the need for liberating intelligence, Robinson merely called for a change of heart. "What we need first is a change of heart and a chastened mood which will permit an ever-increasing number of people to see things as they are, in the light of what they have been and what they might be." [24]

Veblen was more specific than Robinson, but this brought him no closer to practice. For although he went beyond calling for a change of heart and the use of scientific method in social affairs, his most specific proposal was one whose execution he himself tried to show impossible. Since on his view no effective change of society in a progressive direction could be carried out without the initiative and direction of the country's technicians, it was easy for him to prove the impossibility of carrying out his own program. For he simply observed: "Notoriously, no move of this nature has been made hitherto, nor is there evidence that anything of the kind has been contemplated by the technicians. They still are consistently loyal, with something more than a hired man's loyalty, to the established order of commercial profit and absentee ownership." [25] Veblen's formula was quite simple. "In principle, all that is necessarily involved is a disallowance of absentee ownership; that is to say, the disestablishment of an institution which has, in the course of time and change, proved to be noxious to the common good. The rest will follow quite simply from the cancelment of this outworn and footless vested right. By absentee ownership, as the term applies in this connection, is here to be understood the ownership of an industrially useful article by any person or persons who are not habitually employed in the industrial use of it." [26]

Those who speak glibly of Veblen's lack of interest in value

ought to ponder his simple, flat declaration that absentee ownership has proved to be noxious to the common *good*. Nothing
could seem more like a value judgment, if the notion of common
good be construed as it usually is. Why, then, do people insist
on describing Veblen as deliberately amoral, wholly uninter-
ested in good and bad? Clearly the statement quoted above
reveals an interest in ethical, practical questions. Anyone who
is concerned with the problem of making a revolutionary over-
turn in society, as Veblen was, is obviously concerned with a
moral question. The fact that Veblen wrote books to persuade
engineers to take matters into their own hands is itself an indication of a practical, i.e., a moral, interest. But then, of course,
there are the countless disclaimers of moral interest throughout
his writings, particularly in his early work. And even in the
very chapter from which I have taken the quoted passage about
absentee ownership being noxious to the common good, Veblen
added this aside: "There is no doubt that a proposal to disallow
absentee ownership will shock the moral sensibilities of many
persons; more particularly the sensibilities of the absentee
owners. To avoid the appearance of willful neglect, therefore,
it is necessary to speak also of the 'moral aspect.' There is no
intention here to argue the moral merits of this contemplated
disallowance of absentee ownership; or to argue for or against
such a move, on moral or other grounds. Absentee ownership is
legally sound today. Indeed, as is well known, the Constitution
includes a clause which specially safeguards its security. If, and
when, the law is changed, in this respect, what is so legal today
will of course cease to be legal. There is, in fact, not much more
to be said about it; except that, in the last resort, the economic
moralities wait on the economic necessities. The economic-moral
sense of the American community runs unequivocally to the
effect that absentee ownership is fundamentally and eternally
right and good; and it would seem reasonable to believe that
it will continue to run to that effect for some time yet." [27]

Now when we juxtapose this last passage with the earlier one, in which Veblen indicated his belief that absentee ownership was "noxious to the common good," we have a fairly clear idea of the confusion in his own mind about whether he was indulging in morals or not and also a fairly good idea of why his interpreters have insisted on pointing to his lack of interest in "morals" and "ethics." When he says that absentee ownership is noxious to the common good he certainly *seems* to be judging the "moral merits of this contemplated disallowance of absentee ownership." He is saying that it has no social merit. Why, then, does he add his disclaimer of any interest in the moral merits of absentee ownership? Although he really was condemning absentee ownership morally, and hence operating as a moral critic, his confused and confusing statements about the nature of moral judgments succeeded in giving the impression that he was no moral critic at all. In this way he was able to help his more "objective" disciples to perpetuate the myth of his indifference.

Veblen's conclusion in *The Engineers and the Price System* was hardly encouraging. Only the technicians by seizing power could really make society good, and they were not going to do it. Here was a specific proposal of the only road, combined with pessimism about whether the only road would ever be traveled. "By way of conclusion it may be recalled again that, just yet, the production engineers are a scattering lot of fairly contented subalterns, working piecemeal under orders from the deputies of the absentee owners; the working force of the great mechanical industries, including transportation, are still nearly out of touch and out of sympathy with the technical men, and are bound in rival trade organizations whose sole and self-seeking interest converges on the full dinner-pail; while the underlying population are as nearly uninformed on the state of things as the Guardians of the Vested Interests, including the commercialized newspapers, can manage to keep them, and they are consequently still in a frame of mind to tolerate no substantial abatement of absentee ownership; and the constituted authorities are competently occupied with maintaining the status quo. There is nothing in the situation that should reasonably flutter the sensibilities of the Guardians or of that massive body of well-to-do citizens who make up the rank and file of absentee owners, just yet." [28]

Veblen and Robinson present the two extremes of liberal politics in the twenties. On the one hand we find in Robinson an abstract, evangelical respect for concrete intelligence: "I have no reforms to recommend except the liberation of intelligence"; on the other, in Veblen, a specific proposal which he felt would not be carried out "just yet." Here was liberalism oscillating between general cheers for science and impossible scientific reforms. This was the story of liberal political philosophy in the twenties. It was unwilling to be too specific out of a fear of rigidity, and yet when it became specific it proposed admittedly utopian measures.

This same combination appears in other aspects of the liberal mind of the twenties. Dominated by a pragmatic conception of method and science, it was constantly demanding concreteness and specific proposals. But it was also in revolt against formalism, against the espousal of rigidly conceived ends, and means, of social reform. It was this double attitude which emerged in many of Dewey's writings. When polemicizing against the idealists and the cloudy, impractical metaphysicians, Dewey emphasized his own concreteness; but when faced with what he called the "rigid schemes" of less woolly philosophers he was always quick to retreat to a domain of generality which he denied to his speculative opponents. Consider for example some of his own views of Holmes. Dewey has always regarded Holmes with great respect. In *Experience and Nature* (1926) he called him one of America's greatest philosophers, a compliment which Holmes duly repaid in his ecstatic comments on that book.[29] In 1928 Dewey expressed his admiration for Holmes in an article which made of Holmes a Deweyan—the highest accolade, of course. Dewey summed up Holmes' outlook by listing three cen-

tral ideas: his belief in intelligence as the finally directive force
in life, his belief in freedom of thought as necessary to realize
this, and his belief in the experimental character of life and
thought. But these were quite general and incapable of forming
anything like a social philosophy. And Dewey recognized this,
for he quickly admitted that in one sense of "social philosophy,"
Holmes had none. In short, he said, Holmes has "no social
panaceas to dole out, no fixed social program, no code of fixed
ends to be realized." But then in justification of this poverty
Dewey makes a revealing comment on a spectrum of liberalisms.
"As a social philosophy, 'liberalism' runs the gamut of which a
vague temper of mind—often called forward-looking—is one extreme, and a definite creed as to the purposes and methods of
social action is another. The first is too vague to afford any
steady guide in conduct; the second is so specific and fixed as to
result in dogma, and thus to end in an illiberal mind. Liberalism as a method of intelligence, prior to being a method of
action, as a method of experimentation based on insight into
both social desires and actual conditions, escapes the dilemma.
It signifies the adoption of the scientific habit of mind in application to social affairs." [30]

This statement is more revealing of Dewey's outlook than it
is of Holmes'; it reveals Dewey's awareness of the ambivalence
which has been mentioned. Dewey was acutely conscious of the
dilemma of liberalism. How could it escape being fuzzy without
formulating a creed which would be hardened into a rigid and
ultimately reactionary doctrine? But his recognition of the
dilemma is no proof of his having escaped it. Liberalism as
Dewey defines it, in an effort to escape this dilemma, is hardly
more than a proposal that we apply the so-called scientific
method of intelligence to social problems. Dewey refuses to be
vague by calling liberalism a "temper of mind," but he also
fears being too concrete. In a way the hesitation and the fear
are laudable, but they also illuminate difficulties which critical
readers have found in liberal writings. It is very easy to criticize

Dewey in the way that he criticized Kant in *German Philosophy and Politics*. Unlike Kant, Dewey did not hold that moral rules could be tested by purely formal or deductive procedures, but he goes very little beyond advising us to be empirically intelligent, just as Kant went very little beyond telling us that we ought to avoid self-contradiction.

Kant's supreme categorical imperative was meta-moral, because it was not itself a specific rule of moral behavior. Rather it was a rule describing the ways for deciding what our duties are. In the same way the liberal social philosophy which Dewey identifies merely with a belief in the use of scientific procedure for testing social and moral statements is itself a meta-moral theory. Of itself it commits us to no specific course of action; it supplies us with no detail. Now it will be remembered that Dewey was very critical of Kant for presenting an abstract moral rule which could be filled in with the duties deemed necessary by a powerful institution like the Prussian state. But clearly Dewey's general formulation of liberalism as respect for social science is equally subject to this kind of misuse. As Randolph Bourne suggested, Dewey's own philosophy might easily fall into the hands of those willing to cry "science, science" in defense of the most obnoxious ends and means. Liberalism so construed supplies us with no particular or specific political position that can be acted on, only a plea for intelligence. But surely this can only be the first step in the right direction. What is not always clear is whether Dewey thinks greater concreteness is something to be achieved in the future or whether he positively rejects it as doomed to dogmatism and the whole rigid scheme of fixed ends and means. This lack of clarity obscured a good deal of Dewey's political thinking in the twenties.

In devoting this chapter to the twenties I have tried to picture the liberal ideology rising to its highest level of publication and popularity. In examining it I have restricted myself to the broad philosophy upon which it proceeded in social and political matters. What stands out, of course, is the tremendous respect for what Veblen called "matter-of-fact" procedures, and what Dewey and Robinson called "intelligence." There was no doubt about the efficacy of this in producing man's happiness, it would appear. Indeed Dewey's confidence prevented him from formulating a specific program, for he feared losing the leniency and flexibility which a broad program allowed. But when Veblen, who was quite specific, drew political conclusions from his distinction between business and industry, he found himself proposing something which couldn't be put into effect "just yet."

CHAPTER XIII

Is Ethics an Empirical Science?

U P TO now we have been inspecting the intellectual roots and social significance of Beard, Dewey, Holmes, Robinson, and Veblen from the eighteen-eighties to the nineteen-twenties. We have seen their methodological revolt against formalism express itself in many ways, and we have also sampled their political ideas. Having communicated some notion of their work and of the world in which they thrived, we shall turn now to extended critical reflections on a few basic philosophical themes in their writings. By the twenties they were no longer engaged in an infant industry. On the contrary, their ideas had now become full-grown and ripe for critical analysis.

The philosophical problems which were most insistent and which were most seriously considered by them come under the disciplines of logic and ethics, provided we construe these disciplines broadly. If we understand logic as the study which treats of more than deduction and includes what Dewey calls the theory of scientific inquiry, then most of these men have been concerned with logic with varying degrees of seriousness and success. They were interested in the methodology of law, history, economics, and political science, and they speculated on the nature of science in general. The one division of philosophy which they conspicuously avoided was metaphysics. In *Recon-*

struction in Philosophy Dewey tried to convert even that most august of all philosophical disciplines into a branch of ethics or social science. Their lack of interest in speculative philosophy and their distrust of it deserve careful study, but here I can mention them only as part of a general anti-metaphysical strain in American thought of the twentieth century. To the extent to which our thinkers were interested in philosophy they were interested in its bearing on their own disciplines and on practical questions. They were occupied with two closely related problems: (1) the nature of social science and (2) the relation between social science and moral value and obligation. The second was more serious for them, in fact so serious that they went on to it without giving sufficient attention to the first. That the second problem puzzled them and stimulated them greatly is shown by the more specific topics of preceding chapters: Holmes' interest in the relation between law and ethics, Veblen's attack on the idea of progress in classical economics and his constant interest in avoiding explicit moral judgments, Beard's protest about the cool, scientific neutrality of his work (very different from his later views), the new history's worry about whether historians can select according to their values without losing objectivity, Dewey's undaunted conviction that the solution of our social problems lies in the application of science to human affairs.

In the course of their reflections on science and value they tend to divide into two groups. One worries about whether value judgments are reducible to scientific terms, assuming that science is quite objective. But the other refuses to make this assumption and raises the whole question as to whether social science, particularly history, depends on value assumptions of the social scientist himself. By and large Dewey, Holmes, and Veblen fall into the first group and Robinson and Beard, especially Beard, into the second. Dewey, Holmes, and Veblen were primarily interested in finding out whether science is adequate to the solution of all our moral problems; whether judgments of value and obligation are simply matters of empirical knowledge to be settled by social science itself. For example: Is the problem of whether our society is a good society simply to be solved by experiment and observation? Is the problem of whether one *ought* to support a war something to be solved by going through motions similar to those involved in deciding whether the stock market will go up, whether all bodies do attract each other, and whether Julius Caesar did cross the Rubicon? If they are, matters would be relatively easy. Not absolutely easy because they might still involve complicated empirical questions. But to be convinced that they are in principle empirical problems and soluble in the way that physical problems are is to gain confidence, for, after all, physics has progressed, and even economists, sociologists, political scientists, and historians know more than they used to know.

Robinson and Beard created interest in another question. Instead of asking whether the problem of what was good and what ought to be done can be discovered by the methods of history and social science, Beard asked whether history and social science were possible without value assumptions. Obviously it is important to raise this second question, for if you work hard to show that questions of value may be reduced to social science and then it turns out that the social sciences must assume value propositions, you are not getting very far. You are right back where you started. By and large Holmes, Veblen, and Dewey regarded social science as objective and thought it was important to see whether the categories of value could be reduced to it. They emerged with different answers, as we shall see, but they were primarily concerned with the first question. Robinson and Beard, on the other hand, as historians in reaction against Ranke's conception of history as an account of things "as they really happened," led people to ask whether historians needed value assumptions to get started, assumptions which would help them select the important historical facts from the infinite number theoretically available to them.

Holmes and Veblen both held that law and economics were empirical sciences. They wanted to be free of prejudice and belief in final causes; they wanted to make a distinction between what they found and what they wanted to find. Veblen regarded this as a consequence of his Darwinism. Darwin had completed the rout of teleology in the natural sciences, and Veblen continued the fight in the social sciences. It was in this spirit that he criticized "animism" in his predecessors—the view that society was necessarily tending toward some good goal. He criticized those who could not see the difference between describing the economic world in colorless terms and describing a world in which they wanted to live. The same distinction turns up in Holmes' writings, particularly in his conception of legal duty and in his conception of the law itself. Legal duty and ethical duty are sharply distinguished, and the law is stripped of all its moral overtones. But in spite of this distinction between science and valuation Holmes and Veblen urged a connection between them to the point of sounding paradoxical, as we have seen in earlier chapters. To solve this paradox we must state the distinction which they did accept a little more precisely. The point is simply this: what happens is not always liked (valued), but a scientist is expected to describe what happens even when he dislikes it. The economist must predict the course of an economic process that may end in disaster; the lawyer must predict what the court will do in fact even though it is a bad court trying a bad man. And yet, in spite of this distinction, both Holmes and Veblen became involved in and defended the consideration of value *in the course of their scientific investigations.* Let us see how this came about.

The paradox in Veblen is illustrated by the fact that, although he constantly protested his moral indifference, the main thesis of his chief work, *The Theory of the Leisure Class,* was that the leisure class was a wasteful institution. This must be understood in connection with his announcement that a major purpose of the book was to discuss the *value* of the leisure class.

He argued, as we saw in Chapter VI, that the chief activity of the leisure class is wasteful and therefore without value. When he said that it was wasteful he meant that it did not serve "human life or well-being on the whole." He was squeamish about implying that those who indulge in conspicuous consumption don't value it individually, but in calling it wasteful he did not refrain from making a value judgment in one clear sense of that phrase. What he did refrain from judging was whether we ought to abolish an institution which did not serve "human well-being on the whole," but this is another matter. Veblen admitted that those who consumed conspicuously might enjoy and hence value what they consumed. But it must be insisted that he believed that his own judgment of the disvalue, the wastefulness, of conspicuous consumption was scientifically testable. Indeed this was the chief conclusion of that eminently scientific and evolutionary study, *The Theory of the Leisure Class*. In it Veblen did not refuse to make a value judgment; what he refused to do was to compare the lack of value of conspicuous consumption to society as a whole with its apparent value to those who indulged in it. At this point he stopped his analysis for one of several possible reasons, of which we may mention two. Either he felt that it was exceedingly difficult to compare these two value estimates—that of society and that of individual members of the leisure class—or he may have wanted to suggest that, whereas true value statements express empirical knowledge, the decision as to what to do when two valuations conflict is not a matter of empirical knowledge. Veblen was undoubtedly at the brink of a difficult problem, but we cannot glibly say that valuation was not scientific for him. The problem he avoided was that of deciding what ought to be done about the leisure class and not that of deciding whether it lacked or possessed value. On the latter question his answer was firm, clear, and scientifically defended. Whether the evidence was on his side is not in question. What counts is the fact that he thought he was deciding a question on empirical evidence.

The pattern in Veblen's case was duplicated to some extent in the writings of Holmes. In spite of his sharp distinction between the legal and the ethical, Holmes believed in the possibility of scientific valuation in the law. In fact we have seen that he thought it represented the "true science of law," and its task was the establishment of the relative worth of our social ends. When juxtaposed with his insistence on the distinction between law and ethics, this view of valuation as *the* science of law seems to create a paradox. But this is easily resolved when we remember that he was directing his comments to different audiences. The amoral approach is characteristic of his tough advice to business lawyers, who need to know how the judges will behave, while his emphasis on the need for scientific valuation is addressed to the judges themselves. If judges are legislators, as Holmes urged in *The Common Law,* they are often faced with questions of public policy. "Whenever a doubtful case arises, with certain analogies on one side and other analogies on the other, . . . what really is before us is a conflict between two social desires, each of which seeks to extend its dominion over the case, and which cannot both have their way. . . . When there is doubt the simple tool of logic does not suffice, and even if it is disguised and unconscious, the judges are called on to exercise the sovereign prerogative of choice." [1] Now it is clear that a legal scientist may show that one group desires or values one course of action while another values its opposite. But how about the judicial task of measuring their "relative worth"? Did Holmes regard this as scientific? In his more utilitarian moods he did. Presumably he thought it possible to decide empirically which desire comes closer to expressing *public* policy. As a judge he could not help taking something like a utilitarian position on matters of this sort. As a liberal judge he could afford neither the luxury nor the irony of Veblen's refusal to compare the likes of millionaires with the dislikes of society as a whole. To this extent, therefore, he was more scientifically minded about value than Veblen. In theory he held that we could compare the relative worth of warring social proposals, so long as the yardstick of "public policy" was available. But suppose someone questioned the moral claim of society at large as against the desires of even one member, and suppose he asked, not in whose favor the judge or the legislator should decide, but in whose favor the moral philosopher should decide? What would Holmes have said? Would he have maintained an imperturbable utilitarianism, according to which the right act or the obligatory act was *by defi-nition* that which favored society? On this question Holmes is obscure, although there is evidence of his having doubted that it might be decided "scientifically." [2] But this is precisely the question which led Veblen to his silence. Both of them might have adopted a utilitarianism according to which the very meaning of the word "ought" or "right" forced a decision in favor of society at large, but if they had, I doubt whether they could have defended it on purely empirical grounds. The difficulty of doing this was seen by Jeremy Bentham when he asked himself concerning the principle of utility: "Has the rectitude of this principle been ever formally contested?" To which he replied: "It should seem that it has, by those who have not known what they have been meaning." "Is it susceptible of any direct proof?" To which he replied: "It should seem not: for that which is used to prove everything else, cannot itself be proved: a chain of proofs must have their commencement somewhere. To give such proof is as impossible as it is needless." [3] I doubt whether Holmes and Veblen were prepared to support their moral convictions by such subtle table-pounding.

We are now in a better position to formulate as well as to solve the most obvious paradox of Veblen and Holmes on science and value. The paradox arises from the fact that they sharply separate science and value in some of their writings while in others they suggest the possibility of scientific valuation. It is solved by recognizing that they consistently supported the following two contentions: (1) not all empirical statements are statements of value; (2) all statements of value are empirical. The point is that there are vast regions of knowledge which do not make any claims about what is needed, desired, wanted, or valued. That Julius Caesar crossed the Rubicon is not a proposition in which anything is said about his desires or ours (although we might infer from it with some probability that Caesar desired to get to the other side). It is also important to see that every true value statement expresses empirical knowledge. The situation is analogous to one which is obvious enough to be trivial: whereas not all empirical statements are statements about horses, all statements about horses are empirical. The point is that the domain of empirical science is wider than the science of value and embraces it. The mere fact that it is wider than the science of value justifies us in distinguishing science and value, but it does not justify us in denying that all attributions of value are empirical. Every whale is a mammal in spite of the fact that not all mammals are whales. In the same way all knowledge about value is empirical knowledge in spite of the fact that not all empirical knowledge is knowledge of value.

We should not conclude on this triumphal note, lest the impression be given that all problems touching the relation between science and ethics have been solved by Holmes and Veblen. Far from it. A great problem remains in connection with the definition of the notion of "obligation." Holmes and Veblen were scientific naturalists in connection with measuring value conceived as the characteristic of being liked, desired, wanted, satisfying. But they developed ambiguities and hesitations when it came to being naturalistic about the notion of obligation, about what ought to be done when two values conflict, or about what ought to be desired. Veblen thought he could establish empirically how individuals valued conspicuous consumption and he thought he could establish empirically its lack of value to society as a whole. What he failed to answer and what he studiously avoided answering in obviously scientific terms was the question, What ought to be done about conspicuous consumption? In this respect his views resemble those of a contemporary philosopher in the pragmatic tradition who holds that value propositions may be known empirically, but who denies that the following question can be answered empirically: "Whether the individual can be called upon to sacrifice life itself when necessary for the public good; and whether society can justly demand obedience of the individual in contravention of his own moral convictions." [4] On this question Holmes did no more than point out that society *does* sometimes demand this obedience. "The most fundamental of the supposed pre-existing rights—the right to life—is sacrificed without a scruple not only in war, but whenever the interest of society, that is, the predominant power in the community, is thought to demand it." [5]

If the tendencies in Holmes and Veblen were to be made more articulate, I think they would force us to add one more proposition to the list of basic convictions on the matters that concern us: (3) No ethical statements are empirical, where an ethical statement as distinct from a value statement asserts what is right or what is just, what ought to be desired as opposed to what is desired in fact. Whether holding this third proposition would have involved Holmes and Veblen in difficulties depends on whether they held certain other views in epistemology and ethics. But they had no developed ideas on the crucial problems of whether all scientific knowledge is empirical and whether ethical statements do convey knowledge. Obviously they could not consistently maintain (3) if they held that we *know* what ought to be done and that all our knowledge is empirical. Their failure to deal with these questions shows that their philosophical speculation did not go as far as necessary for the solution of problems that concerned them. They were distinguished social scientists who were interested in philosophy, but their thinking stopped at a vital point.

If they believed the three propositions assigned to them, and I think they did, we can explain a great deal of what they said on science, value, and obligation. The first—"not all empirical statements are statements of value"—explains why both Holmes and Veblen could attack the introduction of value considerations where they were irrelevant. It explains Veblen's attack on natural law and animism in classical economics and Holmes' sharp separation of law and ethics. The second—"all statements of value are empirical"—explains why they spoke of scientific valuation. It accounts for the central value thesis of the "scientific" *Theory of the Leisure Class* and Holmes' remarks on the science of measuring social desires. The third—"no ethical statement is empirical"—explains why they did not try to judge between conflicting values on a purely empirical basis. The situation accounted for by this third proposition is more obvious in Veblen than it is in Holmes, but I believe that further analysis would substantiate this interpretation of their work.

If Veblen and Holmes leave us in doubt about whether they believed that ethical statements were or were not empirical, John Dewey does not. Dewey not only holds that judgments of what *is* desired are verifiable scientifically, but also that judgments of what *ought to be* desired are. His agreement with Holmes and Veblen, then, extends only to the first two propositions listed above; he vehemently disputes the third. In 1929 in *The Quest for Certainty* he published one of his clearest statements on the problem.[6] He tried to define the *desirable* (as distinct from the desired) in a way that would demonstrate the empirical, scientific character of judgments of desirability. Behind him there was a series of similar attempts in the history of philosophy, notably that of John Stuart Mill, whose difficulties with this problem are notorious. Dewey's program is essentially that of Mill, for like him he argues that judgments of what ought to be desired can be verified by reference to empirical considerations alone. The question is whether Dewey can do this, and continue to distinguish the desired from the desirable, and avoid Mill's error. Mill's error consisted in having supposed that the desirable was like the visible and the audible. Since we can show that things are audible, visible, and soluble by showing that they have been heard and seen and dissolved, Mill concluded that we can show that things are desirable by showing that they are or have been desired. What he neglected is a simple ambiguity of the "ble" ending in the English language. While "soluble" is synonymous with "can be dissolved," "desirable" is not synonymous with "can be desired," but rather with "ought to be desired." It follows that although everything that dissolves is soluble, not everything that is desired is desirable. Dewey, of course, recognizes this, but in the last analysis his own attempt at defining the desirable is subject to a similar difficulty.

Dewey's argument begins by calling attention to the fact that science does not assign objective properties to things without being sure that certain test conditions are satisfied. Before saying that something is objectively red rather than that it merely *appears* red now, we make sure that the light is correct, that our vision is normal, and so on. We select certain standard conditions of vision and say that the object is really red just if it appears red to us under these conditions. However, if it appears red to us when we have reason to think that the light under which we are viewing it is not white, or that our vision has been affected by some drug, we are not justified in asserting that it *is* red. Now Dewey argues similarly in the case of saying that something is desirable. The mere fact that we desire it without attention to conditions is not enough. A thing is desirable if, and only if, it is desired under conditions which play the same role in the moral life as twenty-twenty vision and good light play in the visual life. It makes no difference at the moment how these latter conditions are in fact formulated. The important point is that Dewey thinks that judgments of *desirability* are simply judgments that something is desired under conditions which have been thoroughly investigated in the way that the scientist checks his test conditions. It should be observed that Dewey neatly avoids the bald error of Mill and he does not say that whatever is desired is desirable. Obviously some things which are desired under "abnormal" conditions cannot be said to be desirable; for example, things desired under the influence of alcohol or drugs or in a state of mental disorder. But there is no point in denying that undesirable things are *desired* under such circumstances, and Dewey doesn't. What he insists is that desires about whose conditions we have not reflected are not to be taken as evidence of desirability any more than immediate reports of sensation are to be taken, by themselves, as evidence of objective physical characteristics. The point is that those who try to establish desirability by reference to desire alone are not being scientific, just as those who take casual sensations as evidence of objective colors are not.

The difficulties in this view are not easy to state but they are considerable. Dewey wants to show that the relation between being desired and being desirable is identical with the relation between appearing red and being objectively red. Except for one difference. To say that something is desirable, i.e., desired under test conditions, is to make what he calls a de facto statement which is at the same time de jure. It not only tells us that something is true of human beings but it also imposes an obligation on them. This distinguishes it from the statement that something is desired now, from the statement that something looks red now, and most important, from the statement that something is objectively red. None of these last three statements has a "de jure" quality for Dewey; none of them states a claim. They are all merely de facto, whereas the judgment that something is desirable is *both* de facto and de jure. Here the cake is had and eaten! Here we have generated a normative or de jure proposition by performing a suitable operation on merely de facto propositions. But if the operation will generate a norm in this case it should generate one in all cases. In other words, if "desirable" is synonymous with "desired under test conditions" just as "objectively red" is synonymous with "appears red under test conditions," why shouldn't judgments about things being objectively red be "de jure"? But obviously they aren't. Saying that something is objectively red does not impose an obligation on anyone, but it should if Dewey is right in his analysis. The relation between "is objectively red" and "appears red" is precisely the same as the relation between "is desirable" and "is desired" for him. But since "desirable" means "ought to be desired," "objectively red" should mean "ought to appear red," which is absurd. The ladder by which Dewey rises from the reports of sense to objective physical properties is the same as that by which he rises from the desired to the desirable. But clearly this ladder does not lead us from the descriptive to the normative in the first case, and therefore it cannot lead us from the descriptive to the normative in the second. The argument against Dewey proceeds by a reductio ad absurdum. Those who share my opinion on this might conclude that any so-called scientific or empirical or naturalistic definition of "ought to be desired" is refuted by an argument like the one just offered, but I am not convinced of this and I want to emphasize that my argument is limited to Dewey's naturalistic ethics. So far as I know we have been considering Dewey's most articulate statement on this issue, and I am not aware of any that supplements the view expressed in his *Quest for Certainty* in a way that obviates the difficulties in it. But if they cannot be obviated, one of the most important of Dewey's doctrines is in serious straits.

There may be readers who do not find this criticism cogent, who do not feel that a strong argument against Dewey has been advanced. They may feel, perhaps, that all true scientific statements impose obligations, that *all* true scientific statements have a de jure quality. It must be admitted that such readers will be left cold by the argument against Dewey presented above, for that argument proceeded by the method of reductio ad absurdum. And if they do not disagree with the conclusion to which Dewey's position has been reduced, my argument will not seem very persuasive to them. But I ask them to consider what they affirm—that *all* objectively true statements are normative in character. Take, for example, the statement that the table upon which I am writing now is actually brown. In what sense is this normative? To be sure it implies that any person with "normal" vision will have the sensation commonly referred to as brown if he looks at my table in white light when he is reasonably close to it. But surely this imposes no *obligation* on anyone. Surely it doesn't oblige anyone to see brown when he looks at my table, and no one who is not close enough to my table to see it will feel any guilt or shame at not seeing brown patches. Nor, I trust, will those people who are color-blind in such a way as to prevent them from "seeing brown." And those who are fortunate enough to have normal vision and to be in my room and to be able to see this table will not feel any peculiar sense of moral probity when they do see it as brown.

Furthermore, if *all* the statements of science, including those of physics, turn out to be normative in the sense in which statements of desirability are normative, we shall have destroyed a useful distinction. Dewey's task, so far as I can understand it, is to show that ethics is a part of science and not that it exhausts science. But if he persists in his views he will have wiped out the very distinction which, as a reformer, he wants to preserve, the distinction between what is and what ought to be. For obviously now every true statement of science will say what ought to be, and all science will have become ethical in character.

With all its defects the version of Dewey's views that I have presented is more plausible than another which seems to turn up in his writing—that is, the interpretation according to which a desired object becomes desirable just in case we know what causes us to desire it and what consequences ensue from the fact that we desire it. In the first interpretation a desire for an object would make it desirable only if we desired it under certain particular circumstances which correspond to normal vision and good light in the case of visual perception. But in this second interpretation *any* condition in which we desire an object will suffice for concluding that it is desirable, provided that we know that condition and what happens as a consequence of our desiring the object. To make this clearer let us consider the analogous doctrine in the case of color vision. Suppose we find that something looks red at a particular moment. We cannot conclude from this alone that it is red. Yet we might be able to say *why* it looked red to us; we might be able to give the causes of its looking red to us. But surely this would not allow us to conclude that it was objectively red. On the contrary, the fact that we could give such an account of the antecedents of our seeing red might lead us to suppose that the object was not really red, for we know that all kinds of objects look red without being red. And yet, on this other view of Dewey's, knowing the causes of our desire of an object seems to lead us to say that we *ought* to desire it. Suppose we desire a smoke of opium and that we know the complicated causes of our desire. Would Dewey have us conclude that we *ought* to smoke the opium on that account? Would Dewey conclude that *this* smoke of opium ought to be desired? Is the medically educated addict *obliged* to smoke? To this Dewey might reply that such knowledge is not sufficient because we must know the consequences as well as the causes of our desire before an obligation is created. But what kind of knowledge of consequences must we have? I suspect that although Dewey urges us to know the consequences of our *desiring* to smoke opium, what he really wants us to know are the consequences of smoking it. But what kind of knowledge must this be? Presumably that this smoke will have certain effects on our system. So let us suppose that we have found out all about the effects of opium. In fact let us suppose that we have found out that the effects are effects which we don't desire. What about the obligation? Is this smoke of opium, about whose causes and consequences we have the most gruesome information, something we ought to desire? I suspect that Dewey's words read literally would lead us to say yes for him, but I think that he wants us to conclude when we find out the effects of smoking opium, not that smoking opium is desirable, but rather that it is undesirable. In other words, something is desirable just in case we know why we desire it and that the consequences of desiring it will be . . . But what shall be put where the dots are? "Desirable"? But in that case our definition is not very successful, for we wanted to define "desirable" and here we use it in the definition. "Desired"? But then Dewey is in another fix, for he is anxious to rest obligations on more than what *is* desired. He wants to rest them on what is *desirable*. And yet after all these efforts to get to a rock that is more substantial than mere desire he has to appeal to it in the end.

This is where I must leave the difficult problem of Dewey's views on ethics. I must conclude that Dewey has not demonstrated that ethics is part of empirical science. But he has tried as seriously as any other philosopher to demonstrate this, and one cannot conclude from his failures that the situation is hopeless. No one failure to construe moral obligation as a scientific concept dooms the program of ethical naturalism. Moreover, no other theory is without its difficulties. And even if it is doomed, a great deal of Dewey's contribution to ethical theory remains. The criticisms leveled against him here are made not in the spirit of dismissal, but rather in the spirit of doubt. Whether we must conclude that statements containing the word "ought" convey propositions involving non-natural characteristics or whether we must conclude that they are primarily expressions of emotive attitudes is still an open question. Dewey has ruled the first possibility out on the basis of his theory of knowledge, but he has never seriously considered the second, and yet the second is consistent with more of his philosophy than he may think.[7]

The previous discussion shows the importance of clarifying the meaning of "desirable" and of "ought to be desired" in Dewey's ethical philosophy. He wants to take a middle course between transcendentalism and extreme naturalism. The first makes the notion of "ought" non-natural while the second grounds obligation on whatever happens to be liked. Dewey wants to connect obligation with desire but he wants to avoid the view that *any* desire, however raw and unreflected on, creates an obligation. The problem, of course, is how to supply the missing link; how to connect obligation with desire without identifying them and without running into the difficulties raised in this chapter. It should be observed that Dewey's ethical theory is hardly "anti-intellectualistic" in the sense in which earlier pragmatic theories were. Today Dewey's theory is distinguished by its intellectualism, its view that mere desire or interest does not confer value or create obligation. Ethical concepts grow out of a combination of desire and reflection. What has been disputed is whether the precise combination has yet been found.

It should be remembered, in conclusion, that Dewey's views differ from those of both Holmes and Veblen, for Dewey is the only one of the three who attempts to reduce statements of what *ought* to be desired to empirical terms; he is the most insistent defender of scientific method. Holmes and Veblen rejected the more theological aspects of natural law, but when they were called upon to analyze the notion of moral obligation in scientific terms they lapsed into either silence (in the case of Veblen) or obscurity (in the case of Holmes). To Dewey belongs the honor of having come to grips with the enemy, but not of having routed him.

CHAPTER XIV

Can History Be Objective?

WHILE Dewey, Holmes, and Veblen asked whether normative judgments and value judgments were in the last analysis descriptive and empirical in character, Robinson and Beard reversed the problem. Because of the peculiarities of historical research, in particular because of its need for selection, they worried about whether our seemingly objective history rests in the last analysis on value judgments. Their concerns in this respect were not of equal intensity, since Beard was more exercised about the matter than Robinson. The result was that the philosophical motivation of the new history as formulated by Robinson and accepted by Beard at the turn of the century was different from that which underlay Beard's methodology in the early thirties.

Robinson and Beard were more interested in questions about the nature and function of history than most American historians. They were amateurs in philosophy who assumed a job which their philosophical colleagues had neglected. Few major philosophers of their generation apart from Dewey dealt seriously with the procedures and aims of history; there were at best a couple of essays by James, a chapter by Santayana, and almost nothing by Peirce or the realists (whether critical or naive). This lack of interest may be explained in many ways. First of all, the philosophy of history has been associated in America with Spengler, Toynbee,

Hegel, and Marx, and hence regarded with a certain coolness by anti-metaphysical pragmatists, naturalists, and realists. When history was approached epistemologically it raised no special problems for American philosophers, since they saw no peculiarities in historical knowledge. They worried so much about knowledge in general that they hardly had time to treat a mere special case. This was one of the reasons, I suspect, why Beard sought help from the Continent—why his later writings are dotted with references to Croce, Mannheim, and Meinecke, from whom he received stimulation and, if he reported them accurately, most of his confusion about history. Beard's ideas about the method of history and social sciences as expressed in later books like *The Nature of the Social Sciences* (1934) and *The Discussion of Human Affairs* (1936) were quite different from those defended by Robinson in *The New History* (1912) and also different from Beard's own early views.

There is one thread of continuity between Robinson's new history of 1912 and Beard's later conception of history—they both opposed the views of Ranke. Both Robinson and Beard were inordinately upset by the dictum that history ought to describe things as they really happened. In the early days they both criticized this view in the same way, as we have seen in previous chapters. Robinson, and Beard in his early writings, however, respected the name "science" and fought for the right to apply it to their own methods and conclusions. The two chief marks of science, as far as they were concerned, were its freedom from special pleading and its interest in causal explanation. Darwin's influence on history was evident in both respects, for Darwin's success emphasized that science did not have to amuse, comfort, or edify the reader, but that it did have to do more than state the facts conceived narrowly. Darwin's triumph consisted in *explaining* the facts of evolution and in presenting a theory of natural selection which would account for things as they are now. Following Darwin, Robinson proceeded to attack Ranke, and thereafter both he and Beard continued to use Ranke as a whipping boy. But the error of Ranke, as they saw it then, was one of omission. He had overlooked a fundamental duty of the historian. The new historians did not mean that historical knowledge achieved in the spirit of Ranke's dictum was unimportant, nor that it should be tested in some new way. They simply meant that a new function should be added—the function of interpreting or explaining.

The earliest attacks on Ranke were made from a relatively simple point of view. Robinson attacked Ranke because the latter conceived the "facts" in a narrow way. Ranke seemed to eliminate the dynamic aspect of history, the aspect that corresponded to Darwin's theory of evolution, and hence conceived of history as the counterpart of Darwin's duller and more "Baconian" efforts. Ranke also seemed to eliminate a number of important facts when he limited himself to political history. In conformity with historicism and organicism Robinson urged that history be construed as the study of all kinds of social facts, whereas Ranke had narrowed the task of the historian first by eliminating what might be called interpretative facts and then by restricting the remainder to those which were political.

At no point did Robinson doubt that the procedure of the historian in establishing either detailed singular statements or interpretations were "objective." At no point did he suggest that the method of confirming them is radically different from that used in confirming empirical statements of common sense or science. He emphasized the similarities between history and natural sciences rather than their differences. Historical knowledge, whether it was interpretative or merely "descriptive," was to be established according to the canons of all reliable knowledge. There might be differences between the method of verifying the bank balance of a member of the Constitutional Convention and the method of verifying Beard's economic interpretation of the Constitution, but these differences were quite analogous to the different methods of verifying the observation reports of a chemist in a laboratory and verifying the theory which explained them. In his *Economic Interpretation of the Constitution* Beard said he was seeking proximate and remote causes, but he certainly thought that the fundamental thesis of that book was objective and factual. The trouble with non-interpretative history from the point of view of Beard's early writings was its narrow conception of a factual statement. According to that conception, the statement "Booth shot Lincoln in 1865" was factual, but the statement "Because Lincoln was assassinated in 1865 the Reconstruction turned out as it did" no longer expressed a fact.[1] Therefore the new historians urged a broader conception of factual statement. They wanted the historian to admit that he could and should give explanations of how and why things came to pass without ceasing to be objective. When Beard enlarged his conception of the historian's duties he found himself defending causal statements like "The Constitution was created *because* certain men wished to protect their economic interests," but causal statements, on his early view, were just as susceptible of objective test as the singular statements which made up his economic biographies of the framers of the Constitution. This is plainly implied in his writing at that time. The interpretative thesis, "Our fundamental law was not the product of the whole people but rather of a group of economic interests which must have expected beneficial results from its adoption," was supported in an objective way. Without raising the question as to whether he proved the thesis conclusively, we must admit that Beard marshaled evidence in its behalf just as zealously as he marshaled evidence in behalf of a statement about the number of slaves owned by Charles Cotesworth Pinckney.

In approaching Beard's later philosophical views it must be remembered that in 1913 he presented an economic interpretation of the Constitution; and interpretations, according to Beard's *later* views, are not subject to the same kind of tests as "Booth shot Lincoln." But originally Beard saw no profound epistemological implications in the process of historical interpretation. In embarking on the new history Beard and Robinson did not believe that they were entering a realm in which the usual canons of scientific procedure no longer applied and in which the values of the historian precluded scientific objectivity. Beard in 1913 and Beard in 1934 both attacked Ranke, but for different reasons. The early attack on Ranke was based on the conviction that the historian could explain, give causes, interpret, and make "syntheses." But in advancing interpretations, and in creating syntheses, Robinson and Beard did not think they were leaving the domain of objective science or distorting in the interest of their values or "schemes of reference." In Robinson's case this was associated with the conviction that the fundamental task of science was dynamic explanation—telling how things came to be as they are; in Beard's case it was associated with the view that causation was the fundamental concept of science. Their interest in connecting the past with the present was not accompanied by any fears or qualms about losing objectivity. I stress this so much because of the change which came over Beard in later years on precisely these questions. While he continued to argue for interpretation and broad syntheses, and connecting the past with the present, a new note emerged in his philosophical writings. He came to feel that precisely this need for synthesis and interpretation leads to a more relativistic position. He came to worry about whether objectivity is possible once we leave the "solid historical knowledge" that Washington crossed the Delaware, and ascend to the value-charged "historical thought" involved in a history of American civilization.

In his later writings Beard came to distinguish between *history as actuality,* that is, the actual historical process "out there," and *historical record, knowledge, and thought,* which are discursive in character and which communicate things *about* history as actuality. Beginning with the records the historian tries to create *history as knowledge,* a "collection of facts verified, authenticated, and generally agreed upon," like "George Washington was the first president of the United States under the Constitution; John Adams succeeded him; and Thomas Jefferson was inaugurated in 1801." [2] But historical *thought,* according to Beard is different from all of this. It involves selection, arrangement, and interpretation of facts based on the records and historical knowledge, and selection takes place only with reference to ideas and purposes in the mind of the historian.

The distinction between historical knowledge and historical thought is most crucial. On it Beard builds his most serious philosophical conclusion. Historical knowledge, it would appear, is a set of propositions which are formally singular, like "Caesar crossed the Rubicon" and "Washington crossed the Delaware," in contradistinction to general propositions like "All bodies attract each other" and "All gases expand when heated." Beard seems to believe that the propositions which make up history as knowledge are relatively easy to discover. History as thought, on the other hand, brings us into the realm of synthesis, interpretation, and selection; and here a new kind of process takes place, a process which is so tinged with the value preconceptions of the historian that we can no longer have the agreement and objectivity possible on the "George Washington slept here" level. The problem for the philosopher is to investigate the comparative objectivity of these two kinds of history: (1) the compendium or conjunction of known historical propositions which constitute Beard's *history as knowledge* and (2) that entity, however describable, which issues as the result of *history as thought*.

Let us forget the Platonic notion of proposition and the vaguer notion of fact for the moment, and let us simply distinguish two kinds of language. One is a chronicle or an almanac; it contains sentences about the dates of office of presidents, about the dates of battles, and other sentences deemed to be true by the historian before he begins to "think" (in Beard's sense), before he begins to select and interpret. A chronicle is a vast logical conjunction of the sentences which compose it. "George Washington was the first president *and* John Adams was the second *and* . . ." and so on. Each one of these component statements is presumably true, and known to be true by the historian. Hence the problem of defining the truth or adequacy of the whole almanac is a relatively simple matter—the almanac will be true just in case every one of its conjuncts is true. One supposes that Beard would have agreed with this since he makes no fuss about our not *knowing* the truth of such elementary statements. But now let us turn to the profound historical synthesis, the product of history as thought, and ask, What is its relation to the elementary statements composing the almanac or chronicle? This is an extremely important question, and so far as one can tell it is the one that bothers most philosophers of history who agree with Beard, although they never formulate it in quite this way. Considering it will give us some idea of the manner in which "thought" is supposed to enter the procedures of the historian.

If selection simply means paring down the original list (known to be true), the result of selection will also be true. Any part of a true conjunction remains true. And surely any reordering of the true statements on the original list will also be true by virtue of well-known properties of conjunction. It makes no difference whether you say "John Adams was the second president of the United States and George Washington was the first" or whether you reverse the order in the sentence (so long as you keep Washington the first president and Adams the second). Surely no problem is created by this kind of selection and ordering, and yet one is sure that followers of Beard will be annoyed and charge that we are missing the point. So let us reformulate the problem in a way that brings us closer to their worries.

Their problem starts on the assumption that we can never have a complete history. The list which would exhaustively formulate all the true singular statements that we want to make is beyond our reach. But if history be construed as the result of selecting and ordering those statements which we *can* lay our hands on, and if we have a limited amount of space in which to write that history down, we are faced with a choice. There are many different alternative sets of statements about the object whose history we are writing which compete with each other, and they are produced with different principles of selection in mind. The situation may best be understood by imagining that two historians decide to write the history of the United States independently in a certain number of sentences of prescribed length. We want to know which is the better history. We check each statement in them and find they are all true. How, then, shall we choose between the two histories? They contain different statements, but as conjunctions they are both true. Obviously the factual truth of the account is not enough of a basis for decision, but what is the extra factor? How shall we decide? I suggest that the answer may be found if we reflect on the purpose of history. The ideal purpose of history, admitted even by some relativists, is to tell the *whole* truth. But we can't tell the whole truth, and so we are reduced to lists of statements which formulate only certain parts of it. The issue then arises as to whether a choice among true parts of the same size can be made in some objective way, a choice which will allow us to say that one history is objectively better than another.

From some of the things Beard said, one may gather that he despaired of ever being able to do this. His point was that relativism is inescapable because selection is made in terms of values, schemes of reference, and purposes which vary from historian to historian. There can be no doubt, of course, that historians are in fact dominated by their values in the course of their investigations. But even Beard speaks of historical thought being "large, generous, universal in range" as opposed to that which is "small, provincial, and personal in nature," [3] so that he had some conviction that some selections are better than others. But can we formulate a neutral standpoint from which one particular judgment of the worth of principles of selection can be made? The mere fact that historians are biased is no argument against the existence of impersonal standards, and it seems absurd to argue from their limitations to standards which would justify their limitations. It has been argued fallaciously that because of the admitted existence of value-dominated selection we must recognize that it is part of the accredited procedure of history. However, it is important to remember that this hurried flight to relativism starts with recognizing that the whole truth is the aim of the historian. And since he cannot attain his ideal, since he cannot record all the true statements, he is advised by relativists to pick out those which accord with his scheme of reference, his interests, and his problems. In short, he is advised to pay no attention to his unattainable ideal; he is advised to forget about it. But this is a non sequitur. Since we cannot present the whole truth we are fallaciously advised to select those truths which interest us. But the net effect of this is not to help the historian approximate his admitted ideal. How can he approximate it if he forswears the task of approximating it and turns to selection guided by his values and prejudices? We cannot deny his right to study what he pleases, but we may point out that he abandons for poor reasons a task which is usually associated with the study of history. Although the historian cannot present the enormous list which would constitute history in the ideal sense, his task remains that of presenting a briefer one which is *representative* of the enormous list. His selection, in other words, is to be justified on the basis of a connection with the ideal history, analogous to (though not identical with) the way in which a good statistical sample is said to represent an infinite population. It may be said that we have pushed the argument one step further back and that we shall now conduct disputes as to which lists are in fact more representative. This is true, but at least it presupposes agreement on a standard. And once standards are agreed on, debates as to which histories satisfy the standard will undoubtedly take place. But here the situation is quite analogous to what goes on in mathematics. The fact that we can formulate laws of logical deduction does not prevent some people from erroneously supposing that their reasoning is logical. It is not maintained that any conception of a representative list is one which is understood perfectly and which has been clarified or defined. On the contrary, its clarification is a great problem for the philosophy of history. But it is maintained that some such standard is implicitly used by historians who try to give objective arguments back and forth in favor of the credibility of different historical works on a given problem. We may conclude that the fact of selection need not of itself drive us into the kind of relativism espoused by Beard. But we must now turn to interpretation. Does interpretation involve value commitments which destroy historical objectivity?

The process of thought which the historian applies to the records and to historical knowledge in Beard's sense is not limited to selecting and ordering. It also involves what is called "interpretation." And if Beard's own work is taken as an example, historical interpretation amounts to adding a kind of statement not present in "historical knowledge." The historian does not merely select and order singular propositions like "George Washington was the first president of the United States," but advances claims like "Our fundamental law was not the product of the whole people but rather of a group of economic interests which must have expected beneficial results from its adoption." But if the latter is typical of what interpretation adds, we must ask whether it is tested in an objective spirit quite like that which dominates (or ought to dominate) the natural sciences. Oddly enough Beard in 1935, just when he came to hold extremely relativistic views, said something that did not fit in with his new philosophy: "An economic analysis may be coldly neutral, and in the pages of this volume no words of condemnation are pronounced upon the men enlisted on either side of the great controversy which accompanied the formation and adoption of the Constitution. Are the security holders who sought to collect principal and interest through the formation of a stronger government to be treated as guilty of impropriety or praised? That is a question to which the . . . inquiry is not addressed. An answer to that question belongs to moralists and philosophers, not to students of history as such." [4] But in 1934, while arguing for his new relativism, he had said: "The assumption that any historian can be a disembodied spirit as coldly neutral to human affairs as the engineer to an automobile . . . [has] been challenged and rejected." [5] He went even further and speculated in a disparaging tone on the social roots of such an attitude. "Written history that was cold, factual, and apparently undisturbed by the passions of the time served best the cause of those who did not want to be disturbed." [6]

This contradiction is typical of Beard's later writings on this subject. But we are easily confused even if we stay with one half of the contradiction—the relativistic half—and ask: Did Beard think that interpretations like his own could be checked by objective methods? Sometimes his answer is "yes." But sometimes he speaks as though scientific method is applicable only in connection with historical *knowledge*. Scientific method is acceptable within limits. "It is when this method, a child of the human brain, is exalted into a master and a tyrant that historical *thought* [my italics] must enter a caveat. So the historian is bound by his craft to recognize the nature and limitations of the scientific method and to dispel the illusion that it can produce a science of history embracing the fullness of history." [7] But this still does not help us. It may be that we can never achieve a science of history in the nineteenth-century sense, but the question remains whether there is any possibility of formulating criteria for deciding about the scientific adequacy of different histories. Beard never gave any evidence of being able to comprehend this problem. He moved around it but never came to grips with it. He suggested that the historian's values prevent him from objectively weighing the evidence for his contentions, and yet did not want to abandon "inquiry into objective realities, especially economic realities." [8] He kept insisting in vaguer and vaguer language that the historian needed frames of reference which included "things deemed necessary," and "things deemed desirable." [9] Such frames could be large, informed by deep knowledge, and illuminated by wide experience. But if they were large, wouldn't they coincide with what has been called the objective attitude? What does "largeness" imply here if not a desire to approximate the whole truth? In the end Beard spoke of the historian's need for faith in a theory of the nature and direction of the movements of world history. Having rejected the scientific attitude of the nineteenth century, Beard was incapable of substantiating his theories on this subject, and so he fell back on an act of faith in one of the most incoherent of all his reflections on the subject. "Does the world move and, if so, in what direction? If he believes that the world does not move, the historian must offer the pessimism of chaos to the inquiring spirit of mankind. If it does move, does it move backward . . . or . . . forward to some other arrangement which can be only dimly divined —a capitalist dictatorship, a proletarian dictatorship, or a collectivist democracy? The last of these is my own guess, *founded on a study of long trends* [my italics] and on a faith in the indomitable spirit of mankind." [10]

Faced with this we must continue to ask calmly whether Beard thought that historical synthesis couldn't possibly be carried out without commitment on these subjects. If he did, of course, we can only be amazed. Certainly his own work on the Constitution did not logically presuppose such a commitment, and he himself has told us how little interested he was in the politics of the Progressive era. Furthermore, it is important to distinguish between a belief that one of these kinds of society will dominate the world and a hope that one will. Apparently Beard thought a choice on both levels was necessary. Historians must say what they deem desirable as well as likely and then trust in faith. But it would seem that a commitment on neither subject is necessary for the successful prosecution of historical inquiry, much less one based on faith. And even if the historian needed such faith in order to get worked up psychologically, there is absolutely no reason to suppose that a fair test of the adequacy of his historical interpretation would depend on the examiner's sharing his faith.

Beard was guilty of a confusion which is typical in the philosophy of history, the confusion between the psychology of historical interpretation and its logic. It may very well be true that a historian has to ally himself with some speculative theory or some morality before he can get interested in historical synthesis. But the fact that he is attached to it does not bear on the truth or credibility or adequacy of his history. As Sidney Hook says: "The possession of bias or passion on the part of the historian does not preclude the possibility of his achieving objectivity in testing his hypothesis any more than a physician's passion to relieve men from the ravages of a disease . . . precludes the possibility of a discovery of a medical . . . truth. The prepossession of Pasteur's work on antitoxins was that God in his infinite goodness could not have created a scourge for mankind without at the same time creating a remedy. And this did not prevent Pasteur from rigorously testing his hypothesis." [11] At best Beard's "faith" may function in the same way. What is most dangerous about such a faith, however, is the way in which it can justify historical distortion. The views of relativists cease to be obscure when they lead to a surrender of the distinction between fact and fable. An historian attached to the present Soviet regime might well erase certain names from the history of the Russian revolution, but one can hardly sympathize with a relativist logician willing to conclude that this was valid or justified in any sense of those words.

In more concrete moments Beard gave a clearer version of historical thought in operation. Medieval history, he said,[12] had two great tasks: the narration of the struggle in which Christianity triumphed over paganism and the task of reconciling the events of the world with the Catholic faith. But consider an attempt to study the way in which Christianity struggled with paganism. This would be a typical developmental account but certainly not above being compared with the evidence. One might still ask whether the account was true or well confirmed, and one would check this by reference to evidence. And when medieval historians "explained the events of the world," when they said that history was a dream revealing the plan of God, couldn't they be criticized in the light of evidence if the hypothesis could be shown testable? The fact that medieval historians had certain theological and moral purposes in no way freed them from being subject to the canons of validity, evidence, and historical truth. The fact that they had their own purposes in writing these accounts no more makes judgment of their work a matter of taste than does the allegedly high purpose of medieval astronomy free it from condemnation by modern science. Beard gives the impression that the peculiar purposes of medieval historians render them free from the critical judgment of those who do not share their purposes. But this, I think, is simply wrong and a plain result of the confusion I have mentioned—the confusion between the psychology and logic of historical interpretation.

Beard's later views on the philosophy of history were more developed than those of almost any other American historian. But they fall short of the intellectual standards set by his work in history and political science. In one respect they represent a different strain from that which I have been examining throughout this book. The later philosophical writings of Beard, in spite of being frequently associated with Dewey's theory of knowledge, are really part of another tradition. It is sounder to say that the new history of Robinson and of Beard in his early years was the expression in the philosophy of history of the movement we have been considering in this book. Beard's later views had more in common with those of Croce and Mannheim, and he absorbed the amount of obscurity from them which one might expect. Of all the philosophical positions examined in this book, Beard's later philosophy of history seems most implausible. It is obscure and contradictory, and it reveals the worst defect of the tradition on which his later philosophical work depended—a lack of respect for logical rigor and clear thinking which is paralleled only by other writings in the philosophy of history. One must be thankful for the fact that Beard's philosophy did not adequately describe his own scientific work, which, at its best, exhibited none of the features he came to regard as the essence of history.

It is misleading to associate Beard's later philosophy of history with the modern theory of scientific method, as so many historians do. The criticism of history conceived as a statement of the facts "as they really happened" was at first merely a protest against narrow conceptions which excluded historical explanation and everything but political facts. And in the later writings of Beard there was another reasonable point which was added— the sound methodological reminder that there are no " 'raw facts' lying around in the world awaiting collection by the historian" and that there is something absurd about "the idea that facts duly assembled, in a library or laboratory, automatically and inexorably suggest or dictate their own conclusions in all cases." [13] Beard had read, with profit, some of the sounder texts on scientific method which emphasized the need for hypothesis and which criticized the limitations of the extreme Baconian aversion to anticipating nature. But his conclusions would have shocked the authors of the texts from which he imbibed this sound advice, for he went on to suggest that the need for hypothesis in history somehow ushered in an initial *value* commitment. But obviously, if hypotheses are necessary for physical research as well as for historical research, physics too has to begin with some kind of alleged value commitment. Yet Beard thought there was a radical difference between physics and history. Physics, he seemed to think, was cold and neutral, while history needed value hypotheses. The attack on Bacon in the nineteenth century on the subject of hypothesis came to an ironic end in Beard. When Bacon was first attacked for refusing to anticipate nature, he was not attacked for the one good point he made, namely, that we ought not to expect nature to behave as we *want* her to behave. What he was attacked for was his alleged failure to see that research cannot get on without hypotheses to guide it. But these hypotheses were not moral or ethical in character. Beard, I think, simply made the one error which Bacon was right in criticizing, and proceeded to justify himself by citing the standard assaults on Bacon.

It should be said in Beard's behalf that he was the only member of the group I have examined who has given a full account of the methods and aims of the social sciences. It is not surprising, therefore, that his ideas should be subject to detailed criticism. He raced around fields where most of the others stepped lightly and infrequently. And very often he says what they really thought, while they merely mumbled it incoherently or kept it to themselves. For all his mistakes and his philosophical confusions, Beard's later work in the methodology of the social sciences remains stimulating. It goes without saying that his errors in philosophy cast no reflection on his work in social science itself. In this respect he takes his position in a long and worthy line of scientists—physical and social—who have worked with standards in philosophy which they dared not use in science.

CHAPTER XV

Yes and No

WE HAVE just examined the development of a group of ideas which dominated American social thought for fifty years or more and which continues to exert an appreciable though diminished influence on our thinking. We have concentrated on the work of five men—Charles A. Beard, John Dewey, Oliver Wendell Holmes, Jr., James Harvey Robinson, and Thorstein Veblen—who supplied the American mind of the twentieth century with the concepts of instrumentalism, progressive education, legal realism, the economic interpretation of politics, the new history, institutional economics, and political liberalism. Their effect has been enormous, extending from the university to the nursery school, from law courts to political parties. Since every one of their fundamental ideas had been formulated by 1930, most of this study has been devoted to the history of the intellectual pattern which they composed from the eighteen-eighties to the early nineteen-thirties. Except for the continued activity of Beard and Dewey, the close of the twenties marked the movement's greatest influence on the intellectual world. The depression came at the end of an intellectual era, symbolized by the death in 1929 of Veblen and of Vernon L. Parrington, the literary historian who absorbed so much from the men we have studied and who hoped to finish his great book on American thought with a systematic examination of their work.

My main purpose, however, is quite different from Parrington's. For although I have tried to show how the views of these men were connected with one another and with the social circumstances in which they appeared, I have not gone into great detail about their contributions to law, history, economics, and political science, nor have I concentrated on the social scene. My main purpose has been to consider the philosophical ideas which underlay their work and which dominated American social thinking for so long. I have neglected many other thinkers who deserve careful treatment because of their influence on these men or because of the influence these men had on them—for example, Parrington himself, William James, Charles Peirce, Brandeis, and Cardozo, to mention only a few. I am aware of the monumental work I have not written. But monuments need bricks, and I have tried to fashion a few with which future historians, critics, and philosophers may build further, or with which they may destroy a few shiny, opaque windows.

The men we have studied share a number of intellectual traits. They all participated in an early revolt against formalism in social science, in a rejection of the patterns which dominated formed logic, classical political economy, formal jurisprudence, and "barren political history." In their positive ideas they showed great respect for science, historical method, economic interpretation, and cultural analysis. It was not so much the logical coherence of their ideas that led people to accept their works as though they were synoptic gospels; it was rather the way in which they all seemed to contribute to the advent of a more rational society. It made no difference that Holmes was a nineteenth-century liberal in his economics and that he made wisecracks about socialism and reformers. It made no difference that Veblen seemed to avoid political commitment. Their followers overlooked such deviations. The followers became pragmatists in epistemology; they tried to apply scientific method to moral and social problems; they sent their children to progressive schools; they defended social justice and civil liberties by citing Holmes' dissenting opinions; they voted Socialist occasionally; they hailed Robinson's history of the Western mind; they interpreted politics economically and poked fun with Veblen at conspicuous consumption and the leisure class. Dewey thought of science as socially productive, and Veblen seemed to refute classical arguments for laissez faire. Robinson was an ally in the humanization of society and knowledge; Beard punctured myths about legal institutions which blocked social change; and Holmes recognized the legislative power of the judges and challenged the view that law was a deduction from divinely ordained principles of ethics.

When the First World War came some of the leaders of liberal thought lost their composure and their popularity, but they recovered quickly and became even more popular in the twenties. In the thirties they were retrospectively honored as the *philosophes,* the encyclopedists of the Roosevelt "revolution." With the period that followed I have not been concerned, except for some reflections on one aspect of the later, non-synoptic gospel according to Beard. By 1930, as I have said, these men ceased to make up an intellectual corps, and therefore I have restricted myself to the golden age of liberalism in America, an age which closed intellectually just when its ideas became weapons again.

From a philosophical point of view there are three important problems on which these men wrote. One was methodological and concerned the nature of science; a second was in the field of ethics; the third in political philosophy.

I. *Science*

In spite of all the enthusiasm which Beard, Holmes, Robinson, and Veblen felt for the methods of science, none of them has written on the subject with great distinction. For all Dewey's admiration of scientific method, his writings up to 1930 contain no impressive reflections on the inner workings of science. Whatever he did say about the methods of science was gained by thinking about how we come to know the ordinary world around us. To be sure *The Quest for Certainty* (1929) appealed to numerous physicists who offered what Dewey thought was substantiation of his views on knowledge. But prior to the appearance of his *Logic,* Dewey's observations on the nature of science were restricted to epistemology and to the kind of informal psychology of inquiry which one finds in *How We Think* (first edition, 1910). There was nothing like the systematic study of scientific method made by Mill, Jevons, Mach, Duhem, and Pearson in the nineteenth century. In 1938 Dewey's *Logic* appeared, and there for the first time he tried to deal intensively with difficult questions like probability, measurement, and classification. But when he spoke of scientific method to the politicians of the twenties, he meant nothing more pretentious than observation, deduction, and experiment. When he urged them to use the methods of science in social affairs, he was not thinking of any peculiar interpretation of science associated with pragmatism or instrumentalism. His disputes with other philosophers about the nature of the knowing process were abstruse and did not bear closely upon the practical advice he gave in *Reconstruction in Philosophy* or *The Quest for Certainty.*

In the case of Beard, Holmes, Robinson, and Veblen the matter was different. So far as I can see, they have never said anything about the logic of scientific procedure which has not been either elementary or obscure. They cannot be taken seriously in their observations about the methods of physics or mathematics, and when they come to talk about the nature of science in general they are reduced to vagueness or dependence on dubious second-hand information. This is particularly true of Beard. Robinson made little show of being informed on this subject; Veblen confined himself to unanalyzed phrases about "theories of cumulative sequence"; and Holmes talked unpretentiously, it should be said, on historical explanation as an example of science in the law. In spite of this vagueness, however, they respected the method of science, admired its results, and wanted their own disciplines to be closely associated with it. Moreover they made an attempt to deal with these problems, and this distinguished them among social scientists and philosophers. While they advanced no original theories about the nature of science, they wrote on it with distinction by comparison with most American philosophers and scientists of their day. And what is most important, they helped to keep alive a philosophical interest in the social sciences.

In revolting against formalism they accomplished a number of salutary effects in the history of social thought. Surely there are no sharp boundaries between the social sciences, as there are no sharp boundaries between the natural sciences. Sciences should follow their subject matters, and their subject matters are notoriously fuzzy at the edges. We may arbitrarily define one discipline on the basis of the terms or words which form its basic vocabulary, but the listing of the terms in this basic vocabulary is not absolutely determined. Only those who believe that there is something called the essence of economics, or the essence of sociology, or the essence of history, can draw hard and fast distinctions between the sciences. In trying to formalize a discipline one must make a decision which cannot be justified by reference to something called "the real nature of the discipline." Even mathematical logic can do no more than enumerate its basic terms and then confess that the enumeration is in the last analysis arbitrary. So it is with the social sciences, and anyone who erects strong barriers which prevent people in one field from looking into others or even from climbing into them is obstructing the advance of knowledge. Divisions among scientists are divisions of labor and like all divisions of labor they can be justified only by an over-all increase of scientific production. The great virtue of the American revolt against formalism was its fostering of a flexible and lenient conception of the relation among the social sciences. This went hand in hand with a distaste for intellectual and moral rigidity, a distaste which was temperamentally associated with the spirit of progressive education and of social liberalism in politics. Attitudes were involved which went beyond scientific method. These men worked in an age which was trying to free itself from the constraints of previous morality and ideology.

Unfortunately they were unable to set limits to this revolt against rigidity and sometimes they allowed it to run wild. It is not exaggerating to say that the revolt was speedily followed by a reign of terror in which precision and logic and analytic methods became suspect. This is typified not only in the animus which institutional economists felt against deductive theory but also in Dewey's persistent failure to see the virtues of logical analysis in philosophy. Nor is it an exaggeration to say that this same fear of rigidity has caused liberalism's anxiety about having principles turn into dogma. It is easy to show how the whole reaction against these anti-formalist liberals in philosophy, politics, economics, and education was part of a search for intellectual vertebrae and not the result of a neurotic quest for certainty. The espousal of deduction and abstract theory need not lead to totalitarianism as some of the wilder anti-formalists have thought. An interest in the precise formulation of philosophical premises and conclusions with the help of formal logic is no sign of reaction. Nor is it necessarily a regression to search for political principles that go beyond simple methodological exhortations to be intelligent in social matters.

The twenties marked the end of this reign of terror. But the result, I fear, was Thermidor and not freedom. Today we have little to choose from except the despair of those who are no longer interested, the cynicism of others who continue to call themselves liberals but who have surrendered their consciences, the nonsense of shameless defenders of reaction in the name of revolution. American social thought has yet to reveal any cohesive successor to the school we have examined, but, if it comes, that successor will do well to preserve the virtues of the older group. It will do well to combine humanitarianism with principles; it must be anti-formalist without being anti-intellectual or opportunist.

II. *Ethics*

It is hoped that the observations of the thirteenth and fourteenth chapters clarify some of the issues which surround the key philosophical question actually faced by these American social thinkers—the question of science and value. Dewey, Holmes, and Veblen, as we have seen, dealt with the question of whether value and obligation are ultimately reducible to concepts of social science. On this they were in partial agreement. All three held that we can scientifically test statements asserting that certain things are desired or wanted. But some of them hesitated about judgments of what *ought* to be desired, of what we are obliged to desire. Veblen in particular seemed to avoid construing judgments of obligation as empirical; Holmes avoided it a little less obviously, but he behaved like Veblen on some occasions. It was Dewey who was most forthright on the subject. It was Dewey who held that a judgment that something is desirable is just as scientific as a judgment that something is desired, if not more scientific. But for all its acuteness I have been forced to criticize Dewey's defense of this position—without, however, inferring the defeat of naturalistic ethics. The cases of Robinson and Beard were quite different, particularly that of Beard. Beard tried to show that history rested on non-scientific value commitments and that scientific history was therefore impossible. But his arguments are unsound, and the philosophy he defended was quite different from that which underlay the new history as it was originally conceived by Robinson and carried out by both Robinson and Beard.

The implications of these observations are clear. None of the basic contentions of this philosophy of social science is beyond question, particularly those dealing with the fundamental problem of science and ethics. But their shortcomings should not lead us to obscure their tremendous leavening effect on American philosophical reflection, if not on American philosophy. These men represent a current in American thought which has not yet spent itself and which may be only temporarily submerged. The problems with which they dealt were real and serious, and their answers set a pattern for one of the few distinct movements of American thought in the twentieth century. Above all, they communicated a respect for freedom and social responsibility which has all but disappeared from the earth. For all their fuzziness and their lack of logic they have been a force for the good in American intellectual life. We would do well to have a generation which would advance some of their causes and implement some of their programs.

III. *Political Philosophy*

Perhaps the most touching indication of the greatness and the defect of the old school is the following exchange adapted from one between Dewey and an impatient admirer: [1]

THE ADMIRER: Instead of many fine generalities about the "method of cooperative intelligence," [you] might well direct [your] attention to this crucial problem of extending our political skill. For political skill can itself be taken as a technological problem to which inquiry can hope to bring an answer. It is obviously dependent on our acquiring the knowledge [of] how to get men to apply the techniques already available for dealing with our social problems, how to enlist the cooperative support of men in doing what we now know how to do. Thus by rights [your] philosophy should culminate in the earnest consideration of the social techniques for reorganizing beliefs and behavior—techniques very different from those dealing with natural materials. It should issue in a social engineering, in an applied science of political education—and not merely in the hope that someday we may develop one.

DEWEY: [I am fully in agreement with what you say] about the importance of developing the skills that, if they were produced, would constitute political technology. The fact—which [you] point out—that I have myself done little or nothing in this direction does not detract from my recognition that in the concrete the invention of such a technology is the heart of the problem of intelligent action in political matters.

Dewey's reply is evidence of his greatness as a human being, but it also raises a question which goes to the heart of his views on politics. In the twelfth chapter we saw how he praised Holmes for refusing to dole out social panaceas, social programs, or codes of "fixed ends." But a political technology does require a program. If we are to reorganize human beliefs and behavior by means of our technology, we must know *how* to reorganize it, and at some point or other we shall have to ask *which* beliefs and *which* behavior we want to encourage. The puzzling thing about Dewey's views on this subject is that sometimes he suggests that the fundamental task of philosophy is to build a political technology and at others suggests that even the modest theorizing, generalizing, and fixing of ends which a technology involves would lead us into rigidity and dogmatism. There are, I suggest, two Deweys. There is the Dewey who revolted against formalism and who feared the consequences of setting up inalienable rights and self-evident principles for political and moral action. Then there is the Dewey who wanted to be a social engineer but did not succeed. One might have hoped that the second Dewey would stimulate students and disciples to build this technology, but where are they? I think the fact that there are few can be attributed, in part, to the first Dewey, the Dewey who inveighed against panaceas, programs, and fixed ends for two generations.

By refusing to formulate ends of social behavior for fear of being saddled with *fixed* ends, Dewey hardly encouraged systematic political engineering. Those of his students who landed on the left were forced to appeal to the tradition of Marx, where they could find more than a methodology of politics. When the

critical admirer in the above dialogue chided Dewey for not
having constructed a political technology his complaint was superficially different from Randolph Bourne's, but he was pointing to the same thing. Bourne had complained of Dewey's failure
to stimulate vision and not of his lack of a technique, for he saw
that we cannot be engineers without knowing what to build.
Only after we know the kind of bridge we want can we start
building it. We may modify our original plans in the light of
further discoveries and snags, but there must be hypotheses to
begin with which will bend to meet the facts. This is the moral
of experimentalism. From it we cannot infer the pointlessness of
political programs, but only the folly of attributing self-evidence
to our empirical assumptions. Ends, Dewey has insisted, are like
hypotheses: they may change with changes in the means at our
disposal. But in attacking the view which makes scientific statements necessary or self-evident, we are not reduced to giving up
hypotheses. Rather we come to see their tentative status. In the
same way the fact that past formulations of ends have degen-
erated into dogma is no argument against formulating ends but
rather against viewing them as sacrosanct.

The ambiguity of Dewey about the possibility of setting up a
social program without lapsing into dogmatism was one of the
chief reasons for the defections from liberalism in the thirties.
But those who left the "wishy-washy" humanitarianism of Dewey
for the brisk and ruthless formulae of totalitarianism now have
evidence like that of Lazarus, yet they cannot tell us all we need
to know. The question today is whether we can salvage more
than a temper in Beard, Dewey, Holmes, Robinson, and Veblen;
but to salvage even their temper would help, for it was a good and
humane temper; it was honest, courageous, rational, and enlightened. There is little point in regarding their books as manuals of
social practice, nor are we justified in tracing all our troubles to
their shortcomings. They should be treated neither as scapegoats
nor as idols but as models of courageous thinking on social matters. American thought has indelibly incorporated many of their

contributions, and American society is considerably in their debt. And although the promise they saw in American life at the turn of the century has not been fulfilled, their example should serve to encourage those social scientists who are more interested in achieving a good society than in measuring attitudes toward toothpaste. The great problem is to build on the sound elements of their work, and this book will have accomplished its immediate purpose if it has communicated some idea of the development of a memorable movement in American social thought as a means of paving the way for an adequate social philosophy.

Notes

CHAPTER I. INTRODUCTION

1. V. L. Parrington, *Main Currents in American Thought* (New York: Harcourt, Brace, 1927-1930), vol. III, p. 401.

2. G. E. Moore, *Ethics* (New York: Holt, 1912), p. 8.

CHAPTER II. THE REVOLT AGAINST FORMALISM

1. See M. G. White, "Historical Explanation," *Mind*, vol. 2, N. S. (1943), pp. 212-29, and "The Attack on the Historical Method," *Journal of Philosophy*, vol. 42 (1945), pp. 314-31. I am aware that these terms have been used differently, and so I must emphasize that I mean only what I say I mean. In the light of their ambiguity I suppose it would be desirable to find something fresh and neutral. I have searched without success. It should be pointed out, however, that the terms do have this much value: they indicate the strong ties which exist between these American thinkers and those whom we should call historicists and organicists without much hesitation.

I have used the word "historicism" differently from Karl Popper in his provocative book *The Open Society and Its Enemies* (London: Routledge, two vols., 1945), since I have not included as essential to historicism a belief in large-scale historical laws or a respect for what he calls "prophecy." To be sure, in some parts of their work the men I am examining hold views which are closely related to those described by Popper as historicist. But the important point is that they believe in what Popper calls piecemeal engineering and do not commit themselves to any doctrines about the inevitable development of society.

2. O. W. Holmes, Jr., *The Common Law* (Boston: Little, Brown, 1881), p. 1.

3. See M. G. White, *The Origin of Dewey's Instrumentalism* (New York: Columbia University Press, 1943), pp. 119-25.

4. See John Dewey, *The Ethics of Democracy* (University of Michigan Philosophical Papers, Second Series, No. 1, 1888).

5. See Joseph Dorfman, *Thorstein Veblen and His America* (New York: Viking, 1934), p. 39.

6. See P. A. Schilpp (ed.), *The Philosophy of John Dewey* (Evanston and Chicago: Northwestern University, two vols., 1939), vol. I, p. 18.

7. See Mark A. de W. Howe (ed.), *Holmes-Pollock Letters* (Cambridge: Harvard University Press, two vols., 1941), vol. I, p. 3; see also H. C. Shriver (ed.), *Justice Holmes: His Book Notices and Uncollected Letters and Papers* (New York: Central Book Co., 1936), p. 21.

8. See John Dewey, *Outlines of a Critical Theory of Ethics* (Ann Arbor, Michigan: Register Publishing Co., 1891) and *The Study of Ethics* (Ann Arbor, Michigan: Register Publishing Co., 1894).

9. Holmes, *The Common Law*, p. 1.

10. John Stuart Mill, in his essay on Austin, says, "The purpose of Bentham was to investigate principles from which to decide what laws ought to exist—what legal rights, and legal duties or obligations, are fit to be established among mankind. This was also the ultimate end of Mr. Austin's speculations; but the subject of his special labors was theoretically distinct, though subsidiary, and practically indispensable, to the former. It was what may be called the *logic of law*" [my italics]. "Austin on Jurisprudence," *Dissertations and Discussions* (Boston: W. V. Spencer, six vols., 1864-67), vol. IV, p. 213. "Jurisprudence, thus understood, is not so much a science of law, as of the application of logic to law." Ibid., vol. IV, p. 220.

11. Holmes, like Dewey, never had a very high opinion of formal constructions. In a letter to Pollock he has the following to say of Hohfeld's attempt to classify jural relations: "Hohfeld was as you surmise an ingenious gent, making, as I judge from flying glimpses, pretty good and keen distinctions of the kind that are more needed by a lower grade of lawyer than they are by you and me. I think all those systematic schematisms rather bores; and now Kocourek in the *Illinois Law Rev[iew]* and elsewhere adds epicycles —and I regard him civilly but as I have written don't care much for the whole machinery." *Holmes-Pollock Letters*, vol. II, p. 64.

12. Holmes, *The Common Law*, p. 1.

13. I am not suggesting that Holmes was not interested in the first question. Indeed he has considered it too. But I wish to suggest that the antiformalism in *The Common Law* was the product of a negative answer to the second question. On this point it may be instructive to examine Mill's comparison of Maine and Austin. The latter is the logician of the law; the former investigates "not properly the philosophy of law, but the philosophy of the history of law." Mill, op. cit., vol. IV, p. 215.

14. Holmes, *The Common Law*, p. 1.

15. It should be pointed out that although Holmes would probably answer the first question in the negative, it is not at all clear that this is entailed by a negative answer to the second. One might formulate the two questions with the word "physics" in place of "law" and conclude that the answer to the second is no, but that the answer to the first is yes. The entire question of Holmes' attitude toward logic in the law is a difficult one. Fearful of the effect that some of his statements may have had in furthering irrationality and illogicality, philosophers like Dewey and Morris R. Cohen have tried to interpret these statements in a manner consistent with their own views. See Dewey's "Justice Holmes and the Liberal Mind," *New Republic*, Jan. 11,

1928, reprinted under the title "Oliver Wendell Holmes" in Dewey's *Characters and Events* (New York: Holt, two vols., 1929), vol. I; and Cohen's "Justice Holmes," *New Republic*, vol. 82, 1935), pp. 206-209. Other problems are raised concerning his relations with C. C. Langdell, often described as the great exponent of inductive method in the law and yet someone of whom Holmes says: "To my mind he represents the powers of darkness. He is all for logic and hates any reference to anything outside of it." *Holmes-Pollock Letters*, vol. I, p. 17.

16. Holmes, *The Common Law*, p. 11, note 1.

17. Ibid., p. 5.

18. Edward Burnett Tylor, *Primitive Culture* (first American edition, Boston: Estes and Lauriat, two vols., 1874), vol. II, p. 453.

19. At a later date Holmes more explicitly announced his sympathy with this point of view. See "The Path of the Law," *Collected Legal Papers* (New York: Harcourt, Brace, 1920), p. 187.

20. I have treated this period in detail in *The Origin of Dewey's Instrumentalism;* see note 3 above.

21. See John Dewey, "The New Psychology," *Andover Review* (September 1884), pp. 278-89.

22. See Dewey, *Psychology* (New York: Harper, 1887).

23. See P. A. Schilpp (ed.), op. cit., vol. I, p. 17.

24. The connections between the later Holmes and the later Dewey are well known. Indeed something of a literature has already grown up on the intellectual links between pragmatism and legal realism. The most recent contribution to this is H. W. Schneider's *History of American Philosophy* (New York: Columbia University Press, 1946), Section 41, entitled "Empirical Radicalism." Dewey has written of Holmes in several places; see M. H. Thomas, *A Bibliography of John Dewey* (New York: Columbia University Press, 1939). Holmes' admiration for Dewey is expressed throughout the Holmes-Pollock correspondence and also in H. C. Shriver (ed.), *Justice Oliver Wendell Holmes: His Book Notices and Uncollected Letters and Papers* (New York: Central Book Co., 1936), see Chapter XII, note 29 below. On some aspects of their intellectual links see M. H. Fisch, "Mr. Justice Holmes, the Prediction Theory of the Law, and Pragmatism," *Journal of Philosophy* (1942), pp. 85-97. It has never been observed, so far as I know, that Dewey was familiar with Holmes' *The Common Law* quite early, and cited it in his *The Study of Ethics* (1894) for Holmes' treatment of legal motive and the "external standard." It is also interesting to examine in this connection Dewey's early essay, "Austin's Theory of Sovereignty," *Political Science Quarterly* (1894), pp. 31-52. In the latter Dewey criticizes Austin in a manner quite consistent with what I have called organicism. He objects to Austin's view that "the residence of sovereignty can be found in a definitely limited portion of political society," and also objects to it for making "a complete gap between the social forces which determine government and that government itself" (ibid., pp. 42, 43). There is a related attack on Maine in *The Ethics of Democracy* (1888) cited note 4 above.

25. John Dewey, "The Present Position of Logical Theory," *Monist*, vol. II (1891), p. 10.

26. Ibid., p. 3. The community which is expressed by these outbursts against formal logic does a good deal to explain the ease with which Roscoe

Pound has united Dewey, Hegel, and Holmes in his own attacks on *mechanical* jurisprudence.

27. For a discussion of certain other aspects of this tendency in American thought, see Schneider, op. cit., Section 33, entitled "Genetic Social Philosophy."

28. John Dewey, "The Evolutionary Method as Applied to Morality," *Philosophical Review*, vol. XI (1902), pp. 111, 113.

29. See John Stuart Mill, *A System of Logic*, Book VI, entitled "on the Logic of the Moral Sciences," in which the various methods are compared.

30. Thorstein Veblen, "Why is Economics Not an Evolutionary Science?" *Quarterly Journal of Economics*, July 1898, reprinted in *The Place of Science in Modern Civilisation and Other Essays* (New York: Huebsch, 1919), p. 56.

31. This appears in Mill's *Essays on Some Unsettled Questions of Political Economy* (London: John W. Parker, 1844).

32. Ibid., pp. 137-38.

33. Ibid., p. 138.

34. Ibid., p. 139.

35. Ibid., p. 140.

36. See below, Chapter V, pp. 60-61.

37. Veblen, op. cit., p. 58; see also J. K. Ingram, *A History of Political Economy* (New York: Macmillan, 1888), on the "realism" of the historical school, especially p. 213. For a recent discussion, see H. Grossman, "The Evolutionist Revolt Against Classical Economics," *The Journal of Political Economy*, vol. 51, Nos. 5 and 6 (1943); this treats the revolts in France and England. H. W. Schneider considers Veblen in his discussion of genetic social philosophy in America, op. cit., Section 33.

38. Naturally, some members of the classical school were sensitive to the growing historicism of the nineteenth century and made many attempts to connect with this tendency; e.g., Mill's attempt to deal with dynamics in the *Political Economy*. But evolutionists and historicists were not satisfied with these overtures. Veblen's attitude on this point is very similar to Dewey's attitude toward the "inductive logicians" of the nineteenth century—e.g., Jevons and Venn—who tried to go beyond formal logic to formulate a theory of scientific method, ostensibly a goal he shared with them. Thus Dewey says that, whereas we might expect empirical logic to advance beyond formal logic, it "virtually continues the conception of thought as in itself empty and formal which characterises scholastic logic." "The Present Position of Logical Theory," *Monist*, vol. II (1891), p. 5; see also M. G. White, *The Origin of Dewey's Instrumentalism*, p. 91.

39. Mill, "On the Definition of Political Economy," *Essays on Some Unsettled Questions of Political Economy*, pp. 142-43.

40. This distinction, it must be urged in fairness to Mill, is not based upon the fact that one method "appeals to experience" and that the other does not. Mill is anxious to disown any mysticism, authoritarianism, or dogmatism. With reference to the phrase "a priori" he says in this essay: "We are aware that this . . . expression is sometimes used to characterize a supposed mode of philosophizing, which does not profess to be founded upon experience at all. But we are not acquainted with any mode of philosophizing, on political subjects at least, to which such a description is fairly applicable"

(ibid., p. 143). A similar point is made in the *System of Logic*, Book VI, Chapter IX, Section 1.

41. In addition to Dorfman's book, see the recent study of John C. Gambs, *Beyond Supply and Demand: A Reappraisal of Institutional Economics* (New York: Columbia University Press, 1946). For a succinct statement of Veblen's "system," see K. L. Anderson, "The Unity of Veblen's Theoretical System," *Quarterly Journal of Economics*, vol. 48 (1933). See also the interesting study by Louis Schneider, *The Freudian Psychology and Veblen's Social Theory* (New York: King's Crown Press, 1948).

42. Dewey delivered a lecture entitled "Ethics" in the series.

43. For a recent discussion of the attitude of American historians on this question and others, see *Theory and Practice in Historical Study: A Report of the Committee on Historiography*, published by the Social Science Research Council (1946), especially Chapter II, by J. H. Randall, Jr., and George Haines, IV, "Controlling Assumptions in the Practice of American Historians."

44. James Harvey Robinson, *History* (New York: Columbia University Press, 1908), p. 14; also see Robinson, *The New History* (New York: Macmillan, 1912), pp. 43-44, where this essay is reprinted, with alterations, under the title "The History of History."

45. Charles A. Beard, *Politics* (New York: Columbia University Press, 1908), p. 14. We must note here the difference between this and Beard's later view concerning the relation between ethics and social science as expressed in *The Nature of the Social Sciences* (New York: Scribner's, 1934). See Chapter XIV of this book.

46. See, for example, his "Logical Conditions of a Scientific Treatment of Morality," *Decennial Publications of the University of Chicago*, First Series, vol. III (1903), pp. 113-39; recently reprinted in Dewey's *Problems of Men* (New York: Philosophical Library, 1946).

47. Robinson, *History*, p. 15.

48. Interestingly enough, Robinson called upon the historical economist Schmoller for support in his polemic against purely political history. See *The New History*, p. 8, note 1.

49. Beard, *Politics*, pp. 5, 6.

50. Ibid., p. 6.

51. See Chapter VIII, notes 20, 21 below.

CHAPTER III. THE AMERICAN SCENE

1. C. A. Beard, *Contemporary American History* (New York: Macmillan, 1914), p. v.

2. Ibid., p. vi.

3. See ibid., p. 4.

4. Ibid., p. 22.

5. Ibid., p. 28.

6. Ibid., p. 32.

7. Ibid., p. 33.

8. Ibid., p. 35.

9. Ibid., p. 36.

10. Ibid., p. 40.

11. Ibid., p. 50.

12. Ibid., pp. 53-54.

13. Ibid., p. 54. Arguing the San Mateo County case of 1882, Conkling, on the basis of the journal of the committee which drafted the amendment, claimed, according to Beard, that "it was not their [the drafters'] intention to confine the amendment merely to the protection of the colored race," but that they wished to extend it to corporations and business interests struggling for emancipation from legislative interference. Ibid., p. 57.

14. Ibid., p. 86.

15. Ibid. p. 87.

16. Ibid., pp. 87-88.

17. Ibid., p. 90.

18. Ibid., p. 164.

19. Ibid., pp. 143-44.

20. Ibid., p. 147.

21. Ibid., p. 169.

22. Ibid., pp. 194, 197, 198.

23. Ibid., p. 199.

24. Ibid., pp. 202-203.

25. Ibid., p. 229.

26. Ibid., pp. 229-30.

27. Ibid., p. 297.

28. Ibid., pp. 303-304.

CHAPTER IV. THE NEW HISTORY AND THE NEW ETHICS

1. J. H. Robinson and Charles A. Beard, *The Development of Modern Europe* (New York: Ginn, 2 vols., 1907-1908), vol. I, p. iii.

2. Ibid., vol. I, p. iv.

3. Ibid., vol. I, p. iv.

4. J. H. Robinson, *The New History* (New York: Macmillan, 1912), p. 15.

5. See John Dewey and James H. Tufts, *Ethics* (New York: Holt, 1908), p. 3.

6. W. I. Thomas, *Source Book for Social Origins* (Boston: R. G. Badger, 1909), p. 3. In a related spirit Dewey enters upon a biological discussion of the origins of inquiry in his *Logic: The Theory of Inquiry* (New York: Holt, 1938).

7. Dewey and Tufts, op. cit., p. 4.

8. Ibid., p. 4.

9. Ibid., pp. 4-5.

10. Ibid., p. v.

11. Ibid., p. v.

12. Robinson and Beard, op. cit., vol. II, p. 375.

13. Ibid., vol. II, pp. 375-76.

14. Ibid., vol. II, p. 376.

15. Ibid., vol. II, p. 380.

16. Ibid., vol. II, pp. 386-87.

17. Ibid., vol. II, p. 405.

18. Ibid., vol. II, p. 407.

19. Ibid., vol. II, p. 421.

CHAPTER V. THE PATH OF THE LAW

1. Thorstein Veblen, *The History of the Leisure Class* (New York: Macmillan, 1899), p. 231.
2. O. W. Holmes, Jr., "The Path of the Law," *Collected Legal Papers* (New York: Harcourt, Brace, 1920), p. 202.
3. Ibid., p. 167.
4. "The Theory of Legal Interpretation," ibid., p. 203.
5. "The Path of the Law," ibid., p. 173.
6. Ibid., p. 168.
7. Ibid., pp. 186-87.
8. Ibid., p. 187.
9. Ibid., p. 175.
10. Ibid., p. 171.
11. Ibid., pp. 170-71.
12. Ibid., pp. 172, 171.
13. Ibid., pp. 176-77.
14. Ibid., pp. 177, 174.
15. Ibid., p. 179.
16. Holmes, *The Common Law* (Boston: Little, Brown, 1881), pp. 35-36.
17. "The Path of the Law," *Collected Legal Papers*, p. 172.
18. Ibid., p. 186.
19. "Learning and Science," ibid., pp. 138, 139.
20. "Law in Science and Science in Law," ibid., pp. 210, 211, 212.
21. Ibid., p. 224.
22. Ibid., pp. 224-25.
23. Ibid., pp. 225-26.
24. Ibid., p. 242.

CHAPTER VI. THE AMORAL MORALIST

1. See J. H. Robinson, *The New History* (New York: Macmillan, 1912), p. 50.
2. Charles A. Beard, *Contemporary American History* (New York: Macmillan, 1914), p. 33, note 1.
3. Quoted in Joseph Dorfman, *Thorstein Veblen and His America* (New York: Viking, 1934) p. 235.
4. Thorstein Veblen, *The Theory of the Leisure Class* (New York: Macmillan, 1899), pp. 19, 10.
5. Ibid., pp. 7-8.
6. Ibid., p. 8.
7. Ibid., p. 9.
8. Ibid., pp. 9-10.
9. See ibid., p. 12.
10. See ibid., p. 12.
11. Ibid., pp. 12-13.
12. Ibid., p. 14.
13. Ibid., p. 15.
14. Ibid., p. 18.

15. Ibid., pp. 25-26.
16. Ibid., pp. 29-30.
17. Ibid., pp. 32, 33.
18. Ibid., p. 35.
19. Ibid., p. 36.
20. Ibid., p. 85.
21. Ibid., p. 34.
22. Wesley C. Mitchell, *What Veblen Taught* (New York: Viking, 1936), p. xix.
23. Veblen, op. cit., pp. 97-98.
24. Ibid., p. 190.
25. Ibid., p. 193.

CHAPTER VII. PROGRESSIVE EDUCATION AND PROGRESSIVE LAW

1. John Dewey, *The School and Society* (New York: McClure, Phillips; Chicago: University of Chicago Press, 1899), pp. 20-21.
2. See ibid., pp. 23-24.
3. Ibid., pp. 25, 25-26.
4. Ibid., pp. 28-30.
5. Ibid., p. 32.
6. Ibid., pp. 38-39.
7. Ibid., pp. 41, 77.
8. Ibid., p. 43.
9. Dewey and Tufts, *Ethics* (New York: Holt, 1908), p. 437.
10. Ibid., p. 438.
11. Quoted in Max Lerner (ed.), *The Mind and Faith of Justice Holmes* (Boston: Little, Brown, 1943), p. 144.
12. Holmes' dissenting opinion in the Lochner case is reprinted in ibid., pp. 148-50; all the quotations in this and the following paragraph are from pp. 148-49.

CHAPTER VIII. HIGH IDEALS AND CATCHPENNY REALITIES

1. Charles A. Beard, *An Economic Interpretation of the Constitution of the United States* (New York: Macmillan, 1913), p. 9.
2. Quoted in ibid., p. 9, note 2.
3. Ibid., p. 8.
4. 18 Yale Law Journal 454, quoted in Max Lerner (ed.), *The Mind and Faith of Justice Holmes* (Boston: Little, Brown, 1943), p. 148.
5. See J. H. Robinson, *The New History* (New York: Macmillan, 1912), chapter II, in which his essay of 1908, *History*, is reprinted with some changes under the title "The History of History."
6. Beard, op. cit., p. 1.
7. Ibid., p. 4.
8. A. M. Simons, *Social Forces in American History* (New York: Macmillan, 1911) p. viii.
9. Charles A. Beard, *Politics* (New York: Columbia University Press, 1908), p. 32.

10. J. H. Robinson, *History* (New York: Columbia University Press, 1908), pp. 17-18.

11. Ibid., p. 18.

12. Beard, *An Economic Interpretation of the Constitution*, pp. 6, 7.

13. Ibid., pp. 16-17.

14. Ibid., p. 17.

15. Ibid., pp. 17, 325.

16. Introduction to J. Allen Smith's posthumous *The Growth and Decadence of Constitutional Government* (New York: Holt, 1930), pp. xiv-xv.

17. See Joseph Freeman, *An American Testament* (New York: Farrar and Rinehart, 1936), p. 106.

18. See also the Introduction to the 1935 edition of Beard's *Economic Interpretation of the Constitution*, pp. ix-x.

19. Ibid., pp. viii-ix.

20. Mark A. de W. Howe (ed.), *The Holmes-Pollock Letters* (Cambridge: Harvard University Press, two volumes, 1941) vol. II, p. 223.

21. Ibid., vol. I, p. 237.

22. *American Law Review*, vol. VII (1873), p. 583, quoted in Felix Frankfurter, *Mr. Justice Holmes and the Supreme Court* (Cambridge: Harvard University Press, 1938), pp. 26-27.

23. Quoted in ibid., p. 51.

24. E. R. A. Seligman, *The Economic Interpretation of History* (New York: Columbia University Press, copyrighted by Macmillan as agent, 1902), p. 3, quoted in Beard, *Economic Interpretation of the Constitution*, p. 15.

25. Ibid., p. 16.

26. Seligman, op. cit., pp. 112, 126.

27. As to the first point: Marx, writing to Joseph Weydemeyer in 1852, said: "No credit is due to me for discovering the existence of classes in modern society nor yet the struggle between them. Long before me bourgeois historians had described the intellectual development of this class struggle and bourgeois economists the economic anatomy of the classes." As to the second he said: "What I did that was new was to prove . . . that *the existence of classes* is only bound up with *particular, historic, phases in the development of production.*" *Karl Marx and Friedrich Engels: Correspondence, 1846–1895*, translated and edited by Dona Torr (New York: International Publishers, 1936), p. 57.

28. See Beard, *The Economic Basis of Politics* (New York: Knopf, 1922), a slightly revised version of four lectures delivered at Amherst College in 1916.

29. Ibid., pp. 44-45.

30. Van Wyck Brooks, *America's Coming-of-Age* (New York: Huebsch, 1915) p. 7.

CHAPTER IX. CREATIVE INTELLIGENCE

1. "The Need for a Recovery of Philosophy," *Creative Intelligence: Essays in the Pragmatic Attitude* by Dewey and others (New York: Holt, 1917), p. 65.

2. Ibid., p. 5.

3. Ibid., p. 7.

4. See, for example, Dewey's "Epistemological Realism: The Alleged

Ubiquity of the Knowledge Relation," *Essays in Experimental Logic* (Chicago: University of Chicago Press, 1916), pp. 264-80.

5. Ibid., p. 1.
6. Ibid., p. 2.
7. *Creative Intelligence*, p. 7.
8. Ibid., p. 25, note.
9. Ibid., p. 68.
10. *Essays in Experimental Logic*, pp. 30-31.
11. *Creative Intelligence*, p. 17.
12. Ibid., p. 18.
13. Ibid., p. 27.
14. Ibid., pp. 28-29.
15. Ibid., p. 29.
16. Ibid., p. 25, note.
17. Ibid., p. 47.
18. Ibid., pp. 47, 48.
19. Ibid., pp. 48-49.
20. All quotations in this and in the preceding paragraph are from ibid., pp. 48-49, 47.
21. Ibid., p. 53.
22. Ibid., p. 60.
23. Ibid., pp. 60-61.
24. Ibid., pp. 61-62.
25. Ibid., p. 62.
26. Ibid., pp. 63-64.
27. See the title essay of Veblen's *The Place of Science in Modern Civilisation* (New York: Huebsch, 1919).

CHAPTER X. GERMAN PHILOSOPHY, POLITICS, AND ECONOMICS

1. John Dewey, *German Philosophy and Politics* (New York: Holt, 1915), pp. 4, 5.
2. Ibid., p. 6.
3. Ibid., p. 7.
4. Ibid., pp. 7-8.
5. Ibid., p. 14.
6. Ibid., p. 20.
7. Ibid., pp. 28, 30-31.
8. Ibid., p. 48.
9. Ibid., pp. 52-53.
10. Ibid., pp. 57-58.
11. Ibid., pp. 58-59.
12. Thorstein Veblen, Preface to *Imperial Germany and the Industrial Revolution* (New York: Macmillan, 1915; Viking, 1939 reprint), p. v; and Joseph Dorfman, Introduction to the 1939 reprint, p. xviii.
13. *Imperial Germany and the Industrial Revolution* (New York: original edition, 1915), pp. 132, 83, 85, 86.
14. Ibid., pp. 226-29.

CHAPTER XI. DESTRUCTIVE INTELLIGENCE

1. Dewey and Tufts, *Ethics* (New York: Holt, 1908), p. 482.

2. See Dewey's "Force, Violence, and Law," *New Republic,* January 22, 1916, and "Force and Coercion," *International Journal of Ethics,* April 1916. Both of these are reprinted in Dewey's *Characters and Events,* edited by Joseph Ratner (New York: Holt, two volumes, 1929), vol. II, pp. 636-41 and pp. 782-89.

3. "Force, Violence and Law," *Characters and Events,* vol. II, p. 637.

4. "Force and Coercion," ibid., vol. II, p. 787.

5. O. W. Holmes, Jr., "The Path of the Law," *Collected Legal Papers* (New York: Harcourt, Brace, 1920), p. 167.

6. John Dewey, "Conscription of Thought," reprinted from the *New Republic,* September 1, 1917, in *Characters and Events,* vol. II, p. 567.

7. Dewey, "Creative Democracy—The Task Before Us," *The Philosopher of the Common Man: Essays in Honor of John Dewey* (New York: Putnam's, 1940), p. 226.

8. Dewey, "In a Time of National Hesitation," *The Seven Arts,* May 1917, pp. 6, 5.

9. See Randolph Bourne, "The Twilight of Idols," which first appeared in *The Seven Arts,* October 1917, and was then reprinted in his *Untimely Papers* (New York: Huebsch, 1919).

10. All of these are reprinted in the second volume of *Characters and Events.*

11. "Conscience and Compulsion" reprinted from the *New Republic,* July 14, 1917, in *Characters and Events,* vol. II, pp. 577, 578-79.

12. "The Future of Pacifism," reprinted from the *New Republic,* July 28, 1917, ibid., vol. II, p. 584.

13. "What America Will Fight For," reprinted from the *New Republic,* August 18, 1917, under the title, "America and War," ibid., vol. II, pp. 564, 565.

14. "Conscription of Thought," ibid., vol. II, p. 568.

15. Randolph Bourne, op. cit., pp. 122, 123, 127-30.

16. Ibid., pp. 132-33.

17. Ibid., p. 137.

18. Max Lerner (ed.), *The Mind and Faith of Justice Holmes* (Boston: Little, Brown, 1943), p. xlii.

19. Mark A. de W. Howe, *Holmes-Pollock Letters* (Cambridge: Harvard University Press, two volumes, 1941) vol. II, p. 36.

20. Lerner, op. cit., p. xliii.

21. O. W. Holmes, Jr., "The Soldier's Faith," an address delivered in 1895 and printed in *Holmes' Speeches* (Boston: Little, Brown, 1913), pp. 62-63.

22. Quoted in Ralph Barton Perry, *The Thought and Character of William James* (Boston: Little, Brown, two volumes, 1935), vol. II, pp. 250-51.

23. See Professor Zechariah Chafee, *Free Speech in the United States* (Cambridge: Harvard University Press, 1941) for a study of this question and for a detailed consideration of Holmes' writings on free speech. See also Lerner, op. cit., for a useful collection of Holmes' important decisions on

civil liberties and a series of introductions concerning the backgrounds of the various cases.

24. Chafee, op. cit., p. 80.

25. 249 U.S. 47 (1919).

26. 250 U.S. 616 (1919).

27. Chafee, op. cit., p. 23.

28. *Masses Publishing Company* v. *Patten,* 244 Fed 535 (S.D.N.Y., 1917).

29. Quoted in Chafee, op. cit., p. 86.

30. *Schenck* v. *U.S.,* quoted in Lerner, op. cit., p. 296. See also ibid., pp. 297-304, and Chafee, op. cit., pp. 85-86.

31. Chafee, op. cit., p. 84.

32. Letter dated Nov. 13, 1917, in *Holmes-Pollock Letters,* vol. I, p. 250.

33. See J. H. Wigmore, "Abrams *v.* U.S.: Freedom of Speech and Freedom of Thuggery in War-Time and Peace-Time," 14 *Illinois Law Review* 539 (1920). For Holmes' reaction to Wigmore's attack, see *Holmes-Pollock Letters,* vol. II, p. 42.

34. Chafee, op. cit., p. 99.

35. "A Statement by Charles A. Beard," *New Republic,* October 1917 (vol. 13), p. 250.

CHAPTER XII. THE TWENTIES

1. In 1920 even Holmes said he loathed war. See Chapter XI, note 19 above.

2. From Simon and Schuster's advertisement of the first crossword-puzzle book; in F. L. Allen, *Only Yesterday: An Informal History of the Nineteen-Twenties* (New York: Harper, 1931; Bantam edition, 1946), pp. 216-17.

3. At this time an extraordinary amount of cross-reference takes place in their writings. See, for example, Veblen's references to Beard, Dewey, and Robinson in *Absentee Ownership;* also Robinson's references to Dewey and Veblen in *The Mind in the Making*. It was also at this time that their work in the fields of education and public opinion served to draw them together. Most of them taught at the New School for Social Research, which was founded during this period, and Dewey and Veblen both served on the editorial staff of the *Dial*.

4. Quoted by Jane Addams in *Peace and Bread in Time of War* (New York: Macmillan, 1922), pp. 250-51.

5. J. H. Robinson, *The Mind in the Making* (New York: Harper, 1921), pp. 180-82.

6. J. H. Robinson, *Medieval and Modern Times: An Introduction to the History of Western Europe* (New York: Ginn, 1918), Supplement, p. xlii.

7. Thorstein Veblen, *The Vested Interests and the State of the Industrial Arts* (New York: Huebsch, 1919), pp. 3, 11, 4, 1.

8. Ibid., pp. 5-6, 6, 7.

9. Ibid., pp. 9, 9-10.

10. Ibid., p. 20.

11. Ibid., p. 27.

12. Ibid., p. 28.

13. Ibid., p. 34.

14. Ibid., pp. 20-21.

15. John Dewey, *Reconstruction in Philosophy* (New York: Holt, 1920), p. 23.

16. Ibid., p. 24.

17. Ibid., pp. 25-26.

18. Ibid., pp. 26-27.

19. See Chapter V, p. 74 and note 23.

20. See J. H. Robinson, *The Humanizing of Knowledge* (New York: George H. Doran, 1923), p. 117, note.

21. Robinson, *The Mind in the Making*, p. 28.

22. Ibid., p. 8.

23. Quoted in ibid., p. 224.

24. Ibid., p. 217.

25. Thorstein Veblen, *The Engineers and the Price System* (New York: Huebsch, 1921), p. 138.

26. Ibid., p. 156.

27. Ibid., pp. 160-61.

28. Ibid., pp. 168-69.

29. Writing to John C. Wu, Holmes said: "Pursuant to your recommendation I sent for Dewey's *Experience and Nature* and am reading it. It makes on me an impression like Walt Whitman, of being symphonic, and of having more life and experience in his head than most writers, philosophers or others. He writes badly and creates more difficulty by his style than by his thought. I could not give a synopsis of what I have read, yet I have felt agreement and delight even when I got only an impression that I could not express. I agree with you that he is a big fellow and I expect to believe when I have finished as I do now that the book is a great work." Letter of December 5, 1926, in H. C. Shriver (ed.), *Justice Oliver Wendell Holmes: His Book Notices and Uncollected Letters and Papers* (New York: Central Book Company, 1936), p. 190.

30. Dewey, "Justice Holmes and the Liberal Mind," *New Republic*, vol. 53 (1929), pp. 210-12; reprinted in *Characters and Events*, vol. I, pp. 100-101.

CHAPTER XIII. IS ETHICS AN EMPIRICAL SCIENCE?

1. Holmes, "Law in Science and Science in Law," *Collected Legal Papers* (New York: Harcourt, Brace, 1920), p. 239.

2. In 1920 Holmes said: "I believe that force, mitigated so far as may be by good manners, is the *ultima ratio*, and between two groups that want to make inconsistent kinds of world I see no remedy except force." *Holmes-Pollock Letters*, vol. II, p. 36.

3. Jeremy Bentham, *An Introduction to the Principles of Morals and Legislation* (London: 1823), chapter I, section XI, p. 6.

4. C. I. Lewis, *An Analysis of Knowledge and Valuation* (La Salle, Illinois: Open Court Publishing Company, 1946), p. 553.

5. Holmes, "Natural Law," *Collected Legal Papers*, p. 314.

6. See especially the tenth chapter of *The Quest for Certainty* (New York: Minton, Balch, 1929).

7. This position has been advanced, with differences, by Bertrand Russell, Rudolf Carnap, and A. J. Ayer. C. L. Stevenson has provided its most elaborate defense in his *Ethics and Language* (New Haven: Yale University

Press, 1944). Stevenson criticizes Dewey's views on the relation between "desired" and "desirable" on grounds similar to those advanced in this chapter.

CHAPTER XIV. CAN HISTORY BE OBJECTIVE?

1. It is rather interesting to observe that many who limit history to singular statements are willing to include as singular (and hence, on their view, as non-causal) statements like "Booth shot Lincoln" and "Brutus killed Caesar." But it is obvious that there is a usage according to which these statements, though singular in form, are in fact causal in content. Killing and shooting are acts in which something is caused to happen. What is required, of course, is some indication of the respects (if any) in which "Brutus killed Caesar" resembles "Brutus killed Caesar because he thought he was ambitious" in being causal, and the respects in which it does not.

2. Charles A. Beard, *The Nature of the Social Sciences* (New York: Scribner's, 1934), p. 50. I suppose it would best be construed as a collection of propositions, rather than as facts. Perhaps a collection of sentences would be better, but such subtleties are never treated by Beard.

3. Ibid., p. 51.

4. Introduction to the 1935 edition of *An Economic Interpretation of the Constitution* (New York: Macmillan), pp. ix-x.

5. C. A. Beard, "Written History as an Act of Faith," *American Historical Review*, January 1934 (vol. 39, no. 2), p. 221.

6. Ibid., p. 221.

7. Ibid., p. 227.

8. Ibid., p. 227.

9. Ibid., p. 228.

10. Ibid., p. 228.

11. Charles A. Beard and Sidney Hook, "Problems of Terminology in Historical Writing," *Theory and Practice in Historical Study* (New York: Social Science Research Council, 1946), p.126.

12. See Beard, *The Nature of the Social Sciences*, p. 53.

13. Ibid., p. 58.

CHAPTER XV. YES AND NO

1. The dialogue which follows is the result of juxtaposing two passages from P. A. Schilpp (ed.), *The Philosophy of John Dewey* (Evanston and Chicago: Northwestern University, 1939), which have been slightly modified. The impatient admirer is Professor J. H. Randall, Jr. See pp. 91, 592, note 57.